PSALMS 1–72

ABINGDON OLD TESTAMENT COMMENTARIES

PSALMS 1-72

RICHARD J. CLIFFORD

Abingdon Press
Nashville

ABINGDON OLD TESTAMENT COMMENTARIES
PSALMS 1–72

Copyright © 2002 by Abingdon Press

Library of Congress Cataloging-in-Publication Data

Clifford, Richard J.
   Psalms 1–72 / Richard J. Clifford.
      p. cm.—(Abingdon Old Testament commentaries)
   Includes bibliographical references.
   ISBN 0-687-02711-X (pbk.: alk. paper)
   1. Bible. O.T. Psalms I–LXXII—Commentaries.   I. Title: Psalms one through seventy-two.   II. Title.   III. Series

BS1430.53 .C57 2002
223'.207—dc21

2002012848

02 03 04 05 06 07 08 09 10 11—10 9 8 7 6 5 4 3 2 1

MANUFACTURED IN THE UNITED STATES OF AMERICA

CONTENTS

Book 2 (Psalms 42–72)

FOREWORD

The Abingdon Old Testament Commentaries are offered to the reader in hopes that they will aid in the study of Scripture and provoke a deeper understanding of the Bible in all its many facets. The texts of the Old Testament come out of a time, a language, and socio-historical and religious circumstances far different from the present. Yet Jewish and Christian communities have held to them as a sacred canon, significant for faith and life in each new time. Only as one engages these books in depth and with all the critical and intellectual faculties available to us, can the contemporary communities of faith and other interested readers continue to find them meaningful and instructive.

These volumes are designed and written to provide compact, critical commentaries on the books of the Old Testament for the use of theological students and pastors. It is hoped that they may be of service also to upper-level college or university students and to those responsible for teaching in congregational settings. In addition to providing basic information and insights into the Old Testament writings, these commentaries exemplify the tasks and procedures of careful interpretation.

The writers of the commentaries in this series come from a broad range of ecclesiastical affiliations, confessional stances, and educational backgrounds. They have experience as teachers and, in some instances, as pastors and preachers. In most cases, the authors are persons who have done significant research on the book that is their assignment. They take full account of the most important current scholarship and secondary literature, while not attempting to summarize that literature or to engage in technical academic debate. The fundamental concern of each volume is analysis and discussion of the literary, socio-historical, theological, and ethical dimensions of the biblical texts themselves.

The New Revised Standard Version of the Bible is the principal translation of reference for the series, though authors may draw upon other interpretations in their discussion. Each writer is attentive to the original Hebrew text in preparing the commentary. But the authors do not presuppose any knowledge of the biblical languages on the part of the reader. When some awareness of a grammatical, syntactical, or philological issue is necessary for an adequate understanding of a particular text, the issue is explained simply and concisely.

Each volume consists of four parts. An *introduction* looks at the book as a whole to identify *key issues* in the book, its *literary genre* and *structure,* the *occasion and situational context* of the book (including both social and historical contexts), and the *theological and ethical* significance of the book.

The *commentary* proper organizes the text by literary units and, insofar as is possible, divides the comment into three parts. The *literary analysis* serves to introduce the passage with particular attention to identification of the genre of speech or literature and the structure or outline of the literary unit under discussion. Here also, the author takes up significant stylistic features to help the reader understand the mode of communication and its impact on comprehension and reception of the text. The largest part of the comment is usually found in the *exegetical analysis,* which considers the leading concepts of the unit, the language of expression, and problematical words, phrases, and ideas in order to get at the aim or intent of the literary unit, as far as that can be uncovered. Attention is given here to particular historical and social situations of the writer(s) and reader(s) where that is discernible and relevant as well as to wider cultural (including religious) contexts. The analysis does not proceed phrase by phrase or verse by verse but deals with the various particulars in a way that keeps in view the overall structure and central focus of the passage and its relationship to the general line of thought or rhetorical argument of the book as a whole. The final section, *theological and ethical analysis* seeks to identify and clarify the theological and ethical matters with which the unit deals or to which it points. Though not aimed primarily at contemporary issues of faith and life, this section should provide readers a basis for reflection on them.

Each volume also contains a select bibliography of works cited in the commentary as well as major commentaries and other important works available in English. A subject index is provided to help the reader get at matters that cut across different texts. Both of these sections can be found in volume 2 of the Psalms.

The fundamental aim of this series will have been attained if readers are assisted not only to understand more about the origins, character, and meaning of the Old Testament writings, but also to enter into their own informed and critical engagement with the text themselves.

Patrick D. Miller
General Editor

LIST OF ABBREVIATIONS

ANEP	*The Ancient Near East in Pictures Relating to the Old Testament.* Edited by J. B. Pritchard. 2d ed. with supplement. Princeton: Princeton University Press, 1969.
ANET	*Ancient Near Eastern Texts Relating to the Old Testament.* Edited by J. B. Pritchard. 3d ed. with supplement. Princeton: Princeton University Press, 1969.
b. Ber.	Babylonian *Berakot*
b. Sukkah	Babylonian *Sukkah*
CBQ	*Catholic Biblical Quarterly*
CCSL	Corpus Christianorum: Series latina. Turnhout: Brepols, 1953–.
CTU	*The Cuneiform Alphabetic Texts from Ugarit, Ras Ibn Hani, and Other Places.* Edited by M. Dietrich, O. Loretz, and J. Sanmartin. Münster, 1995.
LCL	Loeb Classical Library
m. Roš Haš.	Mishnah *Roš Haššanah*
PG	Patrologia graeca [=Patrologiae cursus completus: Series graeca]. Edited by J.-P. Migne. 162 vols. Paris, 1857–1886.
PL	Patrologia latina [=Patrologiae cursus completus: Series latina]. Edited by J.-P. Migne. 217 vols. Paris, 1844–64.
ZAW	*Zeitschrift für die alttestamentliche Wissenschaft*

INTRODUCTION

THE PSALTER AS A BOOK IN THE BIBLE

The English word *psalm* is from Greek *psalmos*, "song accompanied by a stringed instrument; song." This is the term used by the early Greek translation (the Septuagint) for Hebrew *mizmôr*, "melody, song, psalm," which occurs only in the Psalter and is virtually a technical term for "psalm." The Psalter contains 150 psalms arranged in five "books": Psalms 1–41, 42–72, 73–89, 90–106, and 107–50. Each book concludes with a doxology—Pss 41:13; 72:18-19; 89:52; 106:48; and 150:1-6. Rabbinic tradition drew a parallel between the five books of the torah handed down by Moses and the five books of the Psalter handed down by David: "As Moses gave five books of laws to Israel, so David gave five Books of Psalms to Israel" (Braude 1959, 5).

How was the five-book collection formed? There are indications that the five books were formed from already existing collections. Two psalms in Book 1 (14 and part of 40) also appear in Books 2 and 3 (53 and 70, respectively). Books 2 and 3 show a preference for the divine name Elohim over Yahweh, though not with perfect consistency. Certain poems in Book 2 (42–49) and Book 3 (84–88) are attributed to the Korahites, and several in Book 3 (73–83) are attributed to Asaph. Korah and Asaph were apparently considered to be the founders of guilds of Temple musicians. In Chronicles, Asaph is a levitical singer and musician (2 Chron 5:12) and the descendants of Korah have a liturgical role (1 Chron 9:19). Elsewhere in the Psalter, some psalms are clustered by theme, for example, the kingship of God in Psalms 93–99. The superscription "Song of Ascents" prefaces Psalms 120–34. This collection may have been used by pilgrims "ascending" to Jerusalem. Possibly, some psalms and even collections came from ancient shrines such as Shiloh. Evidence for different editions of the Psalter comes from the Dead Sea Scrolls. Three Psalm manuscripts found at Qumrân show an order after Ps 89 that differs from the Masoretic Text. Thus, the Psalter is obviously a collection of collections, though the process of editing cannot be described with any precision.

Recently, scholars have suggested that certain psalms have been purposefully grouped on the basis of their ideas in order to make a theological statement. Some arrangement is indisputable. Psalm 1, for example, is clearly introductory, for it implies that reciting the psalms ("meditate," v. 2) makes one fruitful and prosperous. Other examples of artful arrangement will be pointed out in the commentary. One should not forget that the Psalter is a collection of individual prayers in which ideas are subordinate to prayer. The Psalter is a text of personal piety. Jews and Christians memorized psalms and meditated on them in their *literary* context, which included neighboring psalms. Such meditation might inspire the idea, for example, that the messiah (Ps 2) will rescue one from a myriad of enemies (Ps 3) or that the first exodus that ends Book 4 (Ps 106) becomes the new exodus in the beginning of Book 5 (Ps 107), thus showing the fruitfulness of the exodus event.

There are two systems of numbering the psalms in translations, one dependent on the Hebrew Masoretic Text and the other dependent on the Greek Septuagint. The Septuagint counted Psalms 9–10 and 114–15 as single poems and Psalms 116 and 148 each as two poems, resulting in a discrepancy of one from the Masoretic numbering of Psalms 8–147. The Latin Vulgate and old Roman Catholic Bibles follow the Septuagint numbering. All modern translations follow the Masoretic numbering. There are also two systems of numbering psalm verses. The most common, used by *The New Revised Standard Version* (NRSV), The Revised English Bible (REB), The New International Version (NIV), and The Contemporary English Version (CEV), assigns no verse number to the superscription so that verse 1 is always the first line of the poem. The other system, used by *The New American Bible* (NAB) and *TANAKH: The Holy Scriptures* (NJPS), follows printed Hebrew Bibles in assigning a verse number to the superscription and so is often one verse behind the NRSV verse number.

The superscriptions contain a number of words referring to musical performance. Unfortunately, none can be identified with any certainty. *Selah*, a Hebrew word occurring seventy-one times in thirty-nine psalms, may mark stanza divisions. The phrase "to the leader" *(laměnaṣṣēaḥ)* occurs fifty-five times in Psalms, usually in conjunction with the ascription of the psalm "to/of David." Some terms in the superscriptions may be the names of melodies, for example, "Do not destroy" (Psalms 57–59 and 75) and "Hind of the dawn" (Ps 22). "Shiggaion" in Ps 7 is connected by some to Akkadian *šegû*, "a cry of lamentation," and thus would designate the poem as a lament. General terms for songs appear in the headings: *těhillāh*, "song of praise"; *těpillāh*, "prayer"; *maśkîl* (in the headings of thirteen psalms), "instructive poem(?)"; *mizmôr*, "psalm"; and *šîr*, "song." The commentary will generally not discuss these terms when they occur in the superscriptions.

THE PSALTER AS A REFLECTION OF THE TEMPLE AND ITS WORSHIP

The common designation of the Psalter, "hymnbook of the Second Temple" (520 BCE–70 CE), is a helpful term if one realizes that the Psalms are oriented toward the Temple as God's dwelling rather than accompaniments to Temple ceremonies. The psalms presuppose that the Lord who chose Israel and the Davidic dynasty also chose to dwell on Zion (Jerusalem) and there receive the praise and petitions of Israel. Zion was the privileged place of encounter between Yahweh and the holy people. The reform of King Josiah (640–609 BCE; 2 Kings 22–23 and 2 Chronicles 34–35) heightened the importance of Jerusalem as the center of Israelite worship. During the Second Temple period, the city's central position only increased as a dispersed Judaism aligned its worship with that of the Temple. People prayed in the direction of the Temple (1 Kgs 8:35; Dan 6:10; 1 Esd 4:58) and even entertained the hope that the nations would make a pilgrimage to Zion (Isa 2:1-4; 60–61; 66:18-21).

Superscriptions attributing psalms to David (seventy-three), Solomon (two), and Moses (one) are part of the same democratizing of the Temple liturgy. Fourteen superscriptions associate the psalm with a particular episode in David's life (usually involving suffering), which makes David a model for any individual praying to the Lord. The psalms make it possible for a dispersed Israel to participate in the worship of the people.

Since many psalms reflect ceremonies of the Jerusalem Temple, it is helpful to look briefly at the worship carried out there. The Temple was the central shrine of the twelve tribes (see Psalms 84, 122, 132). Though small by modern standards (approximately 115 feet long, 33 feet wide, and 49 feet high), it was richly furnished. It was exclusively a palace for God, unlike modern synagogues or churches that are also gathering places for the community. The Temple and its courtyard were regarded as an architectural unity. The Lord dwelt in the house, attended by sacred personnel; the people gathered in the courtyard for ceremonies. Like a great potentate, God was honored in beautiful ceremonies, some performed within the house and others in the open-air court where the people could participate. Liturgical song was part of the ceremonial that honored God and instructed the community. Much of that liturgy is reflected in the Psalter.

The psalms provide little direct information about the ritual that originally accompanied them. Ritual texts such as Exodus 35–39 and Leviticus 1–16 do not mention songs, but that does not mean there was no singing; for ritual texts are prescriptions for correct performance, not descriptions of the liturgy of which they are a part. The psalms themselves refer to liturgical actions—feasts (65:1-4; 81:3), visits to the Temple (5:7; 65:4), processions (48:12-14; 118:26-27), sacrifices (4:5; 107:22; 116:17-18), and priestly benedictions (115:14-15; 134:3). Some presume two choirs or a cantor plus choir (Pss 15, 24, 132, 134). The psalms were not recited silently, for Hebrew verbs expressing emotion can refer equally to outward expression as inner feeling; the verb *to rejoice* can mean to shout joyously, and the verb *to meditate* can mean to recite aloud. Musical instruments are frequently mentioned: trumpets or rams' horns, lyres, flutes, drums, and cymbals. Evidence thus points to noisy and communal performances of the psalms.

Zion is the name for Jerusalem as a sacred city. Yahweh, the God of Israel, might appear and act in other places, but Zion was the preeminent place of disclosure and encounter with Israel; only here was Israel fully "before the Lord." Here the Lord was enthroned upon the cherubim (80:1; 99:1) to judge, that is, to govern the people and the nations. Zion was the goal of the three annual feasts of pilgrimage (see below). Though the rest of the universe totter, it remained firm and secure (46:2-3; 48:4-8; 76:3). The songs of Zion (Pss 46, 48, 76, 84, 87, 121–22) celebrate the city as the site of the victory over primordial enemies and the residence of Yahweh, patron of the Davidic dynasty.

The Temple liturgy revolved around the three great feasts of the year: Passover and Unleavened Bread in the early spring; Pentecost at wheat harvest seven weeks later, and Ingathering (also called Booths or simply The Feast) in the early fall. Each was an occasion for celebrating the bounty of the land and the divinely-led history of the people.

Passover commemorated the exodus from Egypt and entry into the promised land (Exodus 12–13). Psalms that celebrate the exodus conquest (e.g., 105, 114, 135–36, and 147) could have been sung appropriately during the feast. The second feast, Pentecost (also called Firstfruits and Feast of Weeks), was associated with the giving of the law by the second century BCE and perhaps much earlier. Psalms 50 and 81 would have been appropriate at this time because they urge observance of the covenant and law given at Sinai. The third feast was Ingathering, which in the early period was the feast of the New Year, when Israel celebrated the Lord's victory over the forces of chaos and subsequent enthronement. The enthronement ceremony was an appropriate background for acclamations of the Lord's kingship (e.g., Pss 47, 93, 95–100) and for celebrations of the Lord's world-establishing victory (e.g., Pss 29, 46, 48, and 76).

THE GENRES AND RHETORIC OF THE PSALMS

Like much ancient literature, especially ancient prayers, the psalms are highly conventional. There are three major categories: hymn, lament, and thanksgiving. The genre of a psalm is usually obvious from its first few verses, and modern pray-ers (that is, those who pray) can learn much from the psalms' own "early warning system." The paragraphs below point out the chief features of each genre.

Purely on the basis of their *form*, more than eighty psalms can be assigned to one of three types: hymn, lament (individual and community), and thanksgiving. About thirty more can be grouped together according to their subject. According to their style and topics, others are reckoned songs of trust (e.g., 23, 91, 121) and wisdom psalms (e.g., 37, 49, 73). Three psalms have the Torah, or law, as their subject (1, 19, 119).

1. *Hymn.* There are twenty-eight hymns (8, 19, 29, 33, 47, 66:1-12, 93, 95–100, 103–5, 107, 111, 113–14, 117, 135–36, 145–50). The structure is extremely simple: There is a *call to worship*, often with the subject named (e.g., "Praise the Lord, all you nations," 117:1*a*) and sometimes with musical instruments mentioned (e.g., "Praise him with trumpet sound," 150:3*a*), and there is an *invitation to praise*, which is often repeated in the final verse. The body of the poem is normally introduced by the conjunction *for* or *because* (Heb. *kî*), giving the basis for the praise.

The basis for praise is usually what God has done. The German scholar Claus Westermann has noticed that comparable hymns in Mesopotamia use "descriptive praise," that is, praising what the god customarily does or is, whereas biblical hymns use "narrative praise," that is, praising God by narrating an act (Westermann 1989). The particular act is often the act by which Israel came into being as a people—the exodus from Egypt and entry into Canaan. References to this one event can be made from either of two perspectives: one using the language of history (historic) with human characters prominent (e.g., Ps 105) and the other using cosmic or mythic language (suprahistoric) with God portrayed as acting directly rather than through human agency (e.g., Ps 114). Sometimes the two perspectives are mingled in one psalm (e.g., Pss 135 and 136).

In the hymn, the verb *to bless (bērak)* occurs frequently, though with a different sense than in English. In the Bible, God blesses human beings and human beings bless God. God's blessing gives to human beings goods they do not possess—health, wealth, honor, and children. But what happens when human beings bless God, who possesses all things? They give the only thing God might lack—recognition by human beings of God's glory. In blessing God, one acknowledges before others God's benefits and widens the circle of God's admirers.

2. *Individual lament. Lament* is the modern term for the genre and is derived from one feature of it: the complaint. A more apt term for the genre is *petition* since the purpose is to persuade God to rescue the psalmist. Individual petitions include Psalms 3–7, 9–10, 13–14, 17, 22, 25–26, 27:7-14, 28, 31, 35–36, 38–39, 41–43, 51, 53–54, 56–57, 59, 61, 63–64, 69–71, 86, 88, 102, 109, 120, 130, 139–43. Some scholars speculate that the original situation of such psalms was a ritual dialogue between a troubled individual and a Temple official, like that between Hannah and the priest Eli at the ancient shrine at Shiloh (1 Sam 1:9-18). At the end of the dialogue, Eli says to Hannah, "Go in peace; the God of Israel grant the petition you have made to him" (1 Sam 1:17), which Hannah takes as a divine assurance and returns home in peace. Laments in the Psalter may simply be literary imitations of such a ceremony, transposing a ritual of healing to personal prayer. Whatever its original situation in life, the lament offers oppressed and troubled individuals a means of unburdening themselves before God and receiving an assurance.

The placement of the elements of the lament was flexible. Each psalm begins with an unadorned cry to the Lord, for example, "Help, Lord!" The *complaint* is a description of the problem or danger, which are variously portrayed as sickness, unfair legal accusation, treachery of former friends, or the consequences of sin such as ostracism from the community. Usually there is a *statement of trust*, uttered despite the overwhelming difficulties, for example, "I am not afraid of ten thousands of people / who have set themselves against me all around" (3:6). The *prayer* is for rescue and often for the downfall of the enemies as well. Finally, there is the *statement of praise*, which contrasts the troubled tone with its serenity and confidence.

The lament pursues a strategy. It portrays a drama with three actors: the psalmist, the enemies ("the wicked"), and God. The *complaint* portrays the psalmist as a loyal client of the Lord, who nonetheless suffers assaults from the wicked or from a threat such as illness. The psalmist's claim of loyalty is not a claim of universal innocence but of innocence in this case. The questions are posed: Will you, just God that you are, allow your loyal client to suffer harm from an unjust enemy? Why do you delay, O Vindicator of the poor, to come to my assistance? The basis of the appeal is not the character of the psalmist but the character of God: *noblesse oblige* (my nobility obliges me to act). The lament enables the worshiper to face threats bravely and learn trust in God.

3. *Community lament.* The following psalms are commonly assigned to this genre: 44, 60, 74, 77, 79–80, 83, 85, 89, 90, 94, 123, 126. The community complains that the Lord has abandoned them to their enemies. In response, they "remember" before God the event that brought Israel into existence in the hope that God will renew or reactivate that event. The foundational event can be described in various ways, for example, driving out the nations (Ps 44), defeating Sea and leading the people to the land (Ps 77), or transplanting a vine from Egypt (Ps 80). The lament aims to persuade God to act by asking, Will you allow another power to destroy what you have created? It appeals to God's character rather than relying on the supposed virtue of the community.

The community remembers God's past action. The verb *to remember* is important in the Psalter. It does not mean to recall what had been forgotten but to make a past event present by describing it. Reciting the story actualizes the event in the liturgy. Translations sometimes obscure the meaning of the verb *to remember*. For example, NRSV Ps 77:12, "I will *meditate* on all your work, / and *muse* on your mighty deeds," is much less satisfactory than NAB (77:13), "I will recite all your works; / your exploits I will tell."

4. *Individual thanksgiving.* Psalms in this category include 18, 21, 30, 32, 34, 40:1-10, 41, 92, 108, 111, 116, 118, 138. In a sense, these psalms are a continuation of the individual lament, for they describe God's response to a plea for help. The thanksgiving is a report to the community of rescue from the hands of the wicked. Like the hymn and the individual petition, it is a transaction between an individual and God: You did me a favor by rescuing me, now I respond by telling of your deed to a circle of admirers.

The thanksgiving genre often uses the verb *hôdû*, "to give thanks, to praise." The customary way of giving thanks in the Bible is not to say "thank you" (there is no equivalent to the phrase in biblical Hebrew), but to tell publicly the beneficial act God has done. An example is Jacob's wife, Leah, whose prayer for a son is finally answered in the birth of Judah. She responds, "This time I will praise *['ôdeh]* the LORD" (Gen 29:35). The thanksgiving psalm reports the act of salvation.

5. *Other categories.* Other psalms can be classed according to their subject matter such as "historical" narratives, festival songs, and liturgies. "Historical" is put in quotation marks because these psalms tell the story of God's mighty acts rather than write history in a modern sense. Such narratives include Psalms 78, 105–6, and 135–36. Israelites would have been sufficiently familiar with their history to note significant variations when it was retold. An example of retelling is Ps 78. Though long and complex, its structure is relatively simple—two parallel recitals displaying a single pattern: gracious act of God (vv. 12-16 and 42-55), a rebellious response by Israel (vv. 17-20 and 56-58), divine anger and punishment (vv. 21-32 and 59-64), and finally, a fresh divine initia-

tive (vv. 33-39 and 65-72). Evidently able to understand the pattern, Israelites would recognize God's new offer of grace after the destruction of the old sanctuary at Shiloh in God's choice of Zion and the Davidic dynasty.

Another simple pattern shapes the long Ps 105. Verses 1-6 invite Israel as descendants of Abraham, Isaac, and Jacob to praise the Lord of the world, and verses 7-11 assert that the Lord is true to the promise given to the ancestors concerning descendants and land. The rest of the poem (vv. 12-45) shows Israel experiencing that promise in different situations before actually receiving it: experiencing the promise as a protected sojourner (vv. 12-15), as a protected prisoner (vv. 16-22), as a protected though oppressed minority (vv. 23-38), and as a protected community on the way to take possession (vv. 39-45).

Another category in the Psalter is the enthronement psalm (24, 29, 47, 93, 95–99). In these the Lord is enthroned as king of heaven and earth. In the opinion of many scholars, these psalms reflect a New Year festival when the fall rains fertilize the land parched from summer heat and dryness, symbolizing God's defeat of chaos and infertility. (The Mediterranean climate of Israel has two seasons: an arid summer from late April to early September and a fertile and wet winter from late September to mid-April.)

In the ancient Near East, the new year was an event of deep religious significance. In Judaism, too, New Year's Day, which falls on the first day of the seventh month (Tishri, September-October) has been observed with solemnity at least as far back as the second century CE *(m. Roš Haš. 1:2)*. Earlier biblical references to an autumn New Year are less explicit but, taken cumulatively, suggest the same. The ancient liturgical calendars in Exodus (23:14-17; 34:22-23) and Deuteronomy (16:13-17) speak of Ingathering or Booths in early autumn as the third of the great pilgrimage feasts. The feast occurs "at the end of the year" (Exod 23:16) and "at the turn of the year" (Exod 34:22), which are ambiguous. The first phrase seems to mean primarily the *end* of the year but can, like the second phrase, refer to the new year that begins as the old ends. In the postexilic period, the celebration of the new year was apparently shifted to the spring, in imitation of the Babylonian calendar.

The Scandinavian scholar Sigmund Mowinckel proposed that the psalms that speak of Yahweh's enthronement as king of the gods and of the universe by reason of his great victory were sung at the fall New Year festival (1967, I:106-92; II: 225-50). Though there are ancient Near Eastern parallels, the best evidence is post-biblical Judaism's celebration of Yahweh's kingship in the autumn festival, including the use of verses from the enthronement psalms. The Septuagint heading (second century BCE) to Ps 29 connects it to the fall Feast of Tabernacles. Similarly, Zech 14:16-19 (sixth century BCE) specifically connects the kingship of Yahweh to the feast of Booths and threatens those who do not keep the festival with loss of rain, which would be an appropriate punishment since the feast coincides with the return of rain.

The New Year fall festival celebrated the Lord who defeated cosmic chaos to become king of the universe. The enthronement cry, "The LORD is king" (93:1; 96:10; 97:1; 99:1) can be equally well translated "Yahweh has become king!" The latter translation does not, of course, presuppose that Yahweh had previously been dethroned. Like the Christian Easter cry, "He is risen," it is a liturgical acclamation. The Lord's kingship is renewed and experienced afresh as the world seems to come back to life after the heat and inertness of summer.

Related to enthronement psalms are the royal psalms (2, 18, 20–21, 45, 72, 101, 110, 144:1-11) and songs of Zion (46, 48, 76, 84, 87, 121–22). When Yahweh was enthroned as king of the world, his regent on earth, the Davidic king, was also celebrated as the Lord's "son" and anointed, for example, "I have set my king on Zion, my holy hill." and "You are my son; / today I have begotten you" (2:6-7). Zion is celebrated as a towering mountain, the residence of the Most High God and a place so secure that enemy kings can only rage helplessly at its base (46:2-3; 48:4-8).

Besides the national psalms mentioned in the previous pages, there are several more personal categories. The song of trust, though a bit vague as a category, is nearest to the individual lament. The genre includes Psalms 11, 14, 16, 23, 27:1-6, 52, 62-

63, 91, 121, 125, and 131. Liturgical actions such as sacrifices and sojourning in the Lord's tent (27:4-6) are mentioned, but these actions have become symbols to express delight and nearness to God.

Another category is Torah (instruction) psalms (1, 19, and 119), in which the psalmist rejoices in the inspired written word. The word or law celebrated in these texts in the course of time was identified with the law of Moses, which became a prominent feature of early Judaism. Originally, however, the reference was to God's word in a more general sense.

The last category to be mentioned, and the most vague, is the wisdom psalms, sometimes called "learned psalmography" or noncultic meditations. Psalms 37, 49, 73, 112, and 127 (sometimes others) are included in this grouping. These compositions contain stylistic or thematic similarities to Wisdom literature (Proverbs, Job, Ecclesiastes, and in the Roman Catholic and Orthodox canons, Sirach and Wisdom of Solomon). Stylistic similarities with Wisdom literature include phraseology such as "happy the one" (1:1), "better . . . than" sayings (37:16), and admonitions (49:16). Thematic similarities to Wisdom literature include contrasts between the doctrine of the two ways (Ps 49) and concern with retribution (Ps 73).

A few psalms do not fit into a genre, or they fit into more than one. On the whole, however, the psalms are ruled by genre and conventions and modern pray-ers are greatly helped by knowing them.

Poetic and Rhetorical Features

The psalms are, first and foremost, poems and make their statement with poetic means. The most distinctive feature of Hebrew poetry is parallelism of lines, for example, "Purge me with hyssop, and I shall be clean; / wash me, and I shall be whiter than snow" (51:7). Both lines say essentially the same thing. Unlike modern poetry, which often strives for a single memorable phrase or image, Hebrew poetry makes two or three parallel statements designed to interact with each other. Its statement is dialectic, one line echoing and completing the other. Though repetition of lines may reflect an oral culture where redundancy was a necessity for communication, the feature retains its charm and beauty even today. It is also one of the few elements of ancient poetry that can be translated without loss into modern languages.

There is no regular rhyme as in English, though when the plural ending -'îm and pronoun suffixes of nouns and verbs are repeated, they produce a rhyming. Another element, often overlooked, is the figure of abstract for concrete, for example,

> For you are not a God who delights in wickedness;
>   evil will not sojourn with you.
> The boastful will not stand before your eyes;
>   you hate all evildoers. (5:4-5)

The first two-line verse uses abstract nouns ("wickedness" and "evil") for concrete nouns (wicked and evil persons), for the verbs "to delight in," and "to sojourn" are appropriate for human beings.

This commentary gives special attention to the psalms as poetry. Several technical terms will be used in the analysis. *Colon,* plural *cola* (Gk., lit. "limb, member") here means a basic metrical or rhythmical unit. It often means the same as *line,* though *line* can be ambiguous. A *bicolon* is two parallel cola (e.g., "Truly God is good to the upright, // to those who are pure in heart" 73:1), and a *tricolon* is three parallel cola. *Chiasm* (Gk. "a placing crosswise," from the name of the Greek letter X, *chi*) is any structure in which elements are repeated in reverse; it may be small-scale (involving two or three cola) or large-scale (involving whole stanzas in a poem). Chiasm appears to have arisen in oral discourse, for it helps hearers keep track of the structure of sections or whole poems. A special form of chiasm is *inclusio* (inclusion, reprise) in which a word at the beginning of a poem or section is repeated at the end, signaling to the reader the section or poem is concluded.

Wordplay is also an important element in Hebrew poetry.

Hebrew words are normally formed from three consonants, for example, the consonants *ktb* can occur in a noun (e.g., "a writing") or a verb (e.g., "to write"). Poets play on these verbal roots for a variety of purposes, including unifying a poem or lending an ironic tone.

OBSERVATIONS ON THE THEOLOGY IN THE PSALMS

It is beyond the scope of this introduction to write a theology of the Psalter. Its beliefs are those of the Old Testament. Several themes, however, are prominent in the Psalter and lend it a tone and direction. The following paragraphs sketch several important themes.

Yahweh the Supreme God of the Universe

Liturgical poetry was not unique to Israel. Ancient Near Eastern temples generally had rituals and ceremonies using the sung word in hymns, petitions, and thanksgivings. What made Israel distinctive was its belief in *one* God, whom they invoked as "God," "Yahweh," and a few other titles. In early Judaism, the title "the Lord" came to be used for the proper name "Yahweh"; this commentary uses "Yahweh" and "the Lord" interchangeably.

Monotheism made Israel's worship distinctive. The Lord, all-powerful and all-knowing, did not require human labor in the way that other deities did. Though extrabiblical cosmogonies invariably depict human beings as abject slaves of the gods, Gen 1 describes them with royal traits ("image of God," "subdue," "have dominion"). Humans—part of the created world yet able to address God in word and music—are by their nature singers before God. The psalms are part of their song. Monotheism also forbids images, for no single being can represent the Creator of all. In Israel's imageless worship the word is privileged: "You heard the sound of words but saw no form; there was only a voice" (Deut 4:12). The words of the psalms thus bring Israel before the Lord in a special way.

Though unlike its neighbors by its worship of a single deity, Israel was like them in believing that the world was made for God not for humans. The belief had rhetorical implications, for the palmists knew that to move God to act they must appeal to God's interest rather than their own. A well-known example is Ps 6:4*b*-5: "Deliver me for the sake of your steadfast love. / For in death there is no remembrance of you; / in Sheol who can give you praise?" Laments put God "on the spot" with their questions, implied or actual: "How can you abandon me who has put all my trust in you? What kind of God would abandon a client nation in their hour of need? How can you, a just God, allow the righteous to suffer and the wicked to prosper?" In short, the psalmists appeal to the divine character. Avowing themselves to be without resources, they portray their enemies as enemies of God. Modern readers should not regard the theocentric strategies of the psalmists as catering to a self-centered and overly sensitive deity. Rather, the strategies simply express a profound sense that the world is God's.

Implied Narratives

Several themes are mentioned repeatedly in the Psalter: divine kingship, the Temple on Mount Zion, the Davidic king, and the "deeds" (sometimes singular, "deed") that God has done. Each of these themes is part of a specific narrative that Israelites knew well and that modern readers need to learn in order to understand the themes.

Psalms 24, 29, 47, 89, 93, 95–99 acclaim Yahweh as king of the universe (e.g., "The LORD is king," 93:1) and supreme over all other heavenly beings (e.g., "Who among the heavenly beings is like the Lord?" 89:6*b*). The poems describe Yahweh's triumphant entry into his palace amid the acclamation of heavenly beings and the nations. Often they go on to say that the Lord establishes equity and justice in the world. What is the story behind these psalms? Modern scholars call the story the combat myth.

The combat myth was a long-lived and influential genre,

attested in Mesopotamia from the late third millennium and in Canaan from 1200 BCE. The extant Mesopotamian texts are the Sumerian epic *Lugal-e,* and the Akkadian poems *Anzu* and *Enuma elish.* The Canaanite texts are the Baal cycle, which is preserved in the Ugaritic texts of pre-1200 BCE, and the Bible. The basic plot of the combat myth can be described, though it must be remembered that every version of the genre is unique. The combat myth states that a force (often depicted as a monster) threatens the cosmic and political order of the universe, instilling fear and confusion in the assembly of the gods. The assembly (or its president), unable to find an army commander among the older gods, turns to a young god to battle the hostile force. He successfully defeats the monster, creates the world (or restores the prethreat order), builds a palace, and is acclaimed king by the gods. In the biblical adaptation of the combat myth, the victory is the creation of the world or the creation of Israel.

The Temple is the earthly palace of God that symbolized kingship. Kingship was dramatic, achieved by the victory. In virtue of the victory, the heavenly beings acclaimed a god king. In the combat myth, the building of the victorious god's palace is the final chapter in the story. It symbolizes the god's kingship and cosmic and political order in the universe. In the Bible, the psalms of Zion (46, 48, 76, 84) mention or presume the victory of Yahweh at the holy mountain ("His dwelling place [has been established] in Zion. There he broke the flashing arrows," 76:2*b*-3*a*) and celebrate the royal rule exercised on the holy mountain ("When God rose up to establish judgment," 76:9*a*). Ancient readers would have viewed this as the final scene of the story.

The royal psalms (e.g., 2, 18, 72) root the Davidic kingship in the kingship of Yahweh. The divine decrees use kinship language to express God's new relationship to the Israelite king: "You are my son; today I have begotten you;" (2:7*b*) and, " 'You are my Father, / my God, and the Rock of my salvation!' / I will make him the firstborn, / the highest of the kings of the earth" (89:26-27). In both psalms, the king is installed after the divine victory. The Davidic king represents the divine king in governing the world, so that the victories of the Davidic king are equated with the primordial victories of Yahweh and those Yahweh will wage in the future. Yahweh protects the king as upholder of divine justice. Psalm 72 prays that the king rule with the justice of God (vv. 1-2); in Ps 101, the king promises to cast out evildoers from the Lord's city. The psalms regarded kingship as a divine institution and assumed that God governed the people through it.

Another instance of an implied narrative is the "deed" of Yahweh. In a large number of cases, especially in hymns and community laments, the deed is the exodus in the broad sense of liberation from Pharaoh, journey through the wilderness, and entry into Canaan. An example is Ps 114, which illustrates several important points.

> When Israel went out from Egypt,
>   the house of Jacob from a people of strange language,
> Judah became God's sanctuary,
>   Israel his dominion.
> The sea looked and fled;
>   Jordan turned back.
> The mountains skipped like rams,
>   the hills like lambs. (vv. 1-4)

This hymn gives praise for a divine deed—God's leading Israel out of Egypt into Judah/Israel (vv. 1-2) through the sea (vv. 3-6) and the wilderness (vv. 7-8). There is little wonder why this act is singled out for hymnic praise; it is the founding event that created Israel as a people with a God, a leader, laws, and land. Several further elements are noteworthy in this and other hymns. The poet is free to select, omit, and configure the narrative. For example, the people in Ps 114 go directly from Egypt to Judah/Israel through Sea/Jordan (vv. 1-4); only later are the wilderness miracles mentioned (v. 8). The poet mixes cosmic and historical language to describe the same event: Sea is personified as a hostile warrior fleeing before the divinely led march of Israel; mountains and seas totter before the victorious Yahweh who transforms the arid waste into fertilizing streams (v. 8). Other hymns such as Pss 135 and 136 also describe the deed of Yahweh as both creation (135:6-7 and 136:5-9) and history (135:8-12 and 136:10-22).

The divine deed as the creation of Israel is clearest in the communal laments. The community, feeling itself on the brink of extinction, recites or "remembers" liturgically the founding event in the hope that the Lord will renew it. In such laments, the historical recital is exactly tailored to fit the lament. Selection of details differs according to what is lamented. Psalm 89, lamenting the defeat of the Davidic king by his enemies, "remembers" Yahweh's sharing the fruits of his cosmogonic victory with David, making him "the highest of the kings of the earth" (89:27b). The lament asks: Are you abandoning your king, the one whom you appointed? Psalm 44 tells of Yahweh's conquest of Canaan as it asks why Israel's enemies move at will through the land. These and other community laments (e.g., 74, 77, 80, 83) remember essentially the same event—the creation of Israel as Yahweh's people—and use both cosmic and historic language.

THE PSALMS AS PRAYER FOR MODERN PEOPLE

Like the prayer "Our Father" in Matt 6:9-13 (Luke 11:2-4), the biblical psalms offer a way of praying. The wide range of genres encourage prayer in every phase of life—happiness and sadness, good health and illness, popularity and disgrace. Though most of the poems are communal, there are many individual laments and songs of trust. Even the latter, however, display a vivid sense of belonging to the holy people. Though the psalmists unhesitatingly take a theocentric view—the world is made for God—they balance it with the conviction that the Lord loves Israel and is passionate about its flourishing. The psalms encourage pray-ers to be honest and transparent before God and to that end portray the full range of emotions—depression, anger, joy, and ecstasy—so that anyone can find their own place within the spectrum.

In the Christian church, the psalms have been used in public worship and private prayer from earliest times. The Psalter is the most cited Old Testament book in the New Testament. Christians praying the psalms have traditionally linked their prayer with

Christ, whose humanity links his prayer to the prayer of the whole human race. Baptism creates a special bond between Christ and the members of his body, the church. In the words of Saint Augustine,

> No greater gift could God give to humans than to make their head the Word through whom he created the universe, and to unite them to him as members so that he might be Son of God and Son of man, one God with the Father, one man with humans. . . . He prays for us as our priest, prays in us as our head, and is the object of our prayer as our God. Let us recognize our voices in his voice and his voice in ours. (Augustine, In Psalmum 85, *Enarrationes in Psalmos, CCSL*, vol. 39, p. 1176, AT)

Though few doubt the splendor and warm humanity of the psalms, some find it difficult to make the psalms their daily prayer. The psalms seem violent and vindictive; their historical detail is excessive and confusing; their logic and rhetoric make them difficult to follow. These three difficulties must be addressed.

Why is there so much violence and war in the portrayal of God? In the Bible the concern is not the existence of God, but the ability of God to bless and save. The issue is power rather than existence. The arena in which power is displayed most clearly is the battlefield. Not surprisingly, therefore, Yahweh is often portrayed as a warrior God, rescuing Israel by defeating its enemies in war. The war imagery is, however, secondary to the main point: God is just and judges (i.e., rules) justly by upholding the faithful and righteous and putting down the wicked and rebellious.

Vindictive psalms are difficult especially for those who view Christianity as uniformly gentle and concerned primarily with the individual soul. "May the LORD cut off all flattering lips" (12:3a) is invoked against God's (and the psalmist's) enemies. Many individual laments pray that God severely punish the wicked. Most notorious is the curse against Babylon: "Happy shall they be who take your little ones and dash them against the rock" (137:9). Such "vindictive psalms" actually pray the just God to redress a here-and-now wrong, for God's power and glory would otherwise remain invisible. These psalms glow with zeal against every injustice disfiguring God's world. That zeal is expressed by poets who think in a nonabstractive manner. They conceive evil as embodied in particular people and wish for the elimination of unjust people, including their potential for living on in their children (cf. "their little ones" of Ps 137). The psalms generally entrust the carrying out of these wishes to God's hands in the conviction that only God can make the world truly just and good. Suffering pray-ers can, however, cry out to God to take action and even use words that appear extreme. Christian hungering and thirsting for divine justice (Matt 5:6) can prompt the praying of these psalms (at least in private) by leaving everything—execution and timetable—in God's hands. One must be cautious, of course, in praying these psalms. One's own enemies and demons are not necessarily God's. Like these psalmists, one must leave judgment to God.

The second difficulty is the detailed recitals of Israel's history in the psalms. Some are retellings of Israel's history, for example, Pss 78, 105-6, and 135-36. Others allude constantly to individual historical events. The psalms presuppose the reader is familiar with the people's history and finds it fascinating. Modern readers have to recognize that Israel encountered God not only in nature but in the events of their history as well. Decisive moments of that history—the journey from Egypt to Canaan, the law giving at Sinai, key battles, the words of leaders—were intensely revelatory for the people. They delighted in their active God and treasured the memory of divine interventions, which they narrated in a variety of versions. Like other ancient Near Eastern peoples, they accepted multiple versions of the same event, were attentive to slight variations in narrative detail, and knew nothing of history "as it exactly happened." Events of their history were sacramental in that they revealed God within the world. Christians are heirs to that history and should learn its main events. The story line can be learned quickly: the creation of the world, the call of Abraham and the story of the ancestral generations; the exodus and conquest; the period of the judges; the institution of the monarchy and the early kings Saul, David, and Solomon, and their successors; and the sixth-century exile and subsequent restoration.

The third difficulty is the dramatic logic of the poems. The psalms have given wonderful phrases and images to the English language: "The heavens are telling the glory of God; / and the firmament proclaims his handiwork" (19:1); "Be still, and know that I am God" (46:10); "Guard me as the apple of the eye; / hide me in the shadow of your wings" (17:8). Though the phrases are haunting, the logic of the poem in which they appear often is unclear. The logic of the psalms is, however, carefully crafted, for it seeks to express wonder and praise memorably and seeks also to persuade God to act. The rhetoric of the poems is sophisticated and repays careful study. This commentary makes a special effort to analyze the psalmists' arguments.

BOOK ONE
(PSALMS 1–41)

PSALM 1

Psalms 1 and 2 together introduce Book 1 and indeed the whole Psalter. Psalm 1 is concerned with the individual facing wickedness in the world, and Ps 2 is concerned with the king (representing Israel) confronting hostile nations. The two poems are linked in theme and vocabulary: Neither has a superscription (only Pss 10 and 33 in Book 1 are also without one); the declaration "happy are" opens Ps 1 and closes Ps 2; the Hebrew phrase rendered by NRSV "the way . . . will perish" in Ps 1:6 occurs again as "perish in the way" in Ps 2:11; the verb *hāgāh* occurs in Ps 1:2 ("meditate") and Ps 2:1 ("plot"). In the Western Greek text of Acts 13:33 a citation from Ps 2 is attributed to "the first psalm." In the Talmud the statement is made that Pss 1 and 2 form one psalm *(b. Ber. 9b)*.

Psalms 1 and 2 are structurally important in Book 1. Psalms 40–41 (a single poem), which close Book 1, echo sentiments and words from Pss 1 and 2. The beatitude "happy is/are" (1:1; 2:11) reappears in Pss 40:4 and 41:1. Psalm 40:8 reprises words from 1:2 in "I *delight* to do your will, O my God; / your *law* is within my heart."

Thematically, Pss 1 and 2 contrast the righteous individual with the wicked. The contrast of the wicked (usually plural) and the righteous (usually singular) is a feature of Wisdom literature and of several psalms. The contrast sometimes occurs as part of the metaphor of the "two ways." The "two ways" metaphor does not assign people to permanent categories of good and bad but rather dramatizes the moral life as two fundamental options that are in polar opposition. By their actions, people put themselves on one of two paths: the righteous (i.e., right with God) path or the wicked path. Each way has an inherent destiny or fate: Those on the right path flourish; those on the wrong path perish. Divine action affecting people on the paths can be expressed directly by verbs with God as subject or indirectly by impersonal or passive verbs ("the divine passive"). Psalms 1 and 2 portray the dualism in dramatic symbols—a flourishing tree versus dry and driven chaff; the true king of the world versus a group of plotting and doomed kings.

The antithesis between righteous and wicked is more frequent in Book 1 than in Books 2–5. Nearly half the Psalter's references to "the wicked" after Pss 1 and 2 occur in the next thirty-nine psalms. The theme of Ps 2—the Davidic king versus the world—occurs throughout the Psalter, as do royal psalms in general (e.g., Pss 18, 20-21, 45, 72, 101, 110, and 144). That the king is important in the Psalter is not surprising, for kingship is a central institution of Israel and symbolizes the kingship of Yahweh.

Literary Analysis

Psalm 1 develops logically from its opening beatitude "Happy are those." The declaration "happy is/are" (v. 1*a*, *'ašrê*; Gk. *makarios*, Lat. *beatus*) should be distinguished from "blessed is/are," which is a blessing of someone. The latter uses a different Hebrew word (*bārûk*; Gk. *eulogētos*, Lat. *benedictus*). A beatitude declares someone fortunate because of a quality possessed or a choice made; it is not a petition that God bless the person. The formula "happy is" occurs five times in Job and Proverbs and about twenty-four times in the Psalter. It is normally followed by the reason for the happiness, for example, "Happy are those whose transgression is forgiven . . . / Happy are those to whom the Lord imputes no iniquity" (32:1*a*-2*a*). Psalm 1:1-2 defines beatitude negatively in three cola (v. 1*bcd*) and positively in two cola (v. 2*ab*). Verse 3 elaborates the beatitude by the metaphor of a well-watered and productive fruit tree. Verses 4-5 elaborate the fate of the wicked by the metaphor of the wind-driven chaff. Verse 6 affirms the outcome of each way or type of behavior.

Verses 1-2 stretch out the "happy is" formula in an unusual fashion. Instead of mentioning the positive conduct declared happy (as in 32:1-2; 33:12; 40:4; 119:1-2), the verses list the actions the "happy" person has *not* done ("those who do *not* follow . . . take . . . sit"). Only afterwards is the positive action mentioned: "but their delight is in the law . . . they meditate." Delaying the positive reason creates a tension in the reader's mind, making the traditional formula seem more forceful. Other instances of unconventional style in verses 1-3 are the repetition of "law" *(tôrāh)* in verse 2 instead of its usual pairing with "word," and the repetition of "way" in verse 6 instead of one of its normal pairings (such as "path"). Also notable are the developed metaphors of the flourishing tree (v. 3) and the driven chaff (v. 4).

Exegetical Analysis

Happy is the righteous person (vv. 1-3)

As is usual in the Wisdom literature, the righteous person is in the singular number and the wicked are in the plural number in order to maximize the contrast between them. NRSV makes the righteous plural in order to make the translation gender inclusive. The primary reason for "happiness" in the psalm is removing oneself from the company of the wicked. The three clauses concerning the wicked in verse 1 make their effect cumulatively. The three activities, which are not sharply distinct, describe a way of life. The wicked are a group whose values and beliefs are not subject to God, so the righteous individual shuns them.

The translation of *tôrāh* in verse 2 is problematic. *Tôrāh* has several distinct meanings in the Bible: a priestly decision or "teaching," an instruction, legal material, and the Pentateuch. Most English translations render the word "law" (NRSV, REB, NIV). The NJPS rendering "teaching" is preferable, however. The antithesis to *tôrāh* in the psalm is the instruction ("advice" and "path") of the wicked (v. 1*bcd*), not their legal commands. In the Wisdom literature, which this psalm resembles, *tôrāh* refers to traditional teaching handed on by the teacher and the parents, not to the law. In the Pentateuch, *tôrāh* refers to narrative and poetry as well as to laws. When *tôrāh* occurs in a fixed word pair, its parallel is often "word" (*dābār*, Isa 2:3; 5:24; Mic 4:2; Zech 7:12). Hence the rendering "law" is too restrictive. The context suggests that *tôrāh* refers to the psalms that follow. The point of the introductory Ps 1 is to show that praying the psalms brings one wisdom and instruction.

"Meditate" (v. 2*b*) is, literally, to "mutter, recite." People in antiquity read aloud or at least moved their lips because the act of reading was not regarded as completely distinct from the act of speaking.

In verse 3 the righteous person is compared to a well-watered and fruitful tree. The same image occurs in Jer 17:7-8. By implication the metaphor compares God's *tôrāh* to life-giving waters. The imagery contrasts the fruitful, firmly rooted tree and barren, driven chaff.

Unhappy are the wicked (vv. 4-6)

In the dramatic perspective of the psalm, the choice is either to follow the will of the Lord or to follow the will of one's own group, the wicked. Only the former are declared "happy" (v. 1), rooted, and alive (v. 3). The wicked, on the other hand, are unrooted, pursued by the wind that drives them away (v. 4). "Drives away" (v. 4*b*) connotes aggressive and usually hostile pursuit as in Deut 28:22; Jer 29:18; and Amos 1:11. Divine activity is expressed indirectly in the wind that pursues the chaff. God is ultimately the agent. The punishment looming over the wicked is that they "will not stand in the judgment" (v. 5a). Though interpreted by a few commentators as judgment after death, the meaning is general and this-worldly; the wicked will not be able to survive a divine visitation. Only the righteous survive, as in Prov 10:25: "When the tempest passes, the wicked are no more, but the righteous are established forever."

The final verse (v. 6) summarizes, differentiating the destiny of the two ways: The Lord knows the way of the righteous, whereas the way of the wicked perishes (divine passive). The verb "knows" expresses a relationship.

Theological and Ethical Analysis

The opening poem of the Psalter declares that person fortunate who shuns the company of the wicked and stays focused on God's word in order to live in accord with it. Just as one must reject profane and wicked conduct to enter a holy area (cf. Isa 55 and Prov 9:1-6), so one must reject wicked companions to pray the sacred psalms. The poem suggests that the teaching ("law," v. 2) includes the entire Psalter. Those who pray it will enjoy life, for they touch its very source. The pray-er becomes like a tree rooted in rich streams of water.

The Fathers of the Church gave much attention to Ps 1. One group of patristic authors viewed the psalm as referring to Christ, for he was the man referred to in verse 1 ("Blessed is the man who walks not in the counsel of the wicked" RSV). This is called the christological interpretation. Among those holding that the "man" in Ps 1 was Christ were Hippolytus, Jerome, Augustine, Cassiodorus, and the later Latin tradition generally. Origen's opinion is uncertain.

Other patristic authors rejected a christological reference because the psalm made Christ obedient to the law (v. 2). For them, the speaker had to be a human being. This is called the ethical view and it seems to have been the majority patristic opinion.

Fathers holding the ethical view include Hilary, Ambrose, Jerome's *Tractates* (disputed attribution), Gregory of Nyssa, Cyril of Alexandria, and the Antiochene School. Most Greek commentators whose work survives, and Latin writers before Augustine, interpret the psalm as referring to human beings called to Christian discipleship. The later Latin tradition depends on Augustine's *Sermons*, which takes *all* the psalms as referring to the whole Christ.

Patristic psalm commentaries are not always a good indicator of the views of ordinary Christians, however. They tend to assume all psalms are christological and demonstrate that thesis in every psalm, often with esoteric ingenuity. Many citations of Ps 1 outside the commentaries take "the man" as every human being, for example, the letter of Ignatius to the Magnesians (XIII.1) and the Epistle of Barnabas (X.10). Such citations show that people then did what people do now: use the psalms primarily to express their own feelings in prayer. Only at a second level of reflection would people use the psalms to express their beliefs about Christ.

PSALM 2

As noted regarding Ps 1, Pss 1 and 2 serve as a preface to the Psalter. Several verbal links occur between the two poems. Psalm 2:11 ends with the same declaration ("happy") with which Ps 1:1 begins. The phrase "the way [of the wicked] will perish" in Ps 1:6 is echoed in Ps 2:11, "you will perish in the way." According to Ps 1, praying the psalms puts one on the right path and endows one with wisdom. According to Ps 2, Yahweh supports the Davidic king and defends Israel from the hostility of the nations.

Literary Analysis

Like Pss 18, 20–21, 45, 72, 101, 110, and 144, Ps 2 is a royal psalm. These psalms extol the king as the Lord's anointed and plead for the king in times of danger. Royal psalms cite the choice of the Davidic dynasty as a motive for God to intervene on the king's behalf. They appeal to the divine honor: Will you allow the nations to defeat the one you put on the throne?

In addition to traditions about the king, Ps 2 draws on traditions about Zion, the mountain of the Lord. Several songs of Zion (Pss 46, 48, 76, 84) tell how the holy mountain was attacked by enemy rulers and then miraculously saved. For example: "Then the kings assembled. . . . As soon as they saw [the divine splendor of Zion], . . . they were in panic, they took to flight" (48:4-5); "[On Zion the Lord] broke the flashing arrows, the shield, the sword, and the weapons of war" (76:3).

Psalm 2 contains a scornful taunt (vv. 1-3) plus a command (vv. 10-11). An oracle (vv. 4-9) intervenes between taunt and command. The taunting question is contemptuous: For what reason would earthly kings rail against the Lord and his anointed? Verse 4 gives the reason for the contempt in the two titles of God: "He who sits in the heavens" and "the LORD." According to the first title, God sits enthroned as king. From the impregnable throne, God roars with a warrior's anger (v. 5, cf. Isa 42:13), reminding the rebels that the Davidic king is legitimately anointed (v. 6). As the Lord's regent, the king dwells on Mount Zion. The scene in Ps 2 is reminiscent of Ps 48:4, where kings similarly stand defiantly at the base of the mountain.

A speaker cites an oracle in verses 7-9. Phrased in the elaborate language of the royal court, the oracle declares the king is the Lord's son and legitimately exercises his rule. Verse 9 gives the mandate authorizing the king to rule the nations. The rebellion of the nations violates the legitimate rule of the king whom Yahweh has placed on the throne. Following the oracle, the command in vv. 10-11 warns the kings to cease rebelling and do obeisance to the king.

Exegetical Analysis

The attack of the nations and their rebellious cry (vv. 1-3)

The nations of the world (v. 1), represented by their rulers (v. 2), are vassals of Yahweh and the Davidic king of Israel. The vassalship of the nations' kings was decided at creation when each nation was given its own deity and Yahweh, the Most High, chose Israel:

> When the Most High apportioned the nations,
>   when he divided humankind,
> he fixed the boundaries of the peoples
>   according to the number of the gods;
> the LORD's own portion was his people,
>   Jacob his allotted share. (Deut 32:8-9)

The sovereignty of the Davidic king is derived from the primordial sovereignty of Yahweh (e.g., 89:1-37).

Yahweh's response and oracle (vv. 4-6)

The Lord laughs scornfully at the rebellion and repeats the ancient decree installing the Davidic dynasty: "I have set my king on Zion, my holy hill" (v. 6). The oracle of sovereignty in verse 6 counters the human statement of independence in verse 3. The identification of the Lord as "He who sits [yôšēb] in the heavens," means "the One who is enthroned in the heavens." The verb yāšab means "to sit as a king" as in 1 Kgs 22:19; Ps 123:1; and Isa 6:1. God angrily denounces the kings as rebels. There is no report of a battle, however. Citing the decree suffices to end the battle. Verse 6 subtly underscores the divine will, as the first person pronouns I or my occur three times in the verse ("I have set," "my king," "my holy hill").

The divine decree installing the Davidic king (vv. 7-9)

After declaring the king to be the son of God (v. 7), the speaker declares that the Lord has given the lands of the nations to him. The king as God's son is mentioned in 2 Sam 7:14 ("I will be a father to him, and he shall be a son to me") and Ps 89:27 ("I will make him the firstborn, / the highest of the kings of the earth"). The Hebrew words for heritage and possession refer to land or territory. The Lord has complete and absolute ownership over the lands of the rebel kings!

The position of the king is extraordinarily exalted. In the ancient Near East, kingship belonged primarily to the gods, and the earthly king was the mediator and agent of the divine order. Elaborate royal ceremonies such as enthronements and anniversaries reinforced the claim to the heavenly origin of kingship. Some scholars postulate a New Year festival in which the kingship of Yahweh was celebrated; the Davidic king would likewise have been affirmed, since his power was derived from Yahweh. Some scholars are skeptical about such a festival, however. It is possible that this psalm is based on a ritual in which enemy kings (represented by officiants) stood outside the walls of the Temple or at the bottom of Mount Zion (cf. 48:4-7) and heard the kind of oracles and warnings found in this psalm. Such a ritual would explain the compact and elliptical descriptions in this and similar psalms (e.g., 46, 48, 114).

Kings of the world, be obedient to the Lord (vv. 10-11)

Since the king has a decree of authorization from the most powerful deity, the rebel kings should take note of it and behave accordingly, that is, withdraw from their impious campaign and submit to the king. They should act as wise kings: "serve the LORD with fear," that is, behave as vassal kings. The verb "to serve" here means political service as a vassal (e.g., Gen 25:23; Deut 28:48; 2 Kgs 25:24).

In verses 11b-12a, three of the four words in the Hebrew text are uncertain, though the general sense is clear from the context. NRSV adopts a common emendation, "kiss his feet." Kissing the feet of an overlord was a gesture of political obedience: "May his foes bow down before him, and his enemies lick the dust" (Ps 72:9; cf. Isa 49:23 and Mic 7:17). The Assyrian king Sennacherib boasts that the kings of Syria and Palestine brought gifts to him and kissed his feet (ANET, 287b). The famous "Black Obelisk" of the Assyrian King Shalmaneser III shows "Jehu, son of Omri" kissing his feet (ANEP, plate 351). If the nations do not submit to the Lord and his anointed, the Lord will destroy them in anger. His anger is already aroused (v. 5) and is liable to flame out again with dire consequences for them.

Theological and Ethical Analysis

The psalm celebrates the sovereignty of the Lord over the nations and the unrivaled prestige of the Lord's anointed. It does so in a narrative of a prototypical attack on the Lord's agent and place, the Davidic king and Mount Zion. The greater the assault, the greater the victory. Against the impious claim of independence from God, the psalmist simply points to the One Enthroned in the Heavens and the decree installing the regent on Zion.

The psalm has had three contexts in the history of the holy community that recited it. The first was when there was a living Davidic king. Though the Davidic Empire was a minor player in international politics for most of its history, Israel prayed the psalm to express its belief that the Lord had chosen Zion and the Davidic dynasty. In the Second Temple period, when Israel had no king, the people prayed the psalm to express its hope that a king would be raised up to deliver it from bondage to the nations. The third context is the Christian community's ongoing confession of the anointed one, the son of God, and his eternal rule.

A book heavily influenced by the imagery of Ps 2 is Wisdom of Solomon, a work of the first century BCE or early first century CE, probably written in Alexandria. It teaches that the Lord rules Gentile kings, though that rule is not yet fully visible.

> Listen therefore, O kings, and understand;
> learn, O judges of the ends of the earth.
> Give ear, you that rule over multitudes,
> and boast of many nations.
> For your dominion was given you from the Lord,
> and your sovereignty from the Most High;
> he will search out your works and inquire into your plans.
> (Wisd of Sol 6:1-3)

Wisdom of Solomon interprets Ps 2 within its own eschatological framework: God's kingdom is revealed through the righteous and wise one, the people of God.

The New Testament cites this psalm more than any other. Acts

4:25-28 view verses 1-2 as fulfilled in the hostility of Jews and Gentiles to "your holy servant Jesus, whom you anointed." Acts 13:33 interprets verse 7 ("You are my son; today I have begotten you") as a prediction of Jesus' resurrection, and Rom 1:4 likewise links sonship and resurrection. The background of the New Testament title "Christ" (NRSV: "anointed"; Heb. *māšîaḥ*, Gk. *christos*) owes something to this psalm, as does his other title "Son of God" (Ps 2:7*b*) in Matt 26:63, John 1:49, and elsewhere. In Rev 19:15 (cf. Rev 12:5), the Word of God strikes down the nations with an iron rod (cf. Ps 2:9). Finally, Heb 5:5 places Pss 2 and 110 together as a witness to the eternal priesthood of Christ.

PSALM 3

Psalm 3 is the first psalm in the Psalter with a superscription. The superscription attributes it to an incident in David's life. All subsequent psalms in Book 1 (Psalms 3–41) are also said to be "of David" except Pss 10 and 33. The mention of David relates this psalm to the preceding Ps 2, which extols the king. Similarly, the "many foes" of verse 1 who attack the psalmist are perhaps intended by the editor to refer to the hostile kings arising against the Lord's anointed in Ps 2. Finally, "his holy hill" (3:4) is the same phrase as in 2:6.

Literary Analysis

In this individual lament a loyal client of the Lord, overwhelmed by the attacks of numerous enemies, dramatizes the situation as a matter of life or death. In psalms of supplication the relationship between the psalmist and God often seems to be modeled after the social relationship of a powerful patron and a dependent client. The psalmist urgently asks God: Will you, my divine patron, allow me, your loyal client, to suffer serious injury or death? The triumph of the enemies makes the patron God look ineffectual and uncaring. The client appeals to the patron's sense of *noblesse oblige* rather than to the client's own virtue. Rather than risk appearing ineffectual, so the psalmist reasons, God will act for the sake of divine honor.

The psalm begins abruptly with a cry to God ("O LORD") followed immediately by the complaint (vv. 1-2). "Many" is used three times to describe the enemies in verses 1-2. They gloat that the psalmist has no "help" *(yĕšû'ātāh)* in God (v. 2b). The Hebrew word will be repeated in verse 8 ("deliverance") and again in the related Hebrew verb *hôšî'ēnî* ("Deliver me") in verse 7. The citation of the enemies' words is a deft touch, a reminder that the enemies are attacking not only the psalmist but God as well.

In verse 3, all three titles applied to God suggest rescue: "shield," "[restorer of] my glory," and "the one who lifts up my head." Despite the enemies' taunt, the psalmist's confidence in God remains unshaken—there *is* help for me in God. Verses 4-6 tell the stories of God's favor: Crying out in prayer in the Temple always elicits a divine response (v. 4), and going to sleep always ends with the psalmist waking safely (v. 5). The psalmist thus does not collapse before "ten thousands" (v. 6). "Ten thousands" *(ribĕbôt)* reflects the same Hebrew root as in "the many" *(rab,* vv. 1-2).

The petition itself is brief. "Rise up" (v. 7) alludes to the enemies' "rising up" in verse 1; "O LORD" reprises the invocations of verses 1 and 3; "deliver me" picks up the Hebrew words for "help" and "deliverance" in verses 2 and 8; "my God" reverses the enemies' use of "God" in verse 2. The last verse (v. 8) places in God's hands the timetable and mode of rescue. It asks for blessings for the psalmist and all the Lord's clients—the people of Israel.

NRSV proposes a five-part structure: verses 1-2, 3-4, 5-6, 7, and 8. Others combine verses 7-8 for a four-part structure. A three-part structure is also possible—verses 1-3, 4-6, and 7-8— and will be followed here. Each of the three sections begins with a prayer and ends with a statement of confidence.

Exegetical Analysis

The superscriptions of several psalms allude to David's flight from Saul, but only this one (and perhaps Ps 63) alludes to David's flight from Absalom's rebellion narrated in 2 Samuel 15–17. It is easy to see why the allusion occurs here since psalm themes appear already in the Samuel account: the mocking of one claiming divine protection (2 Sam 16:5-14), nocturnal danger (2 Sam 17:1), "the many" (2 Sam 15:13 and 17:11), and the diminished "glory" of the psalmist.

The complaint (vv. 1-3)

The cry to God is unadorned and direct. The idiom "rise against" in Pss 54:3 and 86:14 is parallel to "seek the life of." The enemies seek to kill the psalmist. Killing can be taken metaphorically of any danger from hostile people. "The many" in the Psalms and in Wisdom literature is used in opposition to an individual. Generally "the wicked" are in the plural number and "the righteous" is in the singular number. The taunt "there is no help for you in God" means either that the psalmist is excluded from God's protective care because of sin or that the Lord is unable to deliver the psalmist from trouble. Both meanings may be intended; at any rate, "the many" believe the psalmist is alone and helpless.

The psalmist trusts in God and contests the taunt (vv. 4-6)

Challenging "the many" directly, the psalmist invokes God with titles referring to a powerful helper: the "shield" protecting the loyal one (7:10; 18:2, 30, 35; 28:7); "my glory," that is, "one who restores my glory or dignity"; the one who "lifts up the head," meaning "removes one from the power of enemies" (27:6 and 140:9).

The verbs in verses 4-5 are in the imperfect tense, which in Hebrew can express habitual action, a future act, or in some uses, a past act. One can translate them as statements of habitual trust and hope: Whenever I cry to the Lord, he always answers me; whenever I go to bed, I always wake up safely. An indication that verses 4-5 are in fact statements of trust is that the verb in the third and climactic phrase, "I am not afraid of ten thousands of people" (v. 6), is surely an expression of trust. No matter how numerous the enemies, the psalmist refuses to yield to fear.

The psalmist's hope is informed by the experience of God's fidelity. "Holy hill" (v. 4*b*) refers to the site of the Temple. "Whenever I call out in the Temple, God responds. Whenever I lie down to sleep, God will protect me." To lie down and wake again means that God has protected the sleeper from the dangers of the night. It would be hard to imagine a more vivid portrayal of the client-patron relationship. The client is in essence telling God, My loyal trust in you never wavered, even when mobs came claiming you were powerless. You have always been responsive: When I prayed to you, you answered, when I went off to sleep, you let me see another day. Even in this danger, I will not let these enemies cut me off from you.

The petition (vv. 7-8)

Boldly using the verb *qûm* ("to rise up"), which described the rising up of enemies in verse 2, the psalmist cries out to God "Rise up!" And using the same Hebrew root as in "help" in verse 2, the psalmist cries out "Deliver me!" In verse 7*cd*, nearly all translators render Hebrew *kî* "for," but *kî* can introduce the grammatical construction known as the precative perfect, which is best translated in English as an imperative, such as "strike!" rather than NRSV "for you strike." What the psalmist seeks is symmetrical (poetic) justice: Because the enemies wounded me by their words, destroy their organs of speech ("cheek," "teeth"). The sentiment is unyielding, to be sure, but one should note that the psalmist leaves things in the Lord's hands. The just God will not leave genuine acts of injustice unredressed. In verse 8, the last statement, the psalmist moves away from individual concerns to think about the group. As the poem began with a group (the attackers), it ends with a group (the people of Israel), upon whom it asks a blessing.

Theological and Ethical Analysis

The pray-er is overwhelmed by the sheer number of enemies and by their devastating cry: You are beyond help! It is difficult to imagine a more discouraging situation. Endless waves of troubles and no one to help. Astonishingly, the first word out of the psalmist's mouth after the complaint (vv. 1-2) is "you." A relationship with God is immediately established, and the psalmist continues to look at God, expanding "you" with three titles of God as deliverer—shield, restorer of my dignity, and lifter of my head. Having turned first to God, the psalmist can turn to self—self as answered by God, protected in daily life by God, self as resisting fear. So emboldened, the psalmist takes the very words of the enemies and speaks them before God, willing to wait on God's timetable of justice. Such a courageous transaction ends, perhaps inevitably, with prayer for the community, for it is belonging to the beloved community that has made the psalmist trusting in the first place.

This poem is for times when troubles come in waves, each new one diminishing the capacity to cope. Such low points can be a time of grace, however. The psalm directs sufferers to God as a "You" and then toward self as a recipient of gracious moments that serve as reminders of God's commitment and steady strength.

PSALM 4

Psalms 3 and 4 are connected by common words and themes. "My honor" in 4:2 picks up "my glory" in 3:3; "vain words" in 4:2 is the same Hebrew word as "in vain" in 2:1; "answer" occurs in 3:4 and 4:1; "lie down and sleep" in 3:5 and 4:8; "There are many who say" occurs in the Psalter only in 3:2 and 4:6. Psalm 4 is also linked to Ps 2 by its great confidence in God and bold confronting of adversaries.

Literary Analysis

Though generally classed as an individual lament because of its opening cry in verse 1, complaint in verse 2, and statement of trust in verse 8, Ps 4 has elements of a song of trust in its confidence in God, and elements of a thanksgiving in its readiness to teach evildoers (cf. 32:8 and 34:11). Nonetheless, it is closest in type to the individual lament because of the immediate danger that threatens.

The poem begins like other laments—with a call to God for rescue. The complaint is stated indirectly in the spirited address to those attempting to destroy the psalmist's honor with lies (v. 2). The enemies of God are reminded that the psalmist is one of "the faithful" to whom God always shows loyalty and attention (v. 3). Armed with the protection that comes from friendship with God, the psalmist continues to warn all those who attack God's friends: Humbly recognize (v. 4*a*, lit. "tremble," NRSV: "when you are disturbed") the power of God here and show reverence toward it (v. 4). The Lord can be revered in only one way: performing the proper rituals and displaying complete trust. Verses 6-8 continue to make the case for loyalty to the Lord. The phrase, "there are many who say," suggests an individual righteous person (the psalmist) standing in opposition to a crowd. The many want the blessings (to "see some good") granted to the faithful clients of a powerful God and the psalmist does not hesitate to be a model of a prosperous client of the Lord (vv. 7-8).

In structure, the psalm alternates between prayer directed to God (vv. 1, 6-8) and advice directed to other people (vv. 2-5). Though the Hebrew rubric *selah* makes a division after verses 2 and 4, vocabulary and logic within the psalm suggest the subunits are verses 1-3 (the petition and a statement of hope in v. 3), verses 4-6 (an exhortation to others), and verses 7-8 (a statement of hope).

Exegetical Analysis

Plea to God who hears the cry of the faithful (vv. 1-3)

The subunit is marked by the reprise of words from verse 1 in verse 3*b* ("when I call," the divine names "God"/"the LORD," "hear"). "God of my right" (v. 1*a*) is a Hebrew phrase that means God who vindicates me. The verbs *to answer* and *to call* (v. 1*a*) are a fixed word pair, that is, they sometimes occur as near-synonyms in parallel verses. They express communication between God and a human being (e.g., 3:4; 20:9; Jer 7:13). Verses 1-3 show how profound is the human need to hear a response to a request. NRSV "You gave me room" (v. 1*b*) is best taken (with NIV) as a grammatical form that expresses a request: "Give me relief from my distress." NRSV (and many other translations) assume that the psalmist is reminding God of the long and gracious relationship they have enjoyed. In either case, metaphors of physical constraint in verse 1*b* ("distress" meaning "narrowness" and "room" meaning "freedom") show a God who liberates and creates space.

In verse 2, the psalmist's complaint to God is expressed indirectly, by words directed at the enemies. They are accused of destroying the honor of the psalmist, that is, destroying the psalmist's good name. Though modern readers are inclined to undervalue honor as a social good, ancients recognized its absolute necessity for living in a community. The phrases in verse 2*b*, "love vain words" and "seek after lies," are unique in the Bible. They suggest an ardent pursuit of what is contrary to God's will. The psalmist argues, therefore, that the enemies oppose the Lord, not simply the psalmist. Consequently, God should punish them.

Verse 3 is the first of the two statements of hope in the poem (the other being vv. 7-8). "Know" calls the enemies to recognize that the Lord has set apart the psalmist as a *ḥāsîd* ("a faithful one"), that is, one who has been faithful to the relationship with God. As the parallel verse 3*b* explains, the Lord hears the prayers of such a faithful friend. The verbs express habitual actions: When the psalmist cries out in need, God always hears. The singer almost boasts of this close relationship to the enemies, asserting something like "I have a very powerful friend in a high position."

Exhortation to the enemies to honor the Lord (vv. 4-6)

The psalmist urges others (presumably including the enemies) to become a *ḥāsîd*, that is, to be faithful to the demands of the relationship with God. NRSV's emendation of the verb "tremble" to "when you are disturbed" (v. 4*a*) is unnecessary. "Tremble" has the same meaning as in Exod 15:14, Deut 2:25, and Ps 99:1 ("The LORD is king; let the peoples tremble!"), that is, stand in awe. "Ponder it on your beds" (lit. "say to your heart") and "be silent" (be submissive) are commands to repent of persecuting the faithful. Pondering on one's bed symbolizes spontaneous private intent in contrast to commanded ritual performance. Compare Ps 63:6, "when I think of you on my bed, / and meditate on you in the watches of the night."

What constitutes faithfulness is immediately stated in verse 5: Offer the appropriate rituals and trust in the Lord. Worship and commit yourself to God; these are the actions that constitute fear of the Lord. Verse 6 makes its statement indirectly. It implies that the benefits "the many" seek will only be given to those faithful to the Lord. "To see good" is to enjoy prosperity. "The many" are contrasted with the individual righteous person, as often happens in Wisdom literature.

The final statement of trust (vv. 7-8)

The psalmist again (as in v. 3) intentionally becomes an example to "the many" and addresses God directly ("You have put gladness in my heart"). The translation of verse 7*b* is uncertain. NRSV and most translators take it as a comparative ("more than") and assume either that "*their* grain and wine" is the enemies' grain and wine or, more generally, other people's. NJPS translates without the comparative: "You put joy into my heart / when their grain and wine show increase," presumably, "I rejoice when crops abound." Both renderings are syntactically possible.

Verse 8, with its serene statement of trust, brings the reader back to verse 1, where the psalmist expects help from God. Lying down in sleep is a critical moment, for in sleep one cannot see dangers or defend oneself. The psalmist is unafraid, however, because the Lord makes it possible to lie down in safety *(betah)*, a word related to the verb meaning "put your trust in" (v. 5).

Theological and Ethical Analysis

This individual lament is full of serene confidence. Even the opening cry for help is less abrupt than most other laments. The enemies attack, not noting that the object of their attack is a faithful friend of God. They thereby make themselves enemies of God. Instead of calling down God's retaliation, however, the psalmist steps forward as an example of one blessed by the Lord and calls upon the enemies to drop their malicious scheming and direct their energies to being good servants of God. The psalmist seems to say: If you want divine blessings and protection, and wonder how you will attain them, look at me! I trust in the Lord, a living illustration of what it is to live confidently as one faithful to God and enjoy the blessings given to the holy people.

PSALM 5

Psalm 5 is not as closely connected to its surrounding poems as were the preceding four psalms. There are only a few links to earlier psalms. The phrase "all who take refuge in you" (v. 11) is identical to Ps 2:11 and its genre—individual lament—is the same as Pss 3 and 4.

Literary Analysis

The genre is individual lament, containing the usual elements of petition, lament, reference to enemies, and statement of hope. The poem opens with a direct and unadorned cry to the Lord (vv. 1-3), though, unusual for the genre, the plea turns into a kind of hymn, praising the character of God (vv. 4-6). The complaint— enemies are attacking—is in verses 9-10. The prayer is couched in both negative terms (v. 10) and positive terms (vv. 1-3, 11-12). The components of the genre are used with rare artistry.

In essence, the prayer asks protection from the wicked who are keeping the psalmist away from what is most precious and important: the presence of God in the Temple. Verses 1-3 appeal to God to pay attention to the petition. Verses 4-6 have two purposes: (1) They praise the Just One who cannot abide the presence of the wicked and sends them to their destruction, indirectly preparing for the psalmist's own request to enter the protection of the sanctuary in verses 7-8, and (2) the verses subtly remind God that the enemies belong to the wicked and thus should be destroyed (v. 6). Verses 7-8 state the psalmist's intent to enter the Temple (v. 7) and ask for God's help to travel safely to its precincts (v. 8). Verses 9-10 characterize the enemies and beg God to destroy them. The final verses (vv. 11-12) celebrate being in the divine presence.

The progress of thought is largely determined by the alternation of the two themes—seeking/enjoying God's presence and the threat of the wicked. The NRSV paragraph division accurately reflects the alternating themes: verses 1-3, 4-6, 7-8, 9-10, and 11-12.

Exegetical Analysis

In the superscription, NRSV "for the flutes" is a guess for the unique word *hanneḥîlôt*, which is apparently a technical term. NRSV deduces its meaning from etymology, linking the word to *ḥālîl* ("flute"). For the other musical terms, see the introduction.

Give heed to my words, O Lord (vv. 1-3)

All three verses ask for only one thing: to obtain a fair hearing from the God of justice and power. The petition is artfully constructed. Emphasis is given by the repeated address to God (four divine names and two pronouns, "to you") and by the central placement of the double title "my King and my God" between two occurrences of "the LORD" (vv. 1a, 3a). "For to you I pray" (v. 2c) is climactic as the third colon of a tricolon; it summarizes the prior petitions (vv. 1-2b) and brings them to a climax. The verb in verse 3a ("hear") should be interpreted, contrary to

NRSV, as a command ("hear my voice"), continuing the petitions of verses 1-2. The epithets "my King" and "my God" have specific connotations. "My king" implies *acting* like a king by granting favors and winning victories (as in 44:4; 74:12). In the Psalter, "my God" often occurs in contexts of danger where only the Lord can assure safety (e.g., 3:7; 7:1; 18:2). The assumption that God hears prayer in the morning, a special time for divine justice (v. 3; cf. Job 38:12-13, Ps 46:5), is based on the symbolic association of the light of the sun with justice. Thus the psalmist's sleepless night of anguish ends with the dawning light (as in 30:5; 59:16; 143:8). "I . . . watch" (v. 3*b*) expresses the faith-filled expectation of divine intervention as in Hab 2:1: "I will stand at my watchpost . . . / I *will keep watch* to see what [God] will say to me, / and what he will answer concerning my complaint." The mood is both anguished and expectant.

God cannot abide the wicked (vv. 4-6)

The verses praise God's justice through negative statements (vv. 4-5): Using the poetic figure of abstract for concrete ("wickedness" for the wicked person), the psalmist makes the claim that no evil person can stand in the divine sight. Praising God by listing acts abhorrent to divine justice occurs also in 2 Sam 14:14, Job 8:20, Ps 34:16. It is the task of justice to eradicate vice as well as to foster virtue. In Ps 101, for example, the Davidic king promises not only to embrace the good (vv. 1-2) but also to eliminate evil (vv. 3*c*-5, 7-8). "The LORD abhors" (v. 6*b*) often refers to what is ritually unacceptable. The assertion that the Lord will never permit the wicked to draw near to the sanctuary prepares for the psalmist's request to enter the Temple in verses 7-8.

Lead me to your holy sanctuary (vv. 7-8)

The section asserts positively what was asserted in negative terms in verses 4-6—the holiness of God. The place where God dwells, "your house" (v. 7*b*), is the polar opposite of the wickedness just described. To such a God, one must continually pray for a hearing (vv. 1-2). For such a God, one must be prepared to wait throughout the night (v. 3). Admittance to "your house" (v. 7b) is only through God's gracious invitation ("through the abundance of your steadfast love," v. 7a). To enter the holy place one must leave behind the wicked (vv. 4-6). In a world filled with wicked people, divine guidance is necessary to arrive safely at the sacred center. The psalmist prays for this guidance (v. 8).

Let the malicious plans of the wicked come back upon their heads (vv. 9-10)

Continuing the alternation of scenes of taking refuge in God (vv. 1-3, 7-8) and descriptions of the enemies of God and the psalmist (vv. 4-6), this section intensifies the portrait of the wicked by an accumulation of detail and a focus on their deceiving words. Lines 9a and 9d ("mouths" and "tongues") frame lines 9b and 9c ("hearts" and "throats"). NRSV "throats" for *qereb* (v. 9c) is misleading, for *qereb* means "inward part, midst" and is in parallel to "heart" as in Prov 14:33, Jer 4:14, and Ezek 11:19. The chiastic structure of verse 9 (mouths, hearts, inward parts, tongues) communicates that outwardly the wicked flatter while inwardly they plot destruction. In response to such malice and hypocrisy, verse 10 prays that the wicked be caught by their own malicious plans. The sought-for justice is poetic (or symmetrical). The psalmist also points out that their plots are actually directed against God, "for they have rebelled against you." God has a motive to retaliate.

The righteous will rejoice in the presence of the Lord (vv. 11-12)

With verses 11-12, the alternation of positive and negative scenes—taking refuge in God (vv. 1-3, 7-8, 11-12) and depictions of the wicked (vv. 4-6, 9-10)—comes to an end. The final panel portrays the Lord as the refuge of the righteous seeker. The emphasis, however, is not about seeking but enjoying the Lord and receiving blessings. Here all is rejoicing, celebrating, and receiving protection. The poem ends with the Lord blessing the righteous.

Theological and Ethical Analysis

Though the lament ends with an unusually vivid scene of rejoicing and intimacy with God (vv. 11-12), it is far from an idyllic poem. The singer knows first of all how to get the full attention of God in this time of crisis. Verses 1-3 courteously and insistently watch for God "more than those who watch for the morning" (130:6c). Though not panic-stricken, the singer is deeply aware of the malice of enemies and seeks therefore to reach the safety of the Lord's house. Verse 7 states the resolve to travel there. Verse 8, however, is key, for it prays for a safe journey: "Lead me, O LORD, in your righteousness." The pleasant words of the wicked conceal murderous intent. Only those who make the Lord their refuge can be truly safe and able to rejoice.

In one sense, the psalm is about the actual protection that the Temple offers someone in danger. Exodus 21:14 and 1 Kgs 1:51-53; 2:28-29 illustrate how sacred places offered asylum to those in danger of death. The poem uses the security of the sanctuary as a metaphor. The pray-er finds himself or herself in a crisis, surrounded by powerful forces of evil. Should one yield to despair or perhaps join in with the crowd? No, according to this psalm. God is just, and has provided a place of sanctuary in the world; and there is a way to it. Those who make God their refuge will experience protection and peace.

PSALM 6

Literary Analysis

This psalm has the characteristic features of an individual lament, some of them in the same verse: petition (vv. 1-2, 4-5), complaint (vv. 2-3, 6-7), reference to enemies (vv. 8-9), and statement of trust (vv. 8-10). Especially notable is the dramatic shift in tone in verse 8—from lament to serene confidence. This psalm is one of the seven designated as penitential psalms by the church, the others being Pss 32, 38, 51, 102, 130, and 143.

The poem is tightly structured in two major parts, verses 1-5 and 6-10, on the basis of word count (39 words in each) and the person addressed by the psalmist. Verses 1-5 address God, and verses 6-10 address God and the enemies. Each part is further divided into two subsections on the basis of word count and chiastic arrangement: Verses 1-3 and 8-10 have twenty-four words each, and verses 4-5 and 6-7 have fifteen words each. The NRSV paragraphing accurately recognizes the divisions: verses 1-3 (24 words); verses 4-5 (15 words); verses 6-7 (15 words); and verses 8-10 (24 words). The occurrences of pronouns guide the reader through the poem. Sections 1 and 2 have only first person or second person singular pronouns. Sections 3 and 4, on the other hand, have no second person pronouns. In section 1, the psalmist speaks to God about the enemies (and the affliction they cause) and in section 4 speaks to the enemies about God. Sections 2 and 4 are cross-linked by imperative verbs, "turn" (*sûbāh*, with God as object) in verse 4*a*, and "depart" (*sûrû*, with the enemies as object) in verse 8*a*.

Exegetical Analysis

In the superscription, the exact nature of NRSV "stringed instruments" is unknown. "According to The Sheminith" may refer to a melody or to an eight-stringed instrument.

Cease your punishment, for I am exhausted
and terrified (vv. 1-3)

The singer is physically ill ("I am languishing," "my bones are shaking," v. 2) and emotionally exhausted (vv. 6-7). The mention of God's "anger" and "wrath" (v. 1) suggests that the psalmist unquestioningly accepts the illness as punishment for sin. Though God can rebuke and discipline for positive educational purposes (as in Deut 8:5 and Prov 3:12), the rebuking and disciplining in verse 1 are punishment. The eightfold repetition in the poem of the divine name Lord lends an air of intimacy and urgency to the encounter. One need not take the illness literally; it can be a metaphor for any kind of suffering.

The motive proposed in verses 2-3 for God to stop punishing is that the sufferer is physically spent and shaking with terror. There is no part of the sufferer's body or psyche left to strike. This defense is not based on any claim of innocence but on the hope that God will "be gracious" (v. 2a), that is, cease punishing according to strict justice and begin to "heal me." In describing the psalmist's suffering, the poem places in parallel "my bones" (v. 2b) and "my soul" (nepeš, v. 3a); both nouns are subjects of the same verb, "to shake with terror." The two words do not refer to the material and the spiritual aspects of the self, for biblical people conceived the human person not as a body-soul composite but as an animated body. "Soul" literally is the throat area, where life was especially visible in the breath and heartbeat. The literary figure is called metonymy: the use of the name of one thing for that of another of which it is a cause (e.g., eye is the cause of vision). By metonymy, "soul" means "life." The phrases "my bones" and "my soul" mean the whole body.

The question, "How long?" (v. 3b) is a genuine question since divine chastisements were often regarded as imposed for a predetermined period of time. An example is the choice of punishment offered to David in 2 Sam 24:13 of three years, three months, or three days. It helps to bear suffering if one knows how long it will last and that it is not indefinite.

Turn from your anger, O Lord, and allow me to praise you (vv. 4-5)

The section begins with an imperative addressed to God, šûbāh ("turn"). The word will be echoed in verse 8 by another imperative addressed to the enemies, sûrû ("depart"). In the first section, the motive for God to rescue the psalmist was the psalmist's desperate state ("I am languishing"). Here, differently, the motive is "for the sake of your steadfast love" (v. 4b). NJPS translates the phrase "as befits Your faithfulness." The psalmist appeals to God's "steadfast love" (ḥesed), which in this context refers to the claims of the relationship between God and the psalmist. Israel entered into such a relationship with the Lord at the exodus and renewed it regularly. The psalmist now appeals to that relationship between Israel and the Lord. Israel is the special people of Yahweh, the Lord, and has an obligation to praise the Lord. If one is away from Israel and no longer among the living, one cannot give praise. The dead in Sheol (the underworld abode of the dead) exist in a shadowy state and take no part in earthly life including the worship Israel offered (see 1 Sam 28:11-19). For the sake of praise, it is therefore in the Lord's interest to keep the singer from slipping away into Sheol.

Expansion of the complaint (vv. 6-7)

Memorably depicting grief and helplessness, these verses attempt to move God to heal instead of punish. The description of emotion focuses on tears and the damage that constant weeping does to the eyes. Tears were regarded as liquid welling up from the abdomen and making their way through the head as tears. They symbolize interior anguish and communicate to others an individual's pain. The bed is a place where one's deeply personal attitudes and feelings are freely expressed (as in 4:4 and 63:6). When alone, the sufferer pours forth tears of misery.

Verse 7b mentions "my foes" for the first time in the poem and blames the trouble on them. How can this blaming of enemies as the cause of suffering be reconciled with earlier statements that the suffering was caused by illness? Some hypothesize that enemies have put a curse of illness on the psalmist, but there is no evidence for such a curse. The most common explanation is that the enemies are like Job's friends. To them, one afflicted with serious illness is by definition a sinner deserving to be shunned. Perhaps the explanation is more simple and mundane. Illness can diminish anyone virtually to a nonperson. One becomes the object of others' care and is no longer an active agent. The sufferer protests against being reduced to a nonentity by other members of the community.

My return to health will shame my enemies (vv. 8-10)

With verse 8, there is a sudden change of mood from anguish to joyous certainty. Scholars cannot account for the change with confidence. One explanation is that an officiant would have stepped forward at this point in the liturgical ceremony to utter an oracle of salvation to the sufferer, as the priest Eli did to the grieving Hannah in 1 Sam 1:17. The petitioner would have taken it as God's assurance and agreed to live by it. Another explanation is that the very process of lamenting revived the sufferer's spirit, which would have been expressed in such statements as verses 8-10. At any rate, the sufferer is changed, "for the LORD has heard the sound of my weeping" (v. 8*b*), giving a profound sense of assurance (v. 9).

To pray that one's enemies be shamed (v. 10) is basically to pray that they and their plans be frustrated and that this frustration be seen by everyone. "Shame" is not primarily the modern sense of painful consciousness of guilt but something more objective: the humiliation that attaches to those whose confident expectations are dashed. The whole world sees that they placed their hopes on the wrong thing. The enemies hoped for the psalmist's death and annihilation and now they see the psalmist get up from the sickbed and return to the community.

Theological and Ethical Analysis

The simplicity of this psalm is an antidote to excessively complicated prayer. The poem simply accepts the serious illness as coming from God. It prays for relief and healing, proposing two motives for God to act: I am at the end of my rope and you are faithful to our relationship. My life is ebbing away as my enemies watch in approval. Help me and disappoint them!

Two verses of the psalm have been used by New Testament writers. Verse 4 is cited by John 12:27 to illustrate the sufferings of Jesus just prior to his passion. Verse 8 is used in Matt 7:23 and Luke 13:27 of Jesus sending away false followers.

The psalm can be a model for modern pray-ers by its unquestioning acceptance of things that must be, by its frank recording of all the diminishments of sickness (bodily, spiritual, and social), by its childlike appeal to God's interest in preserving a worthy chorister, and by its all-too-human delight at the frustration of malicious enemies. All these experiences are woven into a beautiful poem of enduring value.

PSALM 7

Literary Analysis

In genre, the poem is an individual lament, made distinctive by the oath of innocence and the movement of the prayer from personal justice to world justice. The logic of the poem is not difficult to follow. The psalmist, pursued by enemies, flees to the Lord for refuge, swearing an oath that he or she has not done the act that provoked the pursuit (vv. 1-5). The psalmist urges the Lord to rise up in passionate defense and respect the sincerity of the plea (vv. 6-8). The plea broadens into a prayer that the Lord defend every just person and frustrate the designs of every wicked person (vv. 9-16). The poem ends with a statement of trust that the righteous God will indeed bring about justice (v. 17).

The poem has only a few formal indicators to help readers find their way. "LORD" *(YHWH)* occurs seven times and "God" *('elōhîm)* occurs five times, the latter term in a sense replacing the divine name Yahweh in verses 9-16. Verse 8 seems to mark the halfway point, for there are sixty-five Hebrew words in verses 1-8 and sixty-six in verses 9-17; verses 1-5 are marked off as a section by the repetition of "pursuers/pursue" in verses 1 and 5 and the Hebrew word *napšî* (NRSV: "me") in verses 2 and 5. With verse 9, the petition broadens into a desire for universal justice. The NRSV outline is satisfactory, though one need not make a separate section of verses 9-11 and 12-16.

Exegetical Analysis

Taking refuge in the Lord and swearing an oath of innocence (vv. 1-5)

As noted, verse 5 reprises words from verses 1 and 2, "me" *(napśî)* and "pursuers/pursue," bringing the section to its conclusion. The language suggests that the pray-er is actually being pursued by enemies. Because of the sanctity of the altar, a person who inadvertently committed a crime could touch the altar and claim sanctuary; the privilege could not be claimed for a willful crime (Exod 21:14; 1 Kgs 2:28-35). The palmist's claim of innocence is not recognized by the pursuers. Verse 2 is more vivid than might appear in English translation. The first colon is, literally, "lest (the pursuer) tear my throat *[napśî]* like a lion." Lions go for the throat. "O LORD my God" in verse 3*a* repeats verbatim the divine title in verse 1*a*, closely tying the oath with arrival at the refuge. Verse 4*b* heightens the oath of verse 4*a*, that is, I have neither hurt my friends nor sought vengeance on my foes. The oath has a risk. If the psalmist is not telling the full truth, the enemy can crash into the sanctuary and inflict death with impunity (v. 5).

Plea for personal vindication (vv. 6-8)

The prayer for vindication arises from trust that the pursuer's claim is groundless and that God acts justly. The psalmist's appeal is quite unlike a modern appeal to a judge to hand down a fair and objective verdict. The psalmist wants a divine intervention rather than a neutral verdict. The pleas that God act with anger and wake up (v. 6) ask the Divine Warrior to take quick and effective action. Worshipers sometimes shouted "Wake up!" to God (e.g., Pss 44:23; 59:5; Isa 51:9), presuming that gods, like humans, needed their rest. "Let the assembly . . . be gathered around you" (v. 7): God, like any judge, would be surrounded by petitioners before taking the highest judgment seat. Acknowledging the Lord's role as judge, the psalmist demands action.

Plea for public and universal vindication (vv. 9-16)

The boundary between this section and the preceding is not very clear. NRSV begins a new section, presumably because the perspective becomes broader at this point. The psalmist wants more than personal vindication; the psalmist wants a just *world*. The phraseology is typically biblical: Let the wicked come to an end and the righteous be established (v. 9). Verses 9*d* and 11*a* can be translated in either of two ways, respectively, "O righteous God" and "God is a righteous judge" (NRSV) or "God of the righteous person" and "vindicator of the righteous." At any rate, the justice of God is depicted in its negative aspect of destroying evil rather than upholding what is right: "God who has indignation every day" (v. 11*b*). The harsh tone of the poem was set in the opening verses by the desperation of the asylum seeker.

Verses 12-16 are interpreted in different ways by commentators. Who is the subject of the verbs in verses 12-13? NRSV presumes the wicked are the subject of the first verb, and God is the subject of the remaining verbs. Others (e.g., NIV) understand God as the subject of all the verbs ("If [God] does not relent, he will sharpen his sword"). The renderings of NJPS, REB, and Ehrlich are most persuasive: The wicked person is the subject of all the verbs in verses 12-16. REB, for example, translates verses 12-13 "The enemy sharpens his sword again. . . . It is against himself he has prepared his deadly shafts." Evil actions come back upon the head of the one who does them. Divine causality is here expressed indirectly. God "judges" the wicked by not allowing their wicked plans to succeed; their actions are frustrated. Some psalms show God stopping evil directly, of course, but in this psalm evil is defeated indirectly.

Statement of trust (v. 17)

Individual laments often contain a statement of trust such as this. The troubled psalmist is willing to live as if God had already brought relief, promising songs prior to the rescue in the certainty that God will deliver. Telling of the rescue, even in anticipation, broadens the circle of those who acknowledge God's sovereignty.

Theological and Ethical Analysis

The example of faith is extraordinary. Pursued by enemies, the singer thinks of running to the only refuge, the place where the Lord dwells. Perhaps it is literally the dwelling of the Lord, the Temple in Zion. Perhaps it is metaphorical, the Lord as refuge. There are no human protectors, no police, where the psalmist has taken refuge. The only protector is the Lord who does justice to the innocent and to the wicked. Perhaps the deep faith of the psalmist will rub off on the one who prays this psalm. Perhaps one will begin to trust the Lord and experience one's personal desires growing into a passion that God's will be done in all parts of the world. Perhaps one will learn that God's just purposes are carried out in ways invisible to human eyes, and one will be able to "give to the LORD the thanks due to his righteousness" (v. 17).

PSALM 8

Psalm 8 is a perennial favorite in the Psalter for its remarkable sense of wonder—at the grandeur of the heavens, the artistry of God, and the dignity of human beings. In a sense, it is the biblical version of the famous chorus of the Greek dramatist Sophocles from the fifth century BCE, "Many wonders there be, but naught more wonderful than man" (Sophocles, *Antigone*, line 333, LCL). Psalm 8 portrays glorious creator and wonderful creature. It has the distinction of being the first biblical text to reach the moon, being brought there in the first manned landing by *Apollo 11* on July 20, 1969. Psalm 8 was an apt choice, for it celebrates the majesty of the heavens and the dominion of human beings. (McCann 1996, 710-11)

Literary Analysis

In genre, Ps 8 is a hymn, the first in the Psalter. Hymns invite humans to give praise to God because of something that

God has done. Psalm 8 quickly sweeps the pray-er into rapt appreciation of the glories of heaven and earth. As in many hymns, the opening verse is repeated at the end of the poem. Though several major translations make no stanza divisions, NRSV divides the verses: 1*ab*, 1*c*-2, 3-4, 5-8, 9. Verses 1*ab* and 9 are the frame.

Exegetical Analysis

Wonder at the divine name (v. 1)

God is invoked as Yahweh, Israel's Lord, even though the topic is the human race, not Israel as such. Just as one's own name presents one to others, so the divine name presents God to the world. But where is that name to be found? A god can cause his name to dwell in a place so that worshipers can come and encounter him there. First Kings 8:29 views the Temple as a place where the Lord's name dwells, enabling Israel to meet the Lord there: "My name shall be [in the Temple]." In Ps 8, however, the name of Israel's Lord is not confined to one place; it extends throughout the entire earth. The psalm also says that name of the Lord is "presented" in some fashion by human beings. The divine name *(šēm)* on earth (v. 1*b*) is parallel to the divine splendor *(hôd)* in heaven (v. 1*c*). The same word pair occurs in 148:13, "Let them praise the name of the Lord, / for his *name* alone is exalted; / his *glory* is above earth and heaven."

Verse 1*c* is uncertain. Literally, it reads, "you who endow the heavens with your splendor." Though often placed with the verses following, it is closer in sense to the opening couplet. "How majestic is your name in all the earth, how [. . . ?] your splendor in the heavens." Both heaven and earth belong to the Lord and express divine splendor.

Wonder at the dignity of the human race (vv. 2-8)

Verse 2 is difficult to interpret and may be corrupt. "Foes" and "enemy" may be a reference to the Lord's creation victory over primordial enemies as in Pss 89 and 93. The victory established the Lord's sovereignty over heaven and earth and elicited praise from all beings. In some accounts of the victory (e.g., *Enuma elish,* vi.1-34), the victorious deity immediately created human beings to tend the earth, a detail that would account for the focus on human beings in 8:4-8. The unclear verse 2 has fostered several interpretations. One interpretation is Matt 21:16 where Jesus says to the chief priests and scribes angered by the children's Hosannas: "Yes; have you never read, 'Out of the mouths of infants and nursing babies you have prepared praise for yourself'?" Jesus in Matthew assumes God must be behind the praise because it comes from such an unlikely source.

Verses 3-5 contrast heaven and earth, especially their respective inhabitants, "divine beings" (v. 5, *'elōhîm*) and human beings (v. 4). NRSV renders *'elōhîm* in verse 5a as "God" and prints alternate translations—"divine beings" or "angels"—in the margin. Others translate "a little less than divine" (Delitzsch, NJPS). It is better, however, to follow the majority of translators in rendering *'elōhîm* as "divine beings," which is a well-attested meaning in the Bible (e.g., Gen 6:2, 4; Job 1:6; Ps 97:7). Contemplating the heavens in verse 3, the singer thinks of the dwellers of earth, "human beings" (*'enôš,* lit. "man, human") and "mortals" (*ben 'ādām,* lit. "son of man," i.e., human being). "What are human beings?" is an expression of wonder that in so vast a universe, beings living in only a small part of it have so noble and important a role. Though unfurling the vast reaches of space and directing the movement of the stars and moon, God gives special attention to humans on earth. The psalm gives no reason for God so regarding them. It is simply God's choice to attend to them.

The phrase, "a little lower than divine beings" (NRSV: "God"), has to be interpreted within ancient Near Eastern cosmological conceptions in which heaven and earth are parallel spheres. The heavenly world is ruled by God through heavenly servants. The earthly world, subordinate yet parallel to the heavenly world, is ruled by human servants. The rule of humans is depicted with royal language. They are endowed with glory and honor like the king in 21:5: "His *glory* is great through your help; / *splendor* and majesty you bestow on him." Humans have dominion over the three spheres of earthly life: land, air, and sea (vv. 7-8).

Royal rule by the human race is a startling exception to the role of humans in the ancient Near East. Ancient cosmogonies without exception told how human beings were created as slaves of the gods; their job was to maintain the universe for their divine masters and see to their food, clothing, and honor. Biblical cosmogonies differ. Human beings are not mere slaves because the biblical God is not needy in the same sense as the gods of the extrabiblical cosmogonies. A good example of the biblical difference is Gen 1, which chooses language of kingship to describe human beings: Humans are made in the image and likeness of God; they subdue the earth; they have dominion over its creatures. Psalm 8 shares this view of human beings and their noble vocation.

Wonder at the divine name (v. 9)

The singer now moves from praise of the dignity and task of human beings (vv. 1c-8) to acknowledging the name of the maker of all things, the Lord, powerful over earth.

Theological and Ethical Analysis

This hymn exalts God and human beings in the same breath. Humans have their dignity from God and the very thought of it inspires awe in the psalmist. The poet passes over in silence the vast number of heavenly beings who traditionally were thought to be God's emissaries in governing the world in order to focus on human beings and their royal, albeit delegated, role. "Man is a king," writes Franz Delitzsch, "and not a king without territory; the world around, with the works of creative wisdom which fill it, is his kingdom" (p. 155). "Wonder . . . is the basis of Worship," wrote Thomas Carlyle (*Sartor Resartus*, book 1, chap. 10), and Ps 8 stirs up that wonder and invites praise.

The Bible often focuses on the limits of life and the evil that humans do. Psalm 8 offers a somewhat different perspective: God's beautiful and coherent world with human beings occupying a noble and important place. The grandeur of the universe enhances rather than diminishes their place and vocation. As servants of the Lord, they rule over land, air, and sea. The psalm invites people to wonder at this work of God.

The words of Ps 8:6*b*, "you have put all things under [his] feet," is applied to Jesus in 1 Cor 15:27 and Eph 1:22 in order to affirm all things will be subject to him in the new age. Heb 2:5-9 quotes Ps 8:4-6 to show that "we do see Jesus, who for a little while was made lower than the angels, now crowned with glory and honor because of the suffering of death."

PSALMS 9–10

Psalms 9–10 are actually one psalm and were handed down as a single poem in the Septuagint. The unity of the poem is clear: Ps 10 lacks a heading (one of only four psalms in Book 1 without a heading); Pss 9–10 share vocabulary such as "afflicted, poor, oppressed" (*'onî,* 9:12, 18; 10:2, 9, 12), "forget" (*šākaḥ,* 9:12, 18; 10:11, 12), "seek, call to mind" (*dāraš,* 9:10, 12; 10:13, 15); and, most telling, a single acrostic structure governs the whole. In an acrostic poem, verses begin with a successive letter of the Hebrew alphabet (e.g., Pss 25, 34, 37, 111, 112, 119, and 145). In Psalms 9–10, textual damage has obscured the acrostic sequence; the consonants *d, ḥ, m, n, s,* and *ṣ* are missing. It is easy to understand why scribes arrived at the judgment that there were two poems, since the acrostic structure has been obscured by textual corruption.

Literary Analysis

The acrostic structure in itself does not reveal much about the poetic logic. Genre is a better guide. Psalm 9:1-12 has the appearance of a thanksgiving (though the rescues are general, not particular). Psalm 9:13-20 seems to be an individual lament because its opening verse "Be gracious to me, O LORD" (v. 13) begins other laments (e.g., Pss 56 and 67). The immediately following verses, however, dispel the mood of lament by expressing lively hope in God's vindication (vv. 15-18). Psalm 10 has all the signs of a lament—urgent pleas, portrayals of the wicked and their denials of God's justice, and a statement of trust (10:14-18).

The poem makes highly effective use of contrasts and wordplay. The most obvious contrast is between the oppressor and the oppressed. The oppressors (e.g., "enemy," "nations," "the wicked") are mentioned approximately seventeen times and the oppressed (e.g., "oppressed," "afflicted," "needy," "orphan") about fourteen times. The wicked attack the righteous, of course, but they also attack God by denying divine care for the world (10:3-6, 11-13). An example of wordplay is "forget," which in Pss 9:12, 18; 10:12 refers to God not forgetting the oppressed and in Ps 10:11 is an accusation that God forgets justice. Another wordplay is the Hebrew word *dāraš*, which can mean "to be mindful, seek out, trust in, call to account." In 9:10, 12; 10:15 it is used positively (the poor "put their trust in you," God "is mindful of them," "seek out their wickedness"), and in 10:13 it is used in a negative fashion by the wicked ("[God] will not call us to account"). The psalm is also unified by the repetition of words and concepts. The concept of unlimited duration is expressed nine times in words such as "forever," "always," "throughout all generations," "never," and "no more." It suggests that the flourishing of the wicked will be brief in contrast to the unlimited duration of God's reign. Similarly, "name" occurs in 9:2*b*, 5*b*, and 10*a*. The first and last occurrences refer to the divine name presenting God to the worshiper, whereas the middle occurrence refers to the name of the wicked, which will be destroyed forever (i.e., their descendants).

The psalm was probably composed in the postexilic period when Israel was no longer an independent country. Persian occupation lasted from 539–333 BCE during which time Israel would have learned to count "the nations" (9:5, 15, 17, 19, 20; 10:16) among its oppressors. The poem moves back and forth between Godforsakenness and triumph, exactly what one would expect in a community that believed it was the Lord's people yet experienced itself as a neglected province in a vast empire.

Exegetical Analysis

I give thanks to the Lord who rescues me and judges the world with justice (9:1-12)

The poem begins as a thanksgiving, and praise dominates throughout, even though lament is powerfully represented. The object of praise, "your wonderful deeds" (v. 1*b*), would surely include the exodus. As the founding event of Israel, the exodus implicitly contains the hope that God will be faithful to the founding deed and continue to liberate and upbuild Israel. Psalmic praise is usually grounded in a reason, and this praise is no different. Verses 3-4 mention that God defeated "my enemies" and "sat on the throne giving righteous judgment." Paralleling the personal story of rescue and vindication is the story of national rescue and vindication (vv. 5-8). God has rebuked the nations and "sits enthroned forever" (v. 7*a*). The God who judges (or rescues) the singer is the same God who rebuked the nations and sits enthroned as judge of the world.

Verses 9-10 offer a reflection on the God who protects individuals (vv. 3-4) and the nation (vv. 5-8), concluding that the Lord is a "stronghold" (v. 9), a place to flee for protection when trouble comes. To "know your name" means to use the name of Yahweh in prayer and in oaths. The name of Yahweh is associated with a particular moment in the nation's history, the exodus from Egypt (see Exod 3:13-16), and thus connotes divine mercy and power to liberate. "To know the name" is to have a relationship with this faithful God. Verse 11 echoes v. 1, inviting all the hearers to do what the singer alone did: "sing praises to the Lord, . . . / declare his deeds among the peoples (*'ammîm*)." This last word is different from the word for "the nations" (*gôyîm*), who are regarded as enemies elsewhere in the psalm.

*Have mercy on me that I may recount your justice
in Zion (9:13-20)*

Part 2 begins like other laments with the plea "Be gracious to me," but shifts to a lyrical tone by its promise to give praise "in *the gates* of daughter Zion" (v. 14*b*) to "the one who lifts me up from *the gates* of death" (v. 13*c*). The contrast of "the gates" resembles the other contrasts of "forget" and "seek" noted under Literary Analysis. Instead of the anguished pleading one expects in a lament, the singer simply asserts the working of divine justice in traditional imagery such as nations being caught in the pit they dug to trap others (v. 15). Being caught in the pit shows God is at work, for through this event "The LORD has made himself known" (v. 16). Similar affirmations are found in the two following verses (vv. 17-18). Instead of complaint and petition, one finds confident confession. Part 2 ends with a vigorous prayer (vv. 19-20).

*O Lord, why do you let the wicked flourish?
Act as a judge! (10:1-18)*

With the familiar cry of lament, "why?" (as in 42:5; 44:24; 88:14), the singer begins a lament in full earnest. The specific complaint is the persecution of the poor by the wicked (10:2*a*). The singer can only hope that the self-entrapment of the wicked just asserted in 9:15-17 will actually take place (10:2*b*). The singer now turns to the wicked; verses 3-11 are entirely devoted to describing their malice. Extended descriptions of wicked people are found elsewhere in the Bible (Ps 58:3-5, Prov 6:12-15, Isa 59:4-8). The length and accumulation of detail in such descriptions serve to intensify the malice. The sin of the wicked in verses 3-11 is twofold: persecution of the poor and dismissal of God as uncaring and ineffectual. The dismissal of God is decided in the hearts, that is, the minds of the wicked (10:3-4, 6, 11). Their persecution of the poor is carried out through their actions, which are portrayed by mentioning their bodily organs: lying mouths and tongues (v. 7), stealthy eyes (vv. 8*c*-9), and hands and feet (implied in vv. 9*b*-10*b*). The mention of inner organs (vv. 3-4, 6, 11) alternates with the mention of outer organs.

The cry "Rise up, O LORD" (v. 12a) abruptly breaks the description of pure evil. The psalmist cannot understand how God can let such blasphemous rebellion take place (v. 13). The remainder of the poem is an urgent appeal to act on the "trouble and grief" (v. 14a) that God cannot avoid seeing. Look on the helpless who "commit themselves to you" (v. 14c), "hear the desire of the meek" (v. 17a), "do justice for the orphan" (v. 18a). The acclamation "The LORD is king forever" (v. 16a) not only affirms divine sovereignty but also urges the Lord to *act* like a king by doing justice, in this case, by eliminating the nations from his land. The psalmist believes that it is necessary to bring to the Lord's attention the evil humans do against God and their fellows. When such a powerful being sees, justice will not be long delayed. Describe the malice and God will act.

Theological and Ethical Analysis

The singer records three successive experiences of God. The first (9:1-12) is one of joyous recognition of God's benefits to the singer (9:3-4) and the nation (9:5-8). Salvation functions as judgment, for it is exercised in favor of the psalmist and the people and against the wicked and the nations. Such powerful judgments invite reflection and praise (9:9-12). The second experience is crying for help on the occasion of an attack (9:13-14). The cry for help, however, turns into a serene reflection on the ways of God's justice in the world: God's rule is indirect, evildoers' own malice comes down upon their heads (9:15-18). The third experience is expressed in a genuine lament that is developed at length (10:1-18). The singer is scandalized that God can stand aloof while the wicked exploit the vulnerable and brazenly deny that God will do anything about it. The same singer who exulted earlier in God as helper and just judge (9:1-8) is deeply pained at the divine silence. The third part ends in an inner struggle: refusal to believe God does not see (contrary to the claim of the wicked), insistence that God act now, and assertions that God will be the patron of the orphan.

One who believes in God yet attends to real events in the world will inevitably be drawn into a personal struggle and find in this psalm a model for prayer. On one hand, the pray-er believes that God is present in our lives and in the community's history (Ps 9). On the other hand, one sees vulnerable groups suffering horribly at the hands of exploiters who laugh off appeals to their conscience or threats of divine sanction (Ps 10). This psalmist insists on being faithful to the God who has acted personally and nationally, yet the psalmist is also faithful to the painful realities of injustice and exploitation that mar the world. The result is turmoil, which is reflected in the thanksgivings and the laments that spill over into each other.

PSALM 11

Literary Analysis

Psalm 11 is brief and unusual. It begins with a scornful dismissal of timorous advice and ends with a bold statement of confidence in God. The psalm's counsel to flee like a bird to the mountains and its description of things falling apart ("If the foundations are destroyed, what can the righteous do?" v. 3) linger in the memory as does its uncompromising loyalty to the just God.

The genre is that of a song of trust, which is related to the lament. Laments of an individual normally contain an expression of trust such as "I will give to the LORD the thanks due to his righteousness" (7:17a). The psalm of trust develops this statement of trust into an independent poem.

Interpreters have pointed out a number of problems in the poem: (1) Is the taunt begun in verse 1b confined only to verse 1b, or does it extend to verses 2 and 3? (2) Is "the righteous" person in verse 3b a human being or God? (NRSV translates the singular *ṣaddîq* as plural, "the righteous.") (3) Is verse 6a a wish that God would act or a statement that God will act after examining humankind in verse 4c? (4) Who is the speaker of the psalm: a seeker of asylum in the Temple, a person attacked by enemies, or a poet dramatizing temptation? Regarding question 1, the NRSV quotation marks show that it follows the majority of scholars in extending the taunt to verse 3. Regarding question 2, NRSV again follows the majority position in interpreting *ṣaddîq* in verse 3*b* as a human being. The alternative translation is "What has the Righteous One done?" Regarding question 3, NRSV takes verse 6 as a declaration of what God will actually do. The fourth question will be discussed below.

Is there a thread to guide one through the poem? A number of words are repeated: "the LORD," five times (vv. 1, 4*a*, 4*b*, 5, 7); "the wicked," three times (vv. 2, 5, 6); "the righteous (one)," three times (vv. 3, 5, 7); "the upright," twice (vv. 2, 7); and "love," twice (vv. 5, 7). Though these repeated words reinforce unity, they do not play a significant role in guiding the reader. An exception is "the LORD," which occurs once in the opening and closing lines and twice in the central verse 4. It has also been suggested that "take refuge" *(ḥāsāh)* in verse 1 and "behold" *(ḥāzāh)* in verse 7 echo each other in sound and sense and frame the poem. The surest clue to the structure is the two sections that almost any reader immediately grasps: the sufferer's grand dismissal of the advice of weaker souls (vv. 1-3) and the equally grand declaration that God rules the world (vv. 4-7).

Exegetical Analysis

How can you urge me to run from my enemies? (vv. 1-3)

The psalmist's profound confession, "In the LORD I take refuge" (v. 1*a*), is why the psalmist dismisses counsels to flee. The assertion that one is taking refuge in God is common in the Psalter (e.g., 7:1; 16:1; 25:20; 31:1). At times it refers to seeking refuge in a sanctuary, whereas at other times it is metaphorical, asking for divine protection. "Flee like a bird!" (v. 1) is much more than counsel to remove oneself from a dangerous situation. A fleeing bird is a symbol of panic-stricken flight before hostile forces as in Isa 16:2, "Like fluttering birds, like scattered nestlings, so are the daughters of Moab at the fords of the Arnon," and in Prov 27:8, "Like a bird fleeing from its nest / is anyone fleeing from his place" (AT). A bird does not reflect; it acts by instinct to preserve its life. Danger means flight. A human being, on the other hand, has greater choice and options other than thoughtless flight. The psalmist has made a choice ("In the LORD I take refuge") and does not wish to abandon that commitment.

The dangers that the psalmist's friends describe in verses 2-3 are truly daunting: rampant violence and collapse of moral values. The wicked have the upper hand, and they are armed with the best weapon of the time, the composite bow. The bow was so strong that the archer bent the shaft by pressing with the full weight of his body; "bend the bow" (v. 2) is, literally, "step on the bow." And the arrows from the bow are aimed right at the psalmist! No wonder there are people who see chaos coming and advise everyone to escape any way they can. The phrase, "the foundations are destroyed" (v. 3a) is unique. The verb "destroy" is frequently used to describe destroying structures, cities, or buildings. The chaos is like the chaos that threatened to invade God's own city, as described in Songs of Zion,

> Therefore we will not fear, though the earth should change,
>   though the mountains shake in the heart of the sea;
> though its waters roar and foam,
>   though the mountains tremble with its tumult. (46:2-3)

Psalms 48:4 and 76:3-6 have similar references to threats to the holy mountain. When the foundations totter, what should righteous people do, what should they trust in? Should they flee, or should they stand firm?

Reaffirmation of confidence in the just God (vv. 4-7)

Section 2 gives the answer: Trust in the righteous God dwelling in the heavenly palace. Though dwelling in heaven, God scrutinizes human conduct with ease (vv. 4c-5a), rewarding and punishing in accord with human behavior (vv. 5b-6). The majestic

Lord seated serenely in the heavenly palace (v. 4) contrasts effectively with the violent and agitated scene of verses 2-3. A similar picture is found in Ps 2:4-5, "He who sits in the heavens laughs; / the LORD has them in derision. / Then he will speak to them in his wrath, / and terrify them in his fury." In Ps 11:4, "The LORD" opens both cola, adding to the impression of calm control.

The verses portray a judgment scene. As often in the Bible, judgment consists of differentiation between the wicked and the righteous, putting down one group and upholding the other. The nuance of verse 5 is nicely caught by NAB: "The LORD tests the good and the bad, / hates those who love violence, / And rains upon the wicked." After the mention of the punishment (v. 6) comes the mention of reward, based in God loving "righteous deeds." *Love* and *hate* express acceptance and rejection. God hates the lover of violence (v. 5*b*) and loves the deeds of the righteous (v. 7*b*). Punishment through fire is also mentioned in Gen 19:24 and Amos 7:4; for the image of a cup of judgment see Ps 75:8; Isa 51:17; Jer 25:15. There is no real symmetry between punishments and rewards, however. The reward is seeing the face of God (v. 7*c*), climactically mentioned in the last line of the poem.

The language of seeing God's face suggests the psalmist is in the Temple or seeks to go there. Psalms 27:8-9, 13 and 42:2 mention seeing God's face in the context of the Temple. The Temple is after all the earthly reflection of God's palace in the heavens, which is featured in the very center of the poem (v. 4). Taking refuge in the Lord (v. 1) can mean seeking asylum in the shrine. Moreover, it has already been pointed out that the quaking of the foundations is similar to language used of Mount Zion. All these factors suggest the poem draws on the Zion traditions, though the psalm is not a Song of Zion.

Theological and Ethical Analysis

When serious trouble strikes and people react in panic and confusion, one should not panic and bolt. Rather, the psalm shows how one can take refuge in the dwelling of the Lord. One can take the language literally, of actually going to the house of the Lord, or metaphorically, of trusting in the Lord, utterly transcendent yet found in a particular place.

God has given humans the capacity to choose; they need not act by instinct. God has also given to humans the gifts of courage and trust. As gifts, they can be accepted, that is, put into practice in difficult situations. This psalm is a prayer to accompany the acceptance of these gifts.

PSALM 12

Literary Analysis

This psalm is generally viewed as an individual lament. It takes the usual cast of characters—the sufferer, the wicked, and God—and sets them within a drama. It is unusual, however, in its vehement complaint against the speech of the wicked (v. 2). Their lies are destroying the social fabric and diminishing the number of those loyal to God (v. 1). The poem is also unusual in citing the oracle of salvation (v. 5) upon which the psalmist's hope is presumably based. Many scholars believe that such oracles of salvation were delivered during the "performance" of individual laments. They were not, however, transmitted with the lament texts because they were not regarded as the petitioner's part in the dialogue between sufferer and officiant. Another instance of an oracle transmitted in a lament text is said to be Ps 60:6-8 ("God has promised in his sanctuary . . ."). Unfortunately, we do not know much about the liturgical performance of the psalms. Did they originate in ceremonies in the Temple? Are the present psalms digests of such ceremonies, which have been reworked to enable private worshipers to participate in the liturgy of the Temple?

The genre is disputed. Some view it as an individual lament, and the poem does in fact have all the expected elements of an individual lament: the petition (vv. 1a, 3-4), the complaint (vv. 1-2, 8), and the statement of trust (vv. 6-7). Verse 5 would be, as noted, the oracle of salvation. Another suggestion is that it is a prophetic lament liturgy in which an official cult prophet or charismatic figure makes the declaration in verse 5. Comparable examples are Ps 14 and the book of Habakkuk. The latter begins with a lament liturgy over a crisis (Hab 1:2-4), follows with God's answer in the first person (Hab 1:5-11), and continues with the thankful praise of the community in a liturgical context. Though this suggestion is possible, the view that the psalm is an individual lament plus oracular response is simpler and explains more.

The center of the poem is verse 5, the divine oracle. It contains the middle occurrence of "the LORD" (the third of five in the poem). The verse is also significant in the structure, for it is the verse in which verbs and nouns referring to the speech of the wicked ("utter," "lips," "speak," "lips," "tongue," "say," "tongues," "lips," vv. 2-4) come to an end and are replaced by one verb ("says the LORD"). Verse 5 explicitly answers the opening prayer, reprising from verse 1 the divine name "LORD" and a form of the Hebrew root yš' (NRSV renders the verb as "help" in v. 1 and the noun as "safety" in v. 5c). The whole poem is framed by occurrences of "humankind" in verses 1 and 8. As noted, various nouns and verbs of speech occur often in verses 2-4, always of the speech of the wicked. Beginning in verse 5, however, the only words pertaining to speech (all derived from the same Hebrew root, 'mr) always refer to the speech of God. The meaning of this shift seems to be that God's word silences the words of the wicked and determines the course of history.

The NRSV outline makes sense: complaint of destructive speech and prayer for its removal (vv. 1-4); oracle of salvation and statement of trust in response (vv. 5-6); petition to be preserved from the wicked (vv. 7-8). Another possibility is to divide the psalm into only two sections (as in NJPS): complaint and petition (vv. 1-4) and assurance and thanksgiving (vv. 5-8). In this division, each section has thirty-seven Hebrew words.

Exegetical Analysis

*Complaint of destructive speech and prayer for
its removal (vv. 1-4)*

Like other individual laments, this one begins urgently and
directly, "Help, O LORD." The complaint is that the righteous are
disappearing; presumably they are afraid publicly to practice their
faith and loyalty toward the Lord. The sense is well conveyed by
two proverbs: "When the righteous triumph, splendor abounds,
but when the wicked rise, people hide" (Prov 28:12, AT), "When
the wicked arise, people withdraw, but when they perish, the righteous abound" (Prov 28:28, AT). It is through the righteous that the
body politic flourishes because their loyalty invites God to bless it
with prosperity and peace. The wicked and the righteous, however,
cannot prevail at the same time. The triumph of one means the dis-
appearance of the other.

Modern readers are perhaps surprised at the prominence given
in the psalm to the speech of the wicked. Emphasis on speech is
characteristic of Wisdom literature, especially Proverbs. Life is
conceived as action, and human beings are defined by the organs
of action. Perception, decision, expression, and motion are
expressed by the bodily organs involved: eye, ear, mouth (tongue,
lips), heart, hands, and feet. Of human actions, the most expressive is speech, for it articulates the intentions of the human heart.
This psalm focuses on the essential human act—words. Virtuous
words express the heart. With the wicked, the heart intends one
thing, the tongue expresses something quite different. The
Hebrew idiom in verse 2b is vivid, literally: "with smooth lips
with heart and a heart [i.e., a double heart] they speak." The
wicked go from triumph to triumph. Their words, no longer
telling the true intentions of their hearts, are effective weapons.
Their description of themselves in verse 4 uses the language of
brute power: "we will prevail" and "who is our master?"

It is no wonder that the prayer of the psalmist is that the Lord
destroy the organs responsible for their destructive acts, their lips
and tongue (v. 3). To modern sensibilities, the prayer seems vio-

lent and macabre. The psalmist, however, scarcely expects an avenging angel to cut out the tongues of the wicked. The prayer is that God put an end to their ability to destroy society and persecute the righteous, who are the soul of a flourishing and peaceful community.

Oracle of salvation and statement of trust in response (vv. 5-6)

As if answering the prayer of verses 3-4, the Lord promises to "rise up." Many psalms ask for the same thing, that the Lord rise up and assume a legal or military role (e.g., 3:7; 7:6; 9:19; 10:12). Those whom the Lord will defend are "the poor" and "the needy." The terms are often used in parallel verses (e.g., Deut 15:11; Pss 35:10; 40:17) and designate economic poverty as well as the powerless state that comes from lack of resources. In the present context, the poor and the needy designate those who are left defenseless when the righteous retreat (v. 1) and the arrogant attack (vv. 2-4). Though the poor are powerless in the sight of human beings, they are, by a wonderful biblical paradox, powerful in the sight of God. According to the text, it is precisely their need that provokes God to rise up: "Because the poor are despoiled . . . I will now rise up" (v. 5). "The safety" granted by the Lord (v. 5c) is expressed by the same Hebrew root contained in the opening plea, "Help, O LORD" (v. 1a). The Lord has answered that prayer.

"The promises of the LORD" (lit. "the words of Yahweh," v. 6a) are contrasted with the human words spoken by the arrogant ("utter," "speak" in v. 2; "makes great boasts" in v. 3 plus the mention of lips and tongues). After the two instances of "promises" (lit. "words") in verse 6a, there are no more references to speech in the poem. God's words in verses 5-6 silence all other words. The words of God are pure and are compared to a precious metal—silver—that has been brought to the highest degree of purity. Proverbs 10:20 is similar: "The tongue of the righteous is choice silver; the mind of the wicked is of little worth." Proverbs often declares wisdom to be more precious than gold and silver (Prov 2:4; 3:14; 8:10, 19). The psalmist's usage is different from Proverbs, however: God's promises are precious and reliable, tested in fire.

Petition to be preserved from the wicked (vv. 7-8)

Some commentators regard the last two verses as a continuation of the assurance offered in verses 5-6. NRSV reflects the view in verse 7: "you . . . will protect us; you will guard us." The two verbs in verse 7 are in the imperfect tense, which can be translated as future (NRSV) or as jussive (NAB: "may you protect us"). The jussive makes better sense here because verse 8 states that the danger still exists. The oracle of salvation has not caused it to disappear. "This generation" (v. 7b) refers to the wicked described in verses 2-4. In verse 8b, "humankind" refers back to the complaint of verse 1 that the wicked triumph. The psalm thus ends with a realistic appreciation of a broken world. The psalmist, however, has heard a divine word promising justice and can live in this world.

Theological and Ethical Analysis

The situation is desperate, and the poet portrays it in dramatic terms as the wicked versus the righteous. The wicked have taken over. Their will is law; they have only to state their minds in order to prevail. Those who might be expected to oppose them, "the godly" and "the faithful," have disappeared. The psalmist, cut off from godly allies, can only pray that God will intervene and thwart this capture of public life.

Is the picture extreme, an example of Semitic hyperbole? The answer is no. There have been periods in history when evil did prevail on a massive scale and wipe out all opposition, in antireligious totalitarian regimes, for example. The psalm more likely describes something more limited in scope and closer to our own experience: occasions when corporate behavior or greed or cowardice silenced the gospel so that those who upheld it found themselves isolated and unable to live a common and public life. For this kind of "minority" the psalm is eminently suitable. It turns to God and expects action from the God who is grieved because the poor are despoiled.

PSALM 13

Literary Analysis

This poem is a textbook example of an individual lament. Verses 1-2 are the complaint of the suffering, verses 3-4, the petition, and verses 5-6, the statement of trust and promise of praise. As in Ps 12, the usual cast of three characters (the sufferer, the enemies, and God) act in a drama. The client of the Lord suffers the assaults of an enemy and waits desperately for the Lord, who will punish the wicked and uphold the righteous sufferer. The poem is undatable, for there is no reference to any historical event. Some suggest an early (preexilic) date because it does not wish for the annihilation of the enemy. Such a criterion is, however, not a reliable indicator of date, for holy war oracles (of early date) wish for the annihilation of enemies.

Though the structure of the poem is relatively simple, it gains subtlety by sound echoes between verses 1-2 and 4-6 and by repetition of words. "How long" (*'ad 'ānāh*, repeated four times in vv. 1-2) is echoed in "But I" (*wa'anî* in v. 5a); "sorrow in my heart" (*yāgôn bilbābî*, v. 2b) is echoed in "my heart shall rejoice" (*yāgēl libbî*, v. 5b). Furthermore, several words are repeated: "my enemy" in verses 2c and 4a, "over me/with me" (*'ālāy*) in verses 2c and 6b. The effect of the echoing of sound and of word repetition in verses 1-2 and 4-6 is to connect the complaint (vv. 1-2) to its answer (vv. 5-6). Equivalently, the repetition says the anguished words of the sufferer do not go unheard. A final touch of unity is added by the pattern formed by the use of the divine name: "LORD" appears once in the beginning (v. 1), middle (v. 3), and end (v. 6) of the poem; its middle occurrence is coupled with "my God."

Exegetical Analysis

How long will you ignore me? (vv. 1-2)

"How long," frequent in laments (e.g., 4:2; 6:3; 62:3), is an exclamation of impatience at divine delay. It can also be a real question, because people assumed that divine punishments were inflicted for a specific period of time and sought to learn "how long" their suffering would continue (see comment on 74:9; 90:11-12). In this psalm, "how long" seems to be an exclamation rather than a question. Buffeted by anguish and shame, the psalmist has waited in vain for God to bring relief and salvation and is utterly frustrated. The fourfold "how long" well conveys the exasperation and fear.

"Forget" (v. 1*a*) is more aptly rendered "ignore" with NJPS. "Hide your face from" (v. 1*b*) is a common idiom for God's withdrawal of favor (e.g., Deut 32:20; Job 13:24; Pss 44:24; 88:14). Psalm 104:29 illustrates the idiom: "When you hide your face, [the creatures] are dismayed; when you take away their breath, they die and return to their dust." What is the suffering? It is impossible to reconstruct the situation. As in other laments, the situation is left unspecified so that other pray-ers can make the psalm their own.

The reference in verse 2 to internal suffering and external danger is a reminder that psychological, physical, and social sufferings are often not distinguished in the Psalter. The root danger is, however, external—"the enemy" who is "exalted over me," that is, who is defeating me. The psalmist wishes to win the contest between them. Psalm 27:6 clarifies the psalmist's hope (identical words are italicized): "Now my head is lifted up above my enemies all around me, and I will offer in [God's] tent sacrifices with shouts of joy; *I will sing* and make melody *to the* LORD."

Look at me! Talk to me! (vv. 3-4)

"Look!" is a better translation than NRSV "consider" (v. 3*a*) because it alludes to the complaint in verse 1 that God was not looking at the psalmist: "How long will you hide your face from me?" "To give light to one's eyes" (v. 3*b*) is a Hebrew idiom that means to give vitality and joy (that is, life) to someone (Prov 29:13). The psalmist in verse 3*b* asks for such vitality "or I will sleep the sleep of death" and my enemy will boast of victory. The psalmist portrays the situation in dramatic terms: "on the one side, myself, and on the other, my enemy. Judge us, O God" (that is, intervene justly). "To allow my foes to prevail is to judge them innocent and myself guilty. In that case, they will rejoice, and I will have sorrow in my heart" (v. 2*ab*).

I trust in your love to me and will give thanks in advance (vv. 5-6)

"But I" (v. 5*a*) signals a shift in the poem from anguished complaint (vv. 1-2) and anxious prayer (vv. 3-4) to calm trust (vv. 5-6). The Hebrew word order in verse 5*a* makes the point more clearly than is possible in translation: "But I in your steadfast love (*ḥesed*) trust." The attitude of God (steadfast love) is mentioned before the attitude of the psalmist (trust). The translation "I trust" is preferable to NRSV "trusted," for the latter suggests a past act rather than a present disposition. Nearly every major English translation renders "trust." Parallel with the verb *to trust* is the verb *to rejoice* in the rescue ("salvation") that the psalmist hopes is on the way. The mention of joy (v. 5) leads naturally to the mention of singing to the Lord, that is, giving thanks for the rescue in music.

What accounts for the dramatic change in tone between verses 1-4 and 5-6? As discussed before in relation to Ps 6, some scholars suggest that an officiant in the sanctuary delivered an oracle of salvation to the sufferer after verse 4. For evidence, they point to the dialogue between the distraught Hannah and the priest Eli in 1 Sam 1:9-18, where Eli gives an oracle of salvation to Hannah who accepts it as the word of God. (See under "lament" in the introduction.) Others believe that the very process of complaint and petition has led the psalmist to a deeper faith and hope, making possible the calm statement of verses 5-6. Whatever was the cause, the change is profound, and the palmist now waits serenely for God.

Theological and Ethical Analysis

Though the poet uses traditional material, the poem is vivid and urgent. The four-times repeated "how long" in the complaint quotes a sufferer at the breaking point—emotionally troubled and terrified by the enemy. The petitioner simply asks to be looked at and listened to. The psalmist has the sense to ask in the hour of need. The final statement comes from one who has stayed in the process before the Lord and arrived at a calm state of waiting.

The poem ends with an act of trust and a promise of praise. One has the feeling that the situation has not changed. The psalmist, however, has changed, has glimpsed the God of compassion and justice, and has learned to wait expectantly.

PSALM 14

According to this psalm, there are two basic attitudes to God's governance of the world: either bold denial that God cares anything about justice or courageous affirmation that God is passionately committed to it. The psalm dramatizes human choices by using "either-or" language.

Literary Analysis

The genre of Ps 14, and of its near twin Ps 53, is controverted. According to a few scholars, it is a wisdom psalm because it deals with "fools" (v. 1a) and mentions "any who are wise" (v. 2b) and "knowledge" (v. 4a). Others regard it as "prophetic" because of its denunciation of the rich and defense of the poor (vv. 4-6), while still others suggest it reflects a liturgy using rebuke and threat familiar in the prophetic books.

None of these categorizations are completely satisfactory. The term "wisdom psalm" is somewhat vague and unilluminating; moreover, the word for "fool" is not the usual one in Wisdom literature; the Hebrew word for "knowledge" is likewise general.

"Prophetic" is an unsatisfactory category because rebuke of wicked behavior occurs in liturgies such as Pss 50 and 81. Psalm 14 is best regarded as a song of trust because the singer rejoices in the status of being among "the poor" (v. 6) and taking refuge in the Temple while denouncing the wicked and awaiting God's judgment. Like Pss 36 and 52, it begins by denouncing the wicked and concludes by rejoicing in the protection of God.

There are three sections: the wicked and God's scrutiny of their behavior (vv. 1-3); rebuke of the malefactors (vv. 4-6); and prayer that God extend to all Israel the righteousness given to Zion (v. 7).

Exegetical Analysis

The wicked and God's scrutiny of their behavior (vv. 1-3)

To "say in one's heart" is to operate with a considered judgment, as in 10:6, 11, 13. "Heart" in Hebrew psychology is the organ of thought and decision that expresses itself in deeds; a malicious heart will inevitably give rise to malicious deeds. The "fool," knowingly malicious, is a biblical type. In Proverbs, the fool is often contrasted with the wise person (e.g., Prov 3:35; 10:1; 13:20); in this psalm the fool is a sinner and contrasted with the person who trusts in God. Psalm 14 is not talking about the human race generally, but about a specific group, "the wicked," among whom there is "no one who does good" (v. 3). Typically, the wicked disregard God and attack the devout. "There is no God" reveals their view about God's ability to govern rather than about God's existence. They claim God does not care how the world runs. The poet dramatizes and intensifies the description of the enemies of God in order to pose the question of divine justice more vividly.

In verse 2, Yahweh looks down from heaven to see, firsthand, human misconduct, as in Gen 11:5, "The LORD came down to see the city and the tower, which mortals had built," and Gen 18:21, "I must go down and see whether they have done altogether according to the outcry that has come to me; and if not, I will know." The "wise" is the type contrary to fools and is parallel to those "who seek after God" (2*c*). Although "to seek after God" can also mean seeking an oracle, as in Exod 18:15 and 1 Sam 9:9, such a narrow meaning does not fit here. Finally, the divine judgment is uttered after the investigation: The entire group is guilty (v. 3). Romans 3:10-12 quotes Ps 14:2-3 (plus other psalms and Isa 59:7-8) to prove the entire human race needs divine grace, but Ps 14 in its original meaning is concerned with a particular group—the wicked.

Rebuke of the malefactors (vv. 4-6)

Fools refuse to learn ("no knowledge," v. 4) that there is a God who will *act*, punishing them and rescuing their victims. The metaphor of the wicked devouring the people is also found in Mic 3:1-3: "Listen, you heads of Jacob and rulers of the house of Israel! . . . who eat the flesh of my people, flay their skin off them, break their bones in pieces, and chop them up like meat in a kettle, like flesh in a caldron."

Abrupt shifts in grammatical person like those in verses 4-6 ("my people" and "the LORD," "they" and "you") are not unusual in biblical Hebrew. Though NRSV and other translators render *šam* in verse 5 by its normal meaning, "there," the word can have a temporal meaning, "then," as in 53:5; 66:6; 132:17. When God comes in judgment, the wicked will see their contemptuous statement, "there is no God," proved false. Their denial of God's governance led the wicked to the worst of crimes—exploiting the poor. In verses 5 and 6, "the righteous" is another name for "the poor." The righteous and the poor make God their ultimate hope, foreswearing other resources.

Prayer that God extend to all Israel the righteousness given to Zion (v. 7)

Developing verse 5 ("there they shall be in great terror"), which suggests that judgment takes place in Zion, the final lines ask that the just judgment be extended to all Israel. The phrase "restores the fortunes" occurs in exilic and postexilic literature (e.g., Jer 30:18; Ezek 29:14; Amos 9:14), leading many scholars to suggest that the prayer is an addition. In God's final adjudication, Israel will rejoice.

Theological and Ethical Analysis

Denial of God's authority and exploitation of the defenseless often go hand in hand. With no one to take up their cause, the powerless are at the mercy of exploiters who always find reasons to justify their actions. Bothered by the attitude and actions of the wicked, the psalmist boldly puts up a challenge based on the conviction that God is involved, just, and "coming." God will personally search out and punish those who remake the world to serve their interests at others' expense. For the psalmist, God who looks down from heaven is more real than the wicked who operate in the full sight of all.

Modern readers should not misunderstand the psalm's polar opposition of wicked and righteous as corresponding to those inside and outside the church, or believers and unbelievers. The poet is making use of biblical types, a dramatic way of talking about human activity and its results, in order to encourage confidence in God's justice and identification with the loyal and the poor.

John Calvin comments on this psalm, "By expressing [David's] desire for the deliverance of Israel, we are taught that he was chiefly anxious about the welfare of the whole body of the church, and that his thoughts were more occupied about this than about himself individually. . . . And yet the particular afflictions with which God visits each of us are intended to admonish us to direct our attention and care to the whole body of the Church, and to think of its necessities, just as we see David here including Israel with himself" (Calvin 1999, p. 30).

PSALM 15

Psalms 15–17 are concerned with the Temple. Psalm 15 is an examination of conscience for Temple worshipers; Ps 16 delights in the life offered in the Temple; and Ps 17 wants to behold the face of the Lord, an expression elsewhere signifying a visit to the Temple.

Literary Analysis

Most commentators consider Ps 15 a ritual (or a poem derived from such a ritual), which regulated entrance to the sanctuary. A priest or other official asks those entering if their conduct is in accord with the will of the God they worship. Commentators compare the similar scrutinies in 24:3 ("Who shall ascend the hill of the LORD?") and Isa 33:14b-16 (" 'Who among us can live with the devouring fire? . . .' Those who walk righteously." Entry into ancient Near Eastern sanctuaries was subject to regulation; written warnings posted at shrine entrances are attested. Deuteronomy 23:1-9 and 2 Sam 5:8b also regulate access to the sanctuary. A few scholars, however, deny the ritual context and suggest instead that the psalm is simply a literary expression of the ethical standards required of worshipers. Worship must come from a whole heart to be acceptable to God. These scholars compare such prophetic demands for ethical worship as Isa 1:10-17; Jer 6:20; and Amos 5:21-24.

The opening question, "Who may abide in your tent?" expects an answer like "only a righteous person." The psalm then describes the righteous person in ten actions: The first three are depicted positively with verbs in the participle form (v. 2), the second three, negatively ("not") with verbs in the perfect tense (v. 3); the seventh action is described with one verb in the perfect tense and the other in the imperfect tense (v. 4ab); the last three again depict the actions negatively ("not") with verbs in the perfect tense. The summary verse 5 declares that the one who acts in accord with justice will "never be moved."

Exegetical Analysis

Who may enter the Temple precincts (v. 1)

Since the question (v. 1) is directed to the Lord, the answer (vv. 2-5) must come from the Lord. The Lord's words would have been delivered by a Temple official (if the psalm records an actual ceremony). "Tent" is plural in Hebrew, which connotes an elaborate tent such as the Lord's tent in Jerusalem prior to the construction of Solomon's Temple (2 Sam 6:17; 7:6; Ps 78:60). "Tent" can also be a poetic term for the Temple, as in Pss 27:5 and 61:4. Gods in comparable religious literature might live on holy mountains. Yahweh too lives on a "holy hill." "Abide" and "dwell" suggest participation in the ceremonies that took place in the court surrounding the Temple building. The Temple was the house of God; as such it was not entered by laypersons.

The ideal worshiper (vv. 2-5b)

The ten clauses describing the ideal worshiper are overlapping; they make their effect cumulatively. The first three acts are about personal integrity. "Walk" is a biblical idiom for conducting oneself, and the phrase "walk blamelessly" occurs also in Ps 84:11 and Prov 28:18. "Speak the truth from their heart" (v. 2*c* NRSV) can be taken in either of two ways: "speak the truth *in* their heart" in the sense that one's inmost thoughts are correct; "speak the truth *from* their heart" in the sense that one speaks one's mind accurately and sincerely. NRSV rightly prefers the second meaning. Psalm 28:3*bcd* illuminates the phrase: "workers of evil, who speak peace with their neighbors, while mischief is in their hearts," that is, one's words conceal one's intent. The second cluster of three acts concern one's neighbor. To enter the sanctuary, one must *not* have slandered, harmed one's neighbor, "or borne reproach for [his acts toward] his neighbor" (NJPS). The rendering of the last phrase differs from NRSV and most translations. The Hebrew idiom "to bear reproach" in its other occurrences (Pss 69:7; 89:50; Jer 15:15; 31:19; Mic 6:16) means to suffer scorn, not inflict it. NJPS recognizes the usual meaning and translates accordingly.

The seventh action in the series of ten is the only one described in parallel cola; all the other actions are described in a single colon. Verse 4*a* is, literally, "the one despised in his own eyes is rejected." Most English translations follow the interpretation of the Septuagint that the just person scorns anyone rejected by God. Differently, Delitzsch takes the two verbs ("he is despised" and "he is rejected") in apposition and renders, "despicable is he in his own eyes, worthy to be despised" (p. 214) that is, one humbly recognizes one's unworthiness (cf. 1 Sam 15:17 and 2 Sam 6:22). The majority position is preferable, for it alone offers a satisfactory parallel to verse 4*b*. One can paraphrase: The righteous person despises anyone rejected (by God) and honors those who fear the Lord. Rejecting or honoring others in accord with God's judgment of them is also a theme of ideal (royal) behavior in Ps 101:6-7, "I will look with favor on the faithful in the land, / so that they may live with me. . . . / No one who practices deceit shall remain in my house; / no one who utters lies shall continue in my presence."

The last three actions (vv. 4*c*-5*b*) concern legal and economic integrity. Like the second set of three (v. 3), they are put negatively: not altering a sworn promise, not lending money to a fellow Israelite at interest, and not accepting a bribe to convict an innocent person. Oaths must be kept even when recklessly made, like the treaty with the Gibeonites (Josh 9:14-15, 19-20). Lending to fellow Israelites at interest is forbidden by law (e.g., Exod 22:25; Lev 25:37; Ezek 18:8, 13). Accepting a bribe to convict an innocent person is unthinkable in the biblical conception of justice, for example, "Cursed be anyone who takes a bribe to shed innocent blood" (Deut 27:25).

The declaration (v. 5c)

The last bicolon (v. 5*cd*) assures that "those who do these things shall never be moved." "Be moved" can refer to the quaking of the cosmos, specifically the earth and the mountains that support it over the deep (Isa 24:19; 54:10). Even when the cosmos totters, Zion remains the unshaken center because "God is in the midst of the city; it shall not be moved" (46:5). If one can only be admitted to God's dwelling, one will never be moved. There one finds sanctuary from the collapsing world.

Theological and Ethical Analysis

One can easily imagine a visitor to the Temple being stopped at the gate to the court and asked searching questions. Is your "way," your conduct, in accord with the holiness of the place? Have you acted so as to exclude yourself from the holy community? In the solemn liturgy at Mount Sinai (Exodus 19–20), the Ten Commandments defined the conduct that makes one a member of the holy people. Do them, and you are in; violate them, and you are out. Whenever the people gather, they can expect to hear the constitutive demands. As already noted, it is possible that the psalm does not reflect an actual ceremony, that it is a purely literary expression requiring wholehearted worship. Its authority is no less powerful.

Israel must be holy because God is holy: "Speak to all the congregation of the people of Israel and say to them: You shall be holy, for I the LORD your God am holy" (Lev 19:2). Genuine religion is what one does rather than what one thinks. Righteousness is here expressed as specific actions. The psalm forces one to stop at the gate of God's house and affirm that one's conduct is not at variance with the very object of one's quest.

PSALM 16

The poem associates the Lord with a particular community (Israel) and place (the land of Canaan and the Temple). The mention of the Temple, implied in "path of life" and "in your presence" (v. 11), links the psalm to the preceding and following psalms.

Literary Analysis

The genre of Ps 16 is disputed, which affects the interpretation of the entire poem. Some scholars consider it a prayer accompanying conversion from the worship of many gods to the worship of the Lord (interpreting vv. 3-4 as a rejection of such gods, see below). Others see it as a request for asylum in the Temple (see vv. 1 and 11). Still others regard it as a plea to be cured of mortal illness (see vv. 10-11) or even a thanksgiving for recovery. Much of the difficulty of classifying the poem can be traced to the damaged verse 3. NRSV and REB reflect the majority interpretation that "the holy ones in the land" and "the noble" refer to orthodox believers with whom the pray-er wishes to be associated. Other scholars, however, regard the holy and powerful ones not as pious believers but as gods whom the pray-er rejects. *Qĕdôšîm* (v. 3, NRSV: "holy ones") refers to divine beings in Ps 89:7 ("the council of the *holy ones*") and *'addîrîm* (16:3, NRSV: "nobles") refers to divine beings in 1 Sam 4:8 ("Who can deliver us from the power of these *mighty* gods?"). Among Israel's Phoenician neighbors, two common epithets of gods and goddesses were "holy" *(qiddiš)* and "powerful" *(iddir).*

The textually damaged verse 3 is not a major hindrance to understanding the poem. Verses 1-2 and 4 are comprehensible without it: The poet is choosing the Lord and rejecting other gods. Though it might seem that verses 1-2 are a plea to be rescued from an immediate danger, the verses are better interpreted as an affirmation that the Lord is the psalmist's God. The psalmist expresses the relationship between the patron deity and the human client in a client's typical prayer: Protect me, for you are my only God. Psalm 31:5-7 similarly expresses the relationship in concrete and typical words. In asserting "you are my Lord," the psalmist equivalently accepts Yahweh as personal God. One can assume that the controverted verse 3, which occurs in the midst of this confession-acceptance, is similarly concerned with choosing one God and rejecting other gods. Having chosen the Lord as God, the psalmist goes on to celebrate the benefits of the Lord as divine patron, providing land (vv. 5-6), offering guidance (vv. 7-8), and giving life in the Temple.

Exegetical Analysis

"A Miktam of David" also occurs as a heading in Psalms 56–60; its meaning is unknown.

Avowal of the Lord as my God, rejection of other gods, and prizing of the land as the Lord's gift (vv. 1-6)

Though verses 1-2 look initially like a cry to be rescued from a particular danger, the immediate rejection of other gods suggests the psalmist is rather choosing a deity in the typical words of a client. A similar choosing of a deity is recorded in Gen 28:20-21, at the revelation of the Lord to Jacob. Jacob responds in a vow: "If God will be with me (cf. Ps 16:8), and will keep me (cf. Ps 16:1) in this way that I go . . . then the LORD shall be my God." "Keeping" (protecting) is what a god does (Job 29:2). In Ps 16:2a, the psalmist says to Yahweh, "You are my Lord." The language is typical: The patron deity protects, the client takes refuge in the deity by saying "You are my God."

Unfortunately, the fourteen Hebrew words in verses 2b-4a are damaged, and their sense must to some degree be supplied by the translator. As already noted, NRSV and REB take "holy ones" and "nobles" (lit. "mighty ones") in a positive sense as the holy community into which the psalmist seeks to be admitted. Such a community offers acceptable sacrifice, not the forbidden rites of the alien gods (v. 4bc). As noted above, it is more likely that the holy and mighty ones are gods (as in Ps 89:7 and 1 Sam 4:8) whom the pray-er rejects (as in NAB and NJPS). The uncertain text makes it impossible to choose decisively between the two interpretations on purely linguistic grounds. Both interpretations are compatible with the view that the psalmist is choosing the Lord as his God and rejecting other patron deities.

Verse 4 describes adherence to the Lord negatively, through not worshiping other gods nor using their names in oaths. To name other gods in worship is forbidden in Exod 23:13; Deut 18:20; and Hos 2:17. "Drink offerings of blood" (v. 4c) has occasioned much comment, for blood offerings are attested neither in the Bible (apart perhaps from Isa 66:3) nor in Canaanite religion. Several passages in Jeremiah (e.g., 7:18; 19:13; cf. Ezek 20:28) prohibit drink offerings on the grounds that they are offered to other gods as well as to Yahweh. Psalm 116:13 ("I will lift up the cup of salvation and call on the name of the Lord") may refer to drink offerings. "Blood" may be metaphorical in Ps 16, however, referring to the blood on the hands of the violent (Isa 1:15 and Ps 50:13).

Instead of making offerings to other gods, the psalmist calls on the name of only one—Yahweh (v. 7). This God is experienced in an utterly grace-filled and generous act, the gift of the land that sustains and provides a home for the psalmist. Verses 5-6 clearly refer to the land of Canaan. In Joshua's distribution of the land to the Israelites in Josh 18, for example, the key words in Ps 16:5-6—"portion," "lot," "boundary lines," and "heritage"—occur again and again in the context of land distribution. "Boundary lines" (v. 6a) occur in the sense of land distribution in Josh 17:5, literally, "There fell to Manasseh ten portions" (boundary lines). The psalmist's family land, the very environment of life, is God's gift. As in Deut 6 and 8, the psalmist rejoices that the Lord's power shows itself in the bounty of the land. The next section will elaborate the parallel between the land of Canaan and the land of the Temple (v. 11).

I will bless the Lord, who guides me and lets me experience life in the Temple (vv. 7-11)

The second part of the poem emphasizes the positive response of the individual whose God is now the Lord—giving praise (v. 7), prizing the Lord as one's sole God (v. 8), and rejoicing in the security of nearness to the true God (vv. 9-11). Verses 7-8 "bless" (i.e., acknowledge publicly) God for the wise guidance that brought matters to this point. God's wisdom penetrates so deeply within that one's inner self continues the instruction even in the night (v. 7*b*), that is, in the privacy of sleep. As in Deut 8:5, the Lord instructs the people like a parent, "Know then in your heart that as a parent disciplines [i.e., instructs] a child so the LORD your God disciplines you." Besides giving the praise due the only God, the psalmist resolves to "keep the LORD always before me" (v. 8*a*), which is equivalently heeding the first commandment "you shall have no other gods before me" (Exod 20:3, Deut 5:7). Such nearness to God brings stability (v. 8*b*), intense joy (v. 9*a*), and profound peace (v. 9*b*).

The mention in verse 10 of protection from death and in verse 11 of "the path of life" suggests the psalmist is now speaking of a particular area of the land, the place where the Temple stands. "The path of life" (v. 11) occurs elsewhere only in Proverbs (2:19, 5:6, 10:17, 12:28, 15:24) as the opposite of the path to Sheol. Psalm 16:11*b*, "in your presence," may also be a reference to the Temple.

Acts 2:27 and 13:35 cite Ps 16:10 to demonstrate that the resurrection of Jesus from the dead was predicted by David. Instead of citing the Hebrew text of Ps 16:10*b* ("you do not . . . let your faithful one see the Pit"), Acts followed the Septuagint, which read the verb *šaḥat* ("to be corrupt") for *šaḥat* ("the pit," or the underworld), and translated "neither will you allow your Holy One to see corruption." The meaning is not much affected by the Septuagint interpretation.

Theological and Ethical Analysis

The poem describes a conversion from worshiping several gods to worshiping the Lord alone. The new relationship is not between equals; it is between a needy and vulnerable human being and a protecting and caring God whom one nonetheless addresses as "you" (v. 1). The relationship is freely entered, even though the psalmist is showered with gifts from the choice—a fruitful land, joy from being with a generous and loving God, and protection from a meaningless death. There is here no *quid pro quo* (exchange of one thing for another), no *do ut des* (I give that I may get). Rather, there is a flood of gifts and God's presence when one turns to the God of Israel.

The psalm can be prayed by everyone, young and old, someone new to the community or a longtime member. In a very true sense, one's relationship to God consists in ongoing conversion, turning from false gods and values (no matter how "holy" and "noble") to the living Lord. In conversion, one senses the giftedness of things and of the further promise they contain. One is led finally to exclaim "you show me the path of life!" The prayer might be used at the Easter liturgy where neophytes are received into the church.

PSALM 17

Psalms 15–17 are all concerned in some fashion with the Temple. The first is a liturgical scrutiny that Temple visitors undergo before being admitted to the sacred precincts. Psalm 16 accepts the Lord as patron deity and savors the life to be found in the holy land and the sanctuary. Psalm 17 delights in being transparent before the Lord (v. 3), looks for protection (vv. 6-14), and hopes to "behold your face" and "be satisfied, beholding your likeness" (v. 15), expressions that elsewhere mean visiting the Temple (Ps 11:7, 27:4). In its concern with protection from enemies, Ps 17 anticipates Ps 18.

Literary Analysis

The poem is an individual lament of a petitioner hounded by merciless enemies. The poetic logic is clear: an opening plea for a fair hearing on the grounds of past fidelity (vv. 1-5), the central petition to be saved from present enemies (vv. 6-12), a restatement of the petition (vv. 13-14), and an expression of hope of being rescued (v. 15). Though translations differ regarding stanza divisions (NJPS has three, NAB has four, and NRSV has six), there is little doubt regarding the progression of thought.

The final verse (v. 15) signals the conclusion by repeating words from verses 1-2: *ṣedeq,* "just" in verse 1 and "righteousness" in verse 15; *ḥāzāh,* "see" in verse 2 and "behold" in verse 15; *pānîm,* "from you" in verse 2 and "your face" in verse 15. The description of the enemy in verses 8-11 repeats words from the protestations of innocence in verses 1-5. Whereas the psalmist speaks with "lips free of deceit" (v. 1), "they speak arrogantly" (v. 10); the psalmist has "avoided *(šāmar)* the ways of the violent" (v. 4b) and asks that God "guard *(šāmar)* me as the apple of the eye" (v. 8); the psalmist's "steps have held fast to your paths" (*'aŝur,* v. 5), whereas "they track me down" (*'aŝur,* v. 11); "let your eyes see [my] right" (v. 2), whereas "they set their eyes to cast me to the ground" (v. 11b). The psalmist is portrayed as utterly faithful to God, the mirror image of the lawless enemies. It behooves the just God to act.

Exegetical Analysis

Hear the prayer of someone you know is innocent and worthy of protection (vv. 1-5)

The opening plea is not to be rescued from enemies (that comes in vv. 6-12) but to gain a sympathetic hearing. The same sequence of Hebrew verbs, "hear . . . attend . . . give ear," occurs also in Hos 5:1. The declaration of integrity (vv. 3-5) is necessary because sincerity in worship was demanded of individuals no less than of the nation (as in Isa 1:10-17, 29:13-14; Jer 6:16-21; Amos 5:21-24). "Let my vindication come" (v. 2) compares the judgment of the Lord to the rising sun that scatters evildoers by its morning rays (Job 38:12-13; Pss 19:5-6, 37:6; Hos 6:5). The parallel verse (Ps 17:2b, lit. "let your eyes see the right") continues the metaphor of light as the Lord's authoritative gaze. The other possible interpretation—"my vindication," a decision mediated by a priest, perhaps through the sacred lot shaken from a box—is unlikely, for the psalmist is asking for rescue rather than a legal decision; moreover, the interpretation is not a good parallel to verse 2a.

The verbs of verses 3-5 are in the perfect tense, indicating that God has already tested the psalmist (e.g., NAB: "You have tested my heart"). God knows that the psalmist's claim to be speaking "from lips free of deceit" (v. 1*b*) is true. NRSV translates the verbs of verse 3 as conditional ("if"). Textual uncertainties in verses 3*b*-4 make any translation somewhat tentative, but the gist is clear enough: God has tested, and the psalmist has passed the test with flying colors. The psalmist has been loyal in the relationship and now makes a claim on God.

Rescue me from the enemies who press in on me (vv. 6-12)

Having reminded God of their friendship that has been tested and found true, the psalmist comes to specifics: Act as my God and protect me from the present attack. "You will answer me" (v. 6*a*), for the bond between us is strong. Verse 7 applies a unique epithet to God: "O savior of those who seek refuge" in you (v. 7). "Wondrously show your steadfast love" in verse 7 is a dense phrase meaning something like "display your faithfulness (*ḥesed*) in marvelous deeds." *Ḥesed*, which NRSV usually renders as "steadfast love," is a covenantal term here. The psalmist, having been loyal in deed, now expects God to act loyally in return. Verse 8 is the exact center of the poem, with fifty-eight (Hebrew) words before and after it. Two verbs frame the verse: "guard me . . . hide me." "The apple of the eye" is the delicate and vulnerable center of the eye and face that one protects instinctively (Prov 7:2, Deut 32:10). The metaphor of taking shelter under "the shadow of your wings" (v. 8*b*) is also found in Pss 36:7, 57:1, 61:4, and 91:4. The metaphor is found also in the literature of Israel's neighbors. In Egypt disembodied wings represent divine protection. It is possible that the wings are the wings of the composite animal guardians of ancient Near Eastern thrones, which protect kings from their enemies. In the Bible, such guardians are called cherubim. The enemies' feet march in violence (v. 11), unlike the psalmist's feet that hold fast to God's paths (v. 5). Verse 12 mentions a single enemy as an example of predatory violence (v. 12*a*; NRSV uses the plural), comparing the enemy to a lion ready to spring from ambush (as in Pss 7:2, 10:9, 22:21). The danger is imminent and deadly.

Rise up, destroy the enemy and all offspring (vv. 13-14)

The imperative "rise up, O LORD!" (v. 13) begins a fresh section using vivid verbs of battle and rescue. Though verse 14 is textually uncertain, most take it in a positive sense: God fills the loyal with so many good things that their children enjoy it too (e.g., "May those whom you cherish have food in plenty, may their children be satisfied" REB). The REB translation "cherish" finds support from Ps 83:3b. Differently and rightly, NRSV takes Hebrew ṣpn in Ps 17:14c ("what you have stored up for them") as a punishment and interprets the rest of the verse as saying that the wicked and their children will be sated with the very evil they inflicted on others. The verb śāba' ("to have more than enough," v. 14d) occurs in a reversed sense in verse 15b ("I shall be satisfied") where the psalmist hopes to be sated in seeing the Lord.

The revenge expressed in verse 14 is entrusted completely into the hands of God for its execution. Personalizing evil, the psalmist asks that evil people be destroyed root and branch from God's universe.

The psalmist hopes to see the Lord in the Temple (v. 15)

Most individual laments contain an expression of trust such as this. Though still in danger, the psalmist speaks as if God has already acted, enjoying in anticipation God's gracious act. "Behold your face" describes seeing God in a theophany, as in Exod 24:11. Psalmists long to see God in the Temple in Ps 27:4 and Ps 42:2 ("When shall I come and behold the face of God?"). Seeing God is the anticipated outcome of seeking God's face in 2 Chron 7:14; Ps 24:6; 27:8; and Hos 5:15. The verses aptly conclude the poem. The opening verse asked the Lord to hear the psalmist's voice and give a favorable judgment. In the final verse, the psalmist asks to see the Lord's face (v. 15a) and "likeness" (təmûnāh). The latter word is used in the commandment against making images (Exod 20:4; Deut 5:8). Conversing and seeing are the two privileged modes of divine-human encounter and take place in the Lord's own house.

Theological and Ethical Analysis

Some laments are made in desperation, allowing no time for a reverent approach to the divine throne. Though danger is real in this psalm, the psalmist first asks for an attentive hearing, reminding God of past loyalty and integrity before coming to the specific need of the moment—threatening enemies. At the conclusion, the psalmist is not content with being protected but asks for the complete destruction of the enemies. The psalmist's desires are broader than rescue from an immediate danger. The psalmist desires access to God as a loyal friend and also desires that God's universe be free from the ravages of sinners. The pray-er's ultimate goal is to be with God—being heard, seeing God's face. First comes one's relationship to God, and afterwards, petitions for divine benefits.

The poem is a touching expression of a relationship to God. The singer has a strong expectation of being taken seriously by God, of being known, of being valued as a faithful friend. Building on the covenanted friendship, the psalmist has no hesitation in bringing the most urgent needs to God's attention, confident of God's love and power. Even more than a particular favor, the psalmist hopes for a deeper and more reciprocal relationship to the Lord.

PSALM 18

Psalm 18 shifts the topic from the subject of the three preceding psalms, the Temple, to the king (though the king is often associated with the Temple). It is the third longest poem in the Psalter (after Pss 119 and 78). A nearly identical version is found in 2 Sam 22.

Literary Analysis

If Ps 18 ended at verse 24, it would be easy to classify it as a royal thanksgiving, for the Davidic king praises the Lord in verses 1-3 and 20-24 in response to the Lord's rescue that is narrated in verses 4-19. The king was caught in Sea's toils and the Lord in the guise of Storm God defeated Sea and "took me; he drew me out of mighty waters" (v. 16). The poem continues beyond verse 24, however, as the king describes how the Lord favored him (vv. 25-27) and made him a powerful military leader (vv. 28-42) and head of the nations (vv. 43-45). In verses 46-50, the king once again directly praises the Lord. What added meaning does the second part of the poem provide?

One possible approach is to consider verses 25-45 as the historical description of the Davidic king's military and diplomatic career, corresponding to the heavenly description of divine power in verses 7-19. Other royal psalms such as Pss 2, 18, and 72 mix cosmic and historical language. Verses 25-45 do not, however, have the appearance of a narrative of a specific past event. They describe the Lord's customary behavior toward the king. Verses 31-34a use participles, which in Hebrew describe customary ways of acting, not finite verbs, which are used for specific actions. Only in verse 34b does a finite verb appear, and it is immediately followed by verses 35-45, which describe the characteristics of a successful king rather than a royal victory.

This commentary prefers a slightly different interpretation: The Lord's intervention on behalf of the king (vv. 4-19) is not an ordinary rescue from a crisis but the installation of the king as viceroy after the Lord's world-establishing victory. In Ps 89 the Lord installs the king (vv. 19-28) following his victory over Sea (vv. 5-18). Psalm 89 also opens with a statement of the Lord's love of the king (vv. 1-2; cf. 18:1-3, 46-50), affirms the incomparability of the Lord (89:6-7; cf. 18:31), has the Lord grant the king success in war (89:21-26; cf. 18:29-42), and gives him preeminence among the nations (89:27; cf. 18:43-45).

It is helpful to note here two features of the biblical treatment of origins. The Bible can depict the origin of Israel either in historical language (as is normally the case in the narratives of the Pentateuch), or it can depict the origin in mythic or cosmic language (as in Exod 15 and Ps 89). Sometimes the Bible mixes mythic and historical language, as in Ps 77. Second, the Bible roots biblical kingship not in the historical victories of David and Solomon, but in the cosmic victories of Yahweh over Sea. The biblical tendency is to correlate the victories of Davidic kings with the primordial victory of Yahweh. Because the king's authority was grounded in God's authority, the court poet reminds God of the choosing of David "at the creation" whenever the king suffers defeat: Remember your ancient promise! In Ps 18, the king recalls with intense gratitude not just any merciful rescue but one above all others: the exaltation of David "in the beginning," which is the source of all royal authority. God's choice of David is the basis of the arming and guidance of the king (vv. 25-45).

The poetic structure is visible even in translation. The tenses of the verbs and their subjects are important features. In verses 1-6, the royal "I" is the subject; in verses 7-19, the subject is the Lord, and the verbs are mostly narrative perfects (or equivalent forms); verses 20-24 are separate, framed by verses 20a and 24a ("the Lord rewarded/recompensed me according to my righteousness") and by the return of the royal "I"; in verses 25-34a the psalmist begins to address God in the second person singular, first using the participle form characteristic of hymnic style (vv. 31-34a) and then shifting to the imperfect tense used to describe customary past action (vv. 34b-47). The final verses (vv. 46-50) return to the first person praise of the opening verses (vv. 1-3).

Exegetical Analysis

The superscription locates the psalm in those occasions when David was delivered from the threats of his enemy Saul such as 1 Sam 18:10-30, 19:8-17, 22, 24, and 26. Saul refused to recognize the divine choice of David.

*I acknowledge the Lord who protects me from
my enemies (vv. 1-3)*

The eight metaphors for God in verses 1-2 are all metaphors of power and might, as one expects in a celebration of the Lord as protector of the king. "I call upon the LORD" (v. 3) echoes "I love" (v. 1), for both describe the king's attitude. The verbs refer to habitual acts: The king constantly loves and calls upon the Lord, and the Lord always responds in wonderful reciprocity.

*Caught in Sea's toils, the king called out and
the Lord rescued him (vv. 4-19)*

The section is marked off by its single story of danger, call for help, and the Lord's march to the rescue. The subject of nearly every verb in verses 9-19 is the Lord. Unity comes from the mention of the Sea at the beginning (vv. 4-5) and at the end (vv. 15-16). Verse 19*b* ("because he delighted in me") forms a transition to the next section about the king's loyalty (vv. 20-24).

The drama of verses 4-19 has several scenes: The king, trapped in the morass of Sea (vv. 4-5), calls out to the Lord, who hears from his heavenly palace (v. 6); the Lord responds as God of the storm, accompanied by earth-shaking thunder (vv. 7, 13), lightning (vv. 8, 12, 14), and swift clouds dark with rain (vv. 9*b*, 10*b*, 11, 12). The storm is initially described on its own terms (a rumbling that shakes mountains, v. 7), but then the storm phenomena are applied to the deity. Clouds are the smoke of his nostrils; lightning flashes are glowing coals emanating from him; the swift clouds are his chariot; winds and lightning are his weapons pushing back the waters to expose its depths where the king is trapped. The Storm God's immediate goal is not to annihilate Sea, however, but to rescue the king (vv. 16-17).

Sea threatens as in Pss 46:2, 65:7, 74:13, 77:19, 89:9 and especially Jonah 2:1-6, where Sheol is in "the heart of the seas," and where Jonah complains that "the flood surrounded me; all your waves and your billows passed over me" (Jonah 2:3). In some ancient Near Eastern myths, boundless Sea engulfed the earth until it was pushed back to its present boundaries (the oceans) by the victorious Storm God. Being trapped in Sea is thus an apt metaphor for being in desperate trouble. That the Lord was in "his temple" (v. 6c) suggests he has already vanquished Sea and currently rules, for in the myths the god's palace (temple) was built after the battle to symbolize the cosmic victory. In Ps 18:6, the king's distressful cry rouses the Lord who marches from his heavenly palace with storm weapons to the beleaguered king. The Lord "takes" *(lāqaḥ)*, "draws out," and "delivers" the king from the "mighty waters," a phrase often used of Sea (e.g., Pss 29:3, 77:19, 93:4). The verb "to take" *(lāqaḥ)* develops an ancient Near Eastern and biblical tradition of just individuals taken up to heaven. The antediluvian hero Enoch escaped death in a mysterious manner: "Enoch walked with God; then he was no more, because God took *[lāqaḥ]* him" (Gen 5:24). It is modeled on Mesopotamian antediluvian heroes such as Utnapishtim in *Gilgamesh* (tablet X) who were "taken up" (Akkadian *leqû*) to heaven. Elijah was similarly taken by God to heaven in 2 Kgs 2:1-12 (*lāqaḥ* occurs in v. 10).

The "taking up" of the Davidic king is thus much more than a rescue from an ordinary danger. It is in fact the exaltation of the king, and the psalm functions as a kind of founding legend of the Davidic king. According to the Psalter, the kings' universal authority comes not from the victories of David and Solomon but from the great victory of Yahweh, the patron of the dynasty and guarantor of his dynastic authority. Psalms 2, 46, 48, 72, and 89 presuppose the same dynamic.

The Lord rewarded me according to my righteousness (vv. 20-24)

The last colon of the previous section (v. 19b, "because he delighted in me") provides the transition to this section. Verse 24 echoes verse 20 and marks off the section as distinct. The king's assertion that it is because of his righteousness that God has acted may surprise modern readers accustomed to think of God's choices as utterly gracious and independent of human action. The king here is not talking about his behavior as such but about his relationship to his dynastic patron. The relationship is covenantal: two parties willingly assuming obligations in affectionate mutuality. The king asserts he has fulfilled his obligations in the relationship and waits expectantly upon the Lord, the covenant partner.

Through the Lord I have prevailed and am head of the nations (vv. 25-45)

A new section begins with the shift to the second person singular in verse 25 (reinforced by the repeated second person singular pronoun in vv. 28-29). The second singular pronoun persists until verse 45. Only verses 30-34 speak of the Lord in the third person. The topics follow logically: celebrating the Lord as loyal friend (vv. 25-31), the Lord's arming the king for battle and granting him victory (vv. 32-42), and the installation of the king as head of the kings of the world. The open and trusting relationship of king and God is expressed in verses 25-31; its mutuality should not be viewed as presumption or lack of humility. The king delights in the relationship. Though characterized by mutuality, the relationship is not equal in any literal sense, for it is God who provides the basic realities of life. To "light my lamp" (v. 28a) is to grant prosperity as in 2 Sam 21:17.

Verses 43-45 show the inevitable result of being victorious—the Davidic king becomes preeminent among the kings of the world. The foundation of the preeminence is the cosmic victory of the divine patron of the dynasty, however, not the military exploits of the Judean kings. The kings were not major players in the ancient Near East, being far overshadowed by Egypt, Assyria, and Babylon. The universal sovereignty of the Davidic king was rooted in something greater than human achievement—the universal sovereignty of Yahweh.

I acknowledge the Lord who exalts me over my enemies (vv. 46-50)

Several words from verses 1-3 reappear here, bringing the poem to its conclusion: "my rock," "my salvation," "my deliverer" ("who delivered") and "the LORD." The oath, "The LORD lives" (v. 46) shows the depth of the king's response to the Lord's initiative. It is the only such oath in the Psalter, though it occurs many times in the historical books. The king wants the Lord to be known throughout the world, "blessed" (v. 46a) or acknowledged as great. Since the king was exalted by the Lord (vv. 4-19), he has a corresponding obligation to see that the Lord is honored among the nations.

Theological and Ethical Analysis

The royal psalm is unusual in its portrayal of the king's affectionate loyalty to his Lord. The king owes his very life to the Lord and so glories in the Lord as his shield and strength. The relationship between king and divine patron is intensely mutual, marked on the one side by obedience and praise and on the other by the grant of strength, victory, and authority.

Some modern readers might be uncomfortable with the emphasis laid on military achievement, for example, "I struck them down, so that they were not able to rise; they fell under my feet" (v. 38). One must appreciate, however, that kingship in that period consisted in performance rather than in ceremonials, as with kings today. Divine justice, of which the king was an instrument, was concrete and earthly. It meant upholding the righteous and putting down the wicked. Force was necessary, for only through the implementation of justice did the kingdom and rule of God become visible. In ancient Israel the just God's desire for justice was institutionalized in kingship and realized through the Davidic king. The kings often failed, of course, in which case they endured vigorous criticism and even rejection by the prophets. But kingship should finally be regarded as a holy institution given to Israel for the promotion of faith and justice on earth.

Christians praying this psalm will inevitably think of Jesus, Son of David, whose relationship to God is founded upon God's rescue of him from the power of death. They will think further of

Jesus as the just one who animates the church to be an instrument of peace and justice in the world.

PSALM 19

Psalm 19 is one of three poems in the Psalter on the torah, the others being Pss 1 and 119. It shares with them the conviction that the torah is transformative. Psalm 19 is distinctive in relating the wisdom discernible in the heavens to that discernible in the revealed word. Hebrew *tôrāh* (v. 7*a*) is variously rendered "law" (NRSV, REB, NAB), "teaching" (NJPS), and "torah." The term is broader than "law," for it can refer to narratives and instructions as well as legal materials. Jews, for example, give the name Torah to the Pentateuch, which is a mix of many genres. "Authoritative teaching" is an apt rendering, for it expresses the divine source of the writings, their variety, and their transformative goal.

Literary Analysis

The poem does not fit into the usual psalm genres, though it resembles a hymn in its praise of divine wisdom (vv. 1-11) and an individual petition (lament) in its plea for forgiveness and enlightenment (vv. 12-14). Many scholars regard it as a composite of two poems: Ps 19A (vv. 1-6), about God's revelation through the heavens and the sun, and Ps 19B (vv. 7-14), about the law/teaching that enlightens and purifies the disciple. Parts A and B are often judged to have different origins: a Canaanite hymn to the sun (part A) and a meditation arising from Second Temple "torah piety" (part B). Some scholars regard verses 11-14 as a further addition. Recent commentary, however, has been more concerned with the unified poem than with its sources.

Whatever the details of its composition, the poetic logic is clear: The divine wisdom (meaning ability to govern) discernible in the daily movements of the heavens (vv. 1-4*b*), especially in the sun's course (vv. 4*c*-6), is also visible in the teaching (vv. 7-9) to which human beings have access through humble prayer (vv. 10-14). The focus narrows and intensifies as the poem moves from the heavens praising El (NRSV: "God," v. 1*a*) as creator to the individual praying for light to "my rock and my redeemer" (vv. 11-14). At the center of the movement from the words of the heavens to the words of the servant is the torah (vv. 7-10), which embodies the wisdom of creation and enables human beings to be pleasing to God. The psalmist's feelings of awe and desire inspire the petition of verses 11-14. The poem could serve as an illustration of the famous phrase of Rudolf Otto (1869–1937), *mysterium tremendum et fascinans*, "the mystery that makes one tremble even as it attracts."

Exegetical Analysis

The heavens declare the glory of God (vv. 1-6)

Other psalms mention the heavenly glory of God. Psalm 148 invites the sun and moon, shining stars, and highest heavens to praise the Lord their creator. Psalm 8:3-4 expresses awe that the maker of the heavens should be concerned with lowly earth creatures, human beings: "When I look at your heavens, the work of your fingers, the moon and the stars that you have established; what are human beings that you are mindful of them?" Ps 19 shares these sentiments, but goes further by imagining the heavens themselves "telling the glory." In Ps 96:3, human beings do the telling (Israelites) and the hearing (the nations). In Psalm 19, telling the glory is done through one day (and night) pouring forth speech to the next. How is this done? It is the sun that makes day succeed night. Though the sun will be explicitly mentioned only in verses 4*c*-6, it is already implied in verse 4*ab* by the verb "goes out" (*yāṣāʾ*, used of the sun's rising in verse 5*a*, "comes out") and in the phrase "to the end of the world (used of the sun's course in v. 6*ab*). The sun's course covers "all the earth" and reaches "the end of the world" (see the same use in Pss 50:1; 113:3; Isa 45:6; Mal 1:11). The reader is thus not surprised when the sun is explicitly mentioned in verses 4*c*-6, for vocabulary associated with it has already appeared.

There is a remarkable paradox in the heavenly telling of the glory of God: The heavens do not speak, yet their speech goes out to every corner of the world (vv. 3-4*b*). The paradox will be partially resolved when the sun is introduced in verse 4*c*.

God has made a "tent for the sun" (v. 4*c*), which would have been an elaborate tent dwelling befitting a heavenly personage. The gods in the Ugaritic texts had such tent dwellings, and some biblical texts (e.g., Pss 15:1, 27:5, 61:4) mention the tent of Yahweh. In one Ugaritic myth, the storm god, Baal, complains to the high god El that he has no tent like the other gods, which is an indirect way of asking for an increase in status. That Yahweh makes a tent for the sun demonstrates that the sun is a thoroughly subordinate figure in the heavenly world, a servant (albeit an important one) of the Lord rather than an independent deity.

In two striking metaphors (v. 5), the sun is compared to a bridegroom just emerging from his bridal chamber, radiant and vital, and to a runner rejoicing to run his course at full speed. "Its course," the last Hebrew word in verse 5, is elaborated in verse 6: the sun's course extends from one end of the world to the other (v. 6*ab*), and no area can hide from its powerful burning rays. The sun's energy is unflagging, its brilliance undimmed, its joy unhindered. Joy and exultation may strike readers as odd qualities to ascribe to the sun. The sun, however, brings life to all things on earth and enables their beauty to be seen and appreciated. The qualities of the sun point ahead to the teaching of the Lord, which rejoices the heart and enlightens the eyes (v. 8*bd*).

The teaching that brings benefits to human beings (vv. 7-10)

The first section called God "El" (NRSV: "God," v. 1*a*), a name sometimes associated with creation (e.g., Gen 14:19, 22; Isa 42:5). This section six times calls God "Yahweh," the name associated with the exodus and the giving of the law at Sinai. The seventh occurrence of "Yahweh" will be in the prayer of verse 14. The section also has six synonyms for *tôrāh* (vv. 7-9), which

NRSV renders "law," "decrees," "precepts," "commandment," "fear," and "ordinances." The first four terms (vv. 7-8) transform human beings, "reviving," "making wise," "rejoicing," and "enlightening" them. The effect of the teaching is practical: "reviving the soul" (v. 7a) means to comfort in sadness, to encourage (as in Lam 1:16b, "for a comforter is far from me, one to *revive my courage*"); "making wise the simple" (v. 7b) means to bring the young to maturity (cf. Prov 21:11); "rejoicing the heart" (Prov 27:11) and "enlightening the eyes" mean to give joy and restore vitality (see 1 Sam 14:27, Ps 13:3). The final two descriptions of the teaching are concerned with the teaching itself rather than with its effect on humans (v. 9). The fear of the Lord and the ordinances are everlasting and "righteous," that is, they fully express God's will. Verse 10 declares the teaching to be desirable above all else and points forward to the final prayer by using the language of desire, which is also used of wisdom in Prov 3:15; 8:11.

May the teaching enlighten and cleanse me and
make my poem pleasing to you (vv. 11-14)

The focus has moved from the heavens to instruction and now it is directed to the psalmist. A play on words makes the link: "by them is your servant warned" *(nizhār)*. The same verb (or a homonym) can also mean "be illuminated." The psalmist recognizes the "reward" (v. 11b) of paying attention to and memorizing ("keeping") the teaching. The question of verse 12 ("But who can detect their errors?") reminds one of the brilliance of the sun and the teaching from which nothing is hidden (v. 6c). The prayer is to let *me* see my hidden sins that I may confess and be rid of them. "Errors" and "hidden faults" (v. 12) are unintentional. In ancient Near Eastern culture, an action itself, without reference to human intention, could be reckoned a transgression requiring expiation. "Errors" seem to be actions the psalmist consciously did and only later learned were sins. "Hidden faults" are actions the psalmist unconsciously did and later learned were sinful. "Hidden faults" refers back to "is hid" in verse 6, reminding us that nothing is hidden from the sun and from God. In contrast to the heavens, which praise the Lord directly by their very function, human beings need to be purified before they are able to tell of the glory of the Lord.

Finally, the poet expresses the hope that the psalm itself, "the words of my mouth and the meditation of my heart" (v. 14) be accepted by the Lord as a personal response to the gifts of creation and instruction. As one formed by the protocol of the royal court, the poet elegantly asks for the favor of acceptance.

Theological and Ethical Analysis

Though scholars rightly emphasize the Bible's concern with God acting in history, it is also concerned with God acting in nature, as in this poem. A dichotomous distinction between human beings (history) and nature is modern and not biblical. The Bible uses mythic and historic language for the same event. To take one example, Israel's three pilgrimage feasts celebrated historical and agricultural realities in the same rituals. Psalm 19 paradoxically finds the silent movement of the heavens eloquent in praise and draws an analogy between the sun that illuminates the earth and the divine teaching that illuminates human beings. Awed yet attracted, the poet asks that the revealing and purifying light bring wholeness and make the poem an acceptable offering to God, "my rock and my redeemer."

The poem is a guide for Jews and Christians who find the God of Israel in the marvels of the universe. It is a reminder of God's wisdom in the biblical sense of being able to govern, to organize things great and small and bring them to their appointed ends (vv. 1-6). It also reminds us that God's wisdom is not simply "out there," but is available in the words of torah (vv. 7-10), initiating a discourse that inspires repentance (vv. 11-13) and praise (v. 14). First John 1:5 in a sense comments on Ps 19 in declaring that "God is light and in him there is no darkness at all." Bernard Abbot of Clairvaux (1090–1153) cites verse 4c to show the credibility of God's testimony: "He has gone so far as to pitch his tent in the sun so even the dimmest eyes see him" (PL, Sermo I in "Epiphania Domini," 133:141-43).

PSALM 20

Literary Analysis

The king enjoyed an exalted position in the ancient Near East and in Israel, which is especially celebrated in the psalms. Among the Davidic kings' responsibilities were maintaining the Temple on Mount Zion, seeing that sacrifices were correctly offered in it, and leading the army in battle. These roles form the subject matter of Ps 20. The Temple is where the Lord dwells and from where he will send help. The Lord promised about the Temple that "My name shall be there" (1 Kgs 8:29), and Ps 20 mentions "the name" three times (vv. 1, 5, 7). The singer asks the Lord to remember the offerings the king has made (v. 3). The central petition is that the Lord give victory to the king on the grounds that he trusts in the Lord alone.

The psalm has two equal parts (vv. 1-5, 6-9), each with thirty-three Hebrew words. The first part is a petition, and the second part is the singer's assurance that the prayer has been heard ("Now I know that the LORD will help his anointed") and a final petition. The phrase "the LORD answer you [or us]" occurs as petition (v. 1), assurance (v. 6), and petition (v. 9). The second person singular pronoun (e.g., "the LORD answer you," v. 1) occurs ten times in verses 1-5; in verse 6, the third person pronoun occurs three times; in verses 7-9, the pronoun "we" (the community) occurs twice and the pronoun "us" occurs twice, showing that the king is a representative of the community as well as a figure in his own right.

Exegetical Analysis

May the Lord send you help from Zion, O King (vv. 1-5)

Israelite theologians speak with great care about God's presence in the Temple, avoiding formulations that might imply God lived in the Temple as a permanent resident. This psalm uses Deuteronomic language of the divine name dwelling in the Temple to hear prayer and provide assistance to petitioners to make it clear that God dwells permanently in heaven. Such careful language is found in Deut 14:23, 16:2; 2 Kgs 21:7. King Solomon in 1 Kgs 8:44-45 has in view the very situation of this psalm: "If your people go out to battle against their enemy, by whatever way you shall send them, and they pray to the LORD toward the city that you have chosen and the house that I have built for your name, then hear in heaven their prayer and their plea, and maintain their cause." The "day of trouble" (v. 1) is a military crisis requiring the king to lead the army into battle. The singer asks God to remember to the king's credit all the sacrifices he has commanded to be offered in the Temple (v. 3); they are signs of his devotion as a loyal child and client of the Lord.

Desires of a king (vv. 4-5) were significant (cf. 1 Kgs 3:3-15), for people supposed that as a loyal client of the Lord, he held the interests of the Lord's people—especially their safety—close to his heart. The poet looks forward to a triumphant celebration of a royal victory as is indicated by "shout for joy" and "banners" (v. 5).

Assurance of victory (vv. 6-9)

"Now I know" signals a shift from prayer to pledge. "I know" elsewhere expresses great confidence in God's work (e.g., Job 19:25; Pss 41:11; 56:9). What is the basis of the assurance? It is possible that between verse 5 and verse 6 an officiant delivered an oracle (not transmitted with this psalm) assuring victory, in which case the speaker simply echoes the statement. It is equally possible, however, that verse 6 itself ("Now I know") is the assurance. As if in response to the prayer of verse 1*a*, verse 6*b* asserts that

God "will answer him." In accord with the theology of divine presence mentioned in 1 Kings 8, divine help will come from heaven in the form of victory by God's hand (v. 6bc). Accordingly, king and people renounce trust in the great weapons of the age—chariots and horses—in order to rely wholly on the name of the Lord. Horses and chariots will collapse in battle, but we, strengthened by your name, will stand firm.

The last verse reprises the opening prayer, indicating that actual victory, though promised, still lies in the future. The Masoretic Text can be read as implying that Yahweh is king ("let the King answer us when we call"), whereas the Septuagint and most Christian translations understand the king to be the human king. Such a king needs the prayers of the community.

Theological and Ethical Analysis

Can a prayer originally composed for the Davidic king prior to his going to battle for Israel be prayed by Jews and Christians today? Yes, for the king represented the people, meaning that prayer offered for him was offered for the entire holy people. Second Temple Judaism prayed the psalm to express their hope that a Davidic king would again take the throne and restore Israel. Christians think of the Christ, son of David, who represents the holy community. They pray that God support the church in time of trouble, regarding with favor its offerings and prayers, and granting victory in its witnessing of the gospel to an often hostile world. The church ought to have faith especially in the name (vv. 1, 5, 7) alone and wait for God to answer its prayers (vv. 1, 6, 9). The prayer can also identify the triune God, as the "anointed" (the Christ) trusts in the Lord for rescue.

PSALM 21

This royal thanksgiving is a companion to Ps 20, which prayed for victory for the king setting out for battle. There are verbal links between the two psalms (e.g., 20:4 and 21:2; 20:6; and 21:9, 13) and also between Ps 21 and the great royal Ps 18. The thanksgiving in 18:1-24 resembles 21:1-7, and the equipping of the king in 18:25-45 resembles 21:8-12. The poet's enthusiastic embrace of the institution of kingship contrasts sharply with the prophets' criticism of the kings. The psalms view kingship as a divine gift for the governance and protection of the people; they do not concern themselves with assessing the performance of individual kings.

Literary Analysis

The genre is a royal thanksgiving, which reports the king's victory achieved with the Lord's help. The report is a form of praise because hearers will glorify the Lord upon hearing of the exploits of the king. The structure of the poem is not complex; most scholars discern a thanksgiving in verses 1-7 and a royal commission in verses 8-12, with verse 13 as a concluding prayer. The final verse reprises from verse 1*a* "your strength" and "O LORD." Though most scholars believe verse 7 ends part 1, one can make a case that verse 7 begins part 2 (understanding *kî* as a particle rather than as the conjunction *for*) on the grounds that v. 6 reprises words from part 1 (e.g., "you set/bestow" *[tāśît]* from v. 3; "blessings" from v. 3; "forever" from v. 4; and the root "rejoice/joy" from v. 1). Verses 1-6 seem to be chiastically arranged with verse 3 in the center and verses 2 and 4 paralleling each other.

One can easily imagine the king standing in full regalia before the court while a singer recounts his great achievements and an officiant places a crown on his head (v. 3*b*). His glory is the reflection of divine glory (v. 5). Resplendent in his royal garb, he listens as the court poet promises him further divine help in future wars (vv. 8-12) and asks the Lord to act and to attend to the community's prayer (v. 13).

Exegetical Analysis

O God, you have fulfilled all the king's desires (vv. 1-7)

The verbs "rejoices" and "exults" in verse 1 refer to the display as well as the feelings of joy. The context suggests that "joy" includes songs, processions, and dances, for the psalm celebrates the king's victory (vv. 5a, 6a). One can imagine two possible occasions for the psalm: the king returning from a successful military campaign or an annual liturgy celebrating the king as delegate of the victorious Lord of justice (perhaps a New Year festival). At any rate, the singer attributes the victories as the Lord's granting the king "his heart's desire" and "the request of his lips" (v. 2). As indicated by Solomon's inaugural dream at Gibeon in which God said, "Ask what I should give you" (1 Kgs 3:5), the king was expected to pray to the dynastic God. His task was to protect and rule the people justly so their prosperity would show forth the grandeur of their God. The king would naturally pray for success in war. In praying for military success, the king ultimately was praying that God's justice be done on earth, for battle was not for its own sake but for the implementation of the will of God despite the opposition of the wicked.

The request for life, and the seemingly odd phrase granting "length of days forever and ever" (v. 4) may be responses to the court salutation, "May the king live forever!" (e.g., Neh 2:3; Dan 3:9; 5:10). The concern is for the longevity of the king and the prospect of royal scions. The divine gifts—"blessings," "crown," "glory," "splendor and majesty," "joy," and stability ("not be moved," v. 7b)—show how richly gifted are king and people at this special moment.

Commission of the king and concluding prayer (vv. 8-13)

As noted above, some regard verse 7 as the beginning of part 2. Part 2 is exclusively concerned with equipping the king as a triumphant warrior (cf. Ps 18:25-45). King and patron deity act with perfect synergy, the king's hand finding out his enemies (v. 8) and the Lord swallowing them in wrath (v. 9b). The ultimate purpose of the exploits should be emphasized: to establish divine justice in a world that is hostile to the Lord and the Lord's people. The king is the human instrument of the Lord.

The idiom "your hand will find out" elsewhere means "to do as one judges best" (e.g., Judg 9:33; 1 Sam 10:7; Eccl 9:10). Here the meaning seems to be that the king's sword, held in the hand, will unfailingly reach its target. "When you appear" (v. 9) refers to the dread inspired by the divinely aided king rushing against his enemies. The Storm God's lightning flashes burn them alive (v. 9). The enemies' offspring will be destroyed so that no descendant will carry on their nefarious work (v. 10). NRSV takes verse 11 as a conditional sentence ("if they plan evil"); it is possible also to take it as grounding the preceding ("for they plotted wickedly against you"). Whatever happens, the king will be up to the task (v. 12). The king is portrayed as superhuman. German scholars describe such effusive rhetoric as *Hofstil*, "court style" or ceremonial language.

The final petition (v. 13) makes it clear that the success of the king depends utterly upon the favor of the Lord, the patron of the dynasty. It is the Lord's strength that will bring about divine justice. The king is only an instrument who must wait upon the Lord.

Theological and Ethical Analysis

The institution of kingship (not necessarily any individual king) is here regarded as a divine gift. The holy community and its leader are analogously regarded as instruments of divine justice in the world. The psalm presumes the human community beyond Israel will oppose that justice and even attack the community. It therefore talks of battle and victory instead of talking of the just and prosperous world that the Lord will bring about. The psalm celebrates a moment in the drama of the holy community's role in effecting divine justice: the king's return from a victorious campaign or the king's delegation as the Lord's instrument of justice.

Modern readers, perhaps put off by the attention given to the military role of the king, need to keep in mind the ultimate goal of celebrating the military role of the king: to implement divine justice in an often hostile world. Divine justice, as is often said, means the upholding of the righteous poor and the putting down of the wicked. According to the psalm, the battle is not for national grandeur but for the glory of the Lord. Execution and timetable are in the hands of the Lord. It must be said, however, that the military language can be easily misused. The interests of the people of God are not necessarily those of God, though the people may say otherwise. It is all too easy to brand one's own enemies as God's enemies.

Christian readers will read the psalm in light of the full Christian narrative in which Christ is the Davidic king, the Son whom God has equipped to battle evil and form the community. To him is given "life" and "length of days forever and ever." He is the instrument of justice who upholds the humble and puts down the proud. One can just as well apply the psalm to the Body of Christ, which continues the task of resisting evil and being an instrument of divine peace.

PSALM 22

Psalm 22 is a remarkable blend of expressions of anguish (vv. 1-2, 6-8, 12-18), recollections of God's healing presence (vv. 3-5, 9-11), gratitude for rescue (vv. 22-26), and grand dreams of God's universal sovereignty (vv. 27-31). One could almost take the sections as independent psalms. How the parts fit together is not easy to discern. Especially troublesome to interpreters is the relation of the opening complaint and prayer (vv. 1-21) to the triumphant second part (vv. 22-31). Indeed, the diversity of the sentiments led prominent scholars of a previous generation to conclude that the second part was added later. A good case can be made, however, that the poem was complete from the beginning.

Judaism and Christianity have understood the psalm differently. In one strand of Jewish interpretation, David (mentioned in the superscription) foresees the bleak days of exile in the Persian period, in particular the threat of Haman and King Ahasuerus against the Jews who are represented by Esther. The sufferings in the psalm are therefore corporate as is the eventual triumph. In the New Testament, the psalm was used more than any other to interpret the sufferings of Jesus as those of an innocent and just person vindicated by God (Matt 26:24; 27:35, 39, 46; Mark 15:24, 29, 34; Luke 23:34-36; John 19:24, 28).

Literary Analysis

The poem is an individual lament, though it stretches its conventions. All the components of a lament are present: The cry for help is in verses 1-2; the complaint, which is exceptionally long, is in verses 6-18; the prayer is in verses 1-2, 11, and 19-21. The statement of trust goes beyond convention, for verses 22-31 (a third of the poem) boldly express confidence that God will provide rescue and be acknowledged as supreme by the whole world. It is precisely the length and the triumphant tone of the "statement of trust" that puzzle interpreters.

There are two parts to the long ending, one closely linked to the lament and the other less so. Verses 22-26 are the thanksgiving in response to the troubles depicted in verses 1-21. The sufferer promises to provide this thanksgiving if deliverance is granted. To be sure, the promise is unusually long and elaborate. Verses 27-31 are another matter. The reference to the nations is unexpected in a private thanksgiving. Hence, one must allow for the possibility that the material has been added or, better, that the singer is not a private individual but the king himself. Jewish interpretation, it will be recalled, tended to regard the psalm as corporate rather than private.

In structure, the poem has two parts: verses 1-21 and 22-31. Verses 1-2 are the overture, stating the theme of God's absence in both space ("far") and time ("day" and "night") and establishing a mood of anguish and isolation: I call but there is no response, though you are known as the God who always helped our ancestors (vv. 3-5). Even my enemies recognize that you are my God

(vv. 6-8) and indeed I have called you so from birth (vv. 9-11). Verse 11 (including v. 10*b* "my God") is the midpoint of part 1, pointing back to verse 1 ("my God," "why are you so far") and forward to verse 19 ("You Lord" and "do not be far away"). Verses 12-18 are the complaint proper: Enemies in the form of wild animals circle around, devastating me psychologically (vv. 12-15), *destroying me socially* (vv. 16-18). A prayer, woven from the preceding lament, concludes part 1 (vv. 19-21).

In part 2, the brief statement of trust is expanded into an elaborate promise to proclaim to "my brothers and sisters" the anticipated rescue of the psalmist (vv. 22-24) and to celebrate it liturgically (vv. 25-26). The poem contrasts living with bestial enemies and living with loving kindred. Animal and subhuman imagery dominate the first section (vv. 6, 12-13, 16, 20-21) but gives way to kinship terms and the image of fellow worshipers in the Temple. Verses 27-31 overcome the distance of space and time that previously characterized the relationship to God. Far-off nations will come to Jerusalem to worship Yahweh; those who have gone before and generations yet unborn will serve him.

Exegetical Analysis

The cry, lament, and prayer (vv. 1-21)

In the superscription, "the Deer of the Dawn" is uncertain in meaning; it may be the title of the musical accompaniment. Part 1 consists of verses 1-21, within which are subsections distinguished by the mention of "you" (God) or "I" (the poet) or both together. In verses 1-2, "you" and "I" together play an important role. In 3-5, "you" dominates, and in verses 6-8, "I" is the prevalent pronoun. In verses 9-11, "you" and "I" occur together once again. Verses 9-11 complete the first half of part 1 not only by juxtaposing "you" and "I" but also by reprising "my God" (v. 10*b*) and "near" (v. 11*a*) from verse 1.

In verses 1-2, the psalmist complains of God's absence with a poignant "Why?" "You do not answer" *('ānāh)* in verse 2 will be reprised in "rescued" (lit. "answered," *'ānāh)* in verse 21*b*. The great reversal at the end of the psalm will speak of God's power at work in the sacred space of the Temple (v. 27) and in the time of present (v. 29) and future (vv. 30-31).

Verses 3-5 shift to "you." "Yet you" in verse 3 is matched in verse 6 by "But I." The psalmist has a prayer strategy that is based on the identities and relationship of God and the psalmist. God's role is described by saying: You are holy, a king ("enthroned"), and the patron of Israel whose prayers you always answer. Verses 7-11 will emphasize that I am persecuted precisely because I am your client ("commit your cause to the LORD, let him deliver"). Yet verses 1-2 have already made clear that God is not answering the psalmist's pleas. The psalmist seeks the deliverance that the ancestors routinely obtained from God.

Verses 6-11 shift the perspective yet again, this time from God back to the psalmist. Though the crisis is not detailed (as often seen in individual laments), it involves loss of honor that has led to ostracism and ridicule. The psalmist, considered subhuman and excluded, makes clear that the cause of the ostracism is fidelity to God. Verse 6 reverses the statement in Isa 41:14, "Do not fear, you worm Jacob."

Verse 11 is the transition between the two halves of part 1. It is the conclusion to verses 9-10 (you were near me at birth, do not be far) and to the entire first half of part 1 ("my God" and "far" in vv. 10b-11a point back to v. 1a). Verse 11 also points forward to the second half of part 1 by anticipating the vocabulary and prayer of the last lines of part 1: Verse 11 is the first direct prayer in the psalm ("do not be far") and points to the three petitions in verses 19-21; "do not be far" will appear again in verse 19a.

Verses 12-18 are the complaint proper, though verses 1-2 and 6-8 have already hinted at misery. In an unusually long and sustained metaphor, the enemies are portrayed as wild animals circling the terrified and helpless psalmist. Like the parallelism in verses 1-11, verses 12-18 also show a parallelism: verses 12-15 // 16-18. Each section begins with animals circling (vv. 12-13, 16ab) and ends with the effect upon the psalmist (vv. 14-15, 16c-18). In the first section, the effect is portrayed in more inward terms (psychological and physiological); in the second section, more outward terms are used (the outer surface of the body and loss of honor).

Laments often compare the enemy to a wild animal, for example, "like a lion they will tear me apart" (Ps 7:2) and "I say . . . to the wicked, 'Do not lift up your horn' " (Ps 75:4). The dogs in Ps 22:16 are not scavengers but hunting dogs, which are portrayed on ancient seals attacking humans. Bashan is a region northeast of the Jordan River, its fertile plateau excellent for raising cattle. Hence a bull of Bashan is a paragon of bulls, enormous and dangerous. The circling animals evoke a primitive picture of human beings in terror of animals that stalk them and then, in their own good time, attack. Living constantly with the possibility of attack and with the inability to defend oneself takes its toll: psychological and physical breakdown (vv. 14-15, 16c). The description of emotion in verses 14-15 differs from modern conceptions. Verse 14, "I am poured out like water," refers to tears, which were conceived as liquid welling up from the abdominal region and making their way through the head as tears. Ancients did not always sharply distinguish physical and emotional suffering. Emotions were not regarded as purely interior. They had a communicating function, conveying an individual's pain and joy to others.

In verse 16, the phrase "my hands and feet have shriveled" is an age-old puzzle that has never been satisfactorily explained. The Masoretic Text literally reads, "like a lion my hands and my feet," which is expanded by NJPS "like lions [they maul] my hands and feet" (cf. Isa 38:13). The Septuagint rendered "they have dug my hands and my feet." Though not directly quoted in the New Testament, the verse was applied to Christ's crucifixion by Christian writers as early as Justin Martyr (ca. 100–165). Thereafter it became commonplace with Christian writers who translated either "dug" or "pierced." The masoretic reading "like a lion" is the common Jewish reading today. NRSV's "shriveled" reflects a recent suggestion, but certainty is impossible.

The phrase "I can count all my bones" in verse 17 suggests an emaciated condition. The ribs are exposed because robbers have stripped the psalmist (see v. 18). The Gospels (Matt 27:35; Mark 15:24; Luke 23:34; John 19:24) cite verse 18 to illuminate the casting of dice for Jesus' clothing. The prayer that one expects in an individual lament occurs in verses 19-21. Up to this point, only verse 11 has been a prayer in the strict sense. Verses 19-21 are a summary prayer, referring back to the dog, lion, and wild oxen.

NRSV mistakenly separates verse 21, assigning the first colon to part 1 and the second colon to part 2. The two verbs in verse 21, however, are strictly parallel (as 2 Sam 22:42 equals Ps 18:41 and Ps 20:6, 9). Verse 21b is best interpreted as a precative perfect, "rescue me" (NJPS), rather than a statement of past action.

The response of thanksgiving and praise (vv. 22-31)

The change in tone from part 1 to part 2 cannot be missed even by a casual reader. Instead of being a worm scorned by others (v. 6) and surrounded by hostile animals, the pray-er speaks of "my brothers and sisters" (v. 22a) and stands in the midst of the great congregation, safe at last among fellow human beings, friends, and kin. "Great congregation" elsewhere in the Psalms refers to Israel assembled in the Temple precincts (Pss 35:18; 40:9, 10). To "tell of your name" is to declare to others what God has done (Exod 9:16 and Ps 102:21), thereby encouraging them to praise God. This is exactly what happens in verses 23-24. The psalmist's own rescue is the theme of the proclamation.

What provokes the change of tone and content? Several answers have been proposed: (1) The lament of verses 1-21 has been answered and the psalmist responds with a joyous and magnificent paean of praise in verses 22-31 (implied by NRSV's breakup of v. 21); (2) the psalmist (or someone else) at a later time appended to the original lament the thanksgiving that was eventually sung when the lament was answered, making the whole psalm an account of a whole prayer transaction, like Ps 41; or (3) the psalmist has received an oracle of salvation from an official in the Temple (not recorded here) giving the assurance that deliverance is on the way, which emboldens the psalmist to sing a thanksgiving in advance of the actual deliverance. Each of the three interpretations is possible, though none is completely satisfactory. In the first, the genre would be a "lament plus thanksgiving." Although theoretically possible, in such a reading the lament part loses urgency, for rescue is right around the corner. The second alternative is quite possible, and the similar structure of Ps 41 may be claimed in support. In that case, however, part 1 would no longer be a prayer in the strict sense but a record of a prayer and its answer. The third interpretation is what one would expect according to the conventions of the genre (see introduction) and is the interpretation followed here. One must admit, however, that the length and exultant tone of the thanksgiving-in-advance is very unusual.

The anticipatory thanksgiving consists of two parts of approximately equal length. Verses 22-26 thank God, that is, describe God's wondrous rescue ("for he did not despise or abhor the affliction of the afflicted," v. 24) and its liturgical celebration ("my vows I will pay"; "eat and be satisfied"). Verses 27-31 declare that the ends of the earth will come to worship, even generations yet unborn. Several words occurring earlier in the psalm ("dog," "lion," "count," [sippēr] in vv. 16-17) are reprised in verses 20-22 ("dog," "lion," "tell," "recount" [sippēr]), linking the two parts through imagery and sound. Verse 22 illustrates what rescue means: One goes from a subhuman level of being a worm and being surrounded by predatory animals to the human act of speaking of God to one's own kin. One is restored to one's brothers and sisters and to the congregation of Israel worshiping in the Temple. To praise in the Bible is to tell what God has done, and so the poet invites all the people to acclaim God, who has not hidden face or ear from a poor wretch (vv. 23-24). God does not despise (v. 24a) what human beings despised (v. 6)—a client in need. The bitter complaint of being forsaken and unheard that opened the poem (v. 1) is addressed.

Verses 25-26 locate the ultimate source of the divine praise in Yahweh, who has both performed the rescue and made possible a response. With verses 27-28 the perspective moves from the Temple to the nations, expressing the hope that the nations may also turn to Yahweh and come to the Temple. The phrase "to turn to Yahweh" is unique in the Psalter, being found elsewhere only in the Deuteronomistic history and prophets. The reason for their turn is that universal kingship is Yahweh's alone. The Hebrew of verse 29 is uncertain. NRSV follows an emended text that supposes that even the dead will acknowledge Yahweh's sovereign power. A single thought is developed: All the living (v. 27), all the dead (v. 29), and all those yet unborn (vv. 30-31) will give praise.

Theological and Ethical Analysis

No other psalm more heavily influenced the passion accounts and early Christian reflection on the meaning of Christ's sufferings than Ps 22. The earliest followers of Jesus found the notion scandalous that any servant of God could die in the pain and dishonor of crucifixion: "How then is it written about the Son of Man, that he is to go through many sufferings and be treated with contempt?" (Mark 9:12). Thus they looked in the Scriptures to find examples of servants of God who died in disgrace. One such Scripture text was Isa 53 (cf. Acts 8:27-35); another was Ps 22, which must have seemed to early Christians an accurate prediction of the troublesome passion of Jesus. Mark 15:34 and Matt 27:46 record that Jesus died reciting Ps 22. The wording of the derision hurled at Jesus on the cross (Matt 27:39; Mark 15:29; Luke 23:35-36) has been influenced by Ps 22:7; "I am thirsty" of John 19:28 may allude to Ps 22:15, "my mouth is dried up like a potsherd." The casting of lots for Jesus' garments (Matt 27:35; Mark 15:24; Luke 23:34; John 19:24) was prefigured in Ps 22:18. Hebrews 2:12 also quotes Ps 22:22.

The psalm is the painful cry of a loyal friend of the Lord who is persecuted and ostracized for being loyal. It is that passionate loyalty that is responsible for both the terrible pain of separation described in part 1 and for the exultant hope of part 2.

PSALM 23

The "Good Shepherd Psalm" is the most beloved and popular poem in the Old Testament, being used in both private and liturgical prayer. In funeral rites, the psalm's evocation of the compassion and power of God is especially consoling to mourners, as is the hope for eternal life in traditional renderings of the last line, "I shall dwell in the house of the LORD forever."

Literary Analysis

Psalm 23 is a song of trust in the divine shepherd. Though it is often read as a pastoral idyll, evil (embodied in human beings) lurks at the margin (vv. 4a, 5b), and "nature" is occasionally dangerous (v. 4). The song of trust is, after all, closely related to the personal lament. The structure is largely determined by the successive images of God in the poem—shepherd (vv. 1-4) and host (v. 5)—and by the successive pronouns used for God, he (vv. 1-3) and you (vv. 4-6). The poem's turning point is the middle verse (v. 4). From the experience of being safely guided (vv. 1-3), the psalmist resolves to put aside fear ("I fear no evil") and trust the divine Shepherd even in the worst imaginable danger, out of the conviction that "you are with me" (v. 4c). The image of God changes in verse 5 to a host honoring a guest and serving a meal. The final verse functions like verse 4, for it too is a reflection on being cared for by God; from experiencing God as host, the psalmist concludes that "goodness and mercy shall follow me."

Though the poem is about an individual, it has a strong communal dimension. It contains allusions to exodus traditions, in particular to the new exodus that envisioned a new march through the wilderness, a new covenant, and a new settlement in the land. Psalm 23 employs traditions such as those in Ps 78:43-55, where the divine shepherd leads the exodus from Egypt to the holy hill: "he led out his people like sheep, / and guided them in the wilderness like a flock. / He led them in safety, so that they were not afraid" (Ps 78:52-53a). Traditional covenant language is reversed in verse 6a, "goodness and mercy shall follow me." *Rādap* ("follow") is normally used of hostile pursuit, as in Ps 7:5-6 and Hos 8:1-3, where the covenant curse is expressed as enemy pursuit of covenant-breakers. Psalm 23, however, boldly turns such language on its head and expresses the hope that covenant blessings will "pursue" the psalmist. Michael Barré and John Kselman (1983, 97-127) suggest that the banquet in verse 5 adapts the motif of a sacred banquet at which God affirmed the promise made to the king. That royal banquet is here democratized and interpreted as a feast for the people. It will be recalled that during the exile, at least in some circles (cf. Isa 55:1-5), the promises to David were extended to the whole people. The psalm is a skillful interplay of individual and communal elements. God is my shepherd as well as the shepherd of my people.

Exegetical Analysis

The Lord is my shepherd (vv. 1-4)

The metaphors of the Lord as a shepherd and the people as a flock are familiar ones, being found, among other places, in Pss 80:1, 95:7, 100:3; Isa 40:11; Jer 10:21; and Ezek 34:11-16. Shepherd was a favorite title for ancient Near Eastern kings, symbolizing the king's compassionate care for his people, especially the most vulnerable. The proper parallelism and translation of verse 1 is best shown by paraphrase: It is Yahweh who is my shepherd; / that is why I lack nothing. The next three clauses (vv. 2a, 2b, and 3a) are parallel to each other: The Lord enables me to graze in rich pastures, drink from safe water, and maintain my strength. "Still waters" are those not swiftly running so the sheep can keep their footing as they drink. The traditional rendering, "waters of repose," paints an excessively romantic picture. The phrase "Restores my soul" means to maintain strength, as in Lam 1:19, "my priests and elders perished in the city while seeking food to revive their strength." "Right paths" are paths that lead in the right direction, the opposite of wrong or dangerous paths. The Septuagint, followed by the Vulgate and KJV, rendered the Hebrew idiom with misleading literalness, "paths of righteousness." The meaning of the phrase "for his name's sake" (v. 3*b*) is that Israel, as the elect people, advertises to the world God's ability to make Israel prosper. Psalm 106:8 makes the point clearly: "Yet he saved them for his name's sake, / so that he might make known his mighty power."

Verse 4 imagines life with God in the future. Even in the worst-case scenario, the psalmist will not be controlled by fear. "Do not fear" often prefaced oracular responses, and the psalmist interprets the protection provided so far as the equivalent of such an assurance. "Rod" and "staff" are, respectively, a club for beating away wild animals and a rod to keep sheep from wandering off. "They comfort me" because a properly armed shepherd makes the sheep feel secure.

God hosts the banquet as the psalmist hopes for
the full blessings of the covenant (vv. 5-6)

The same sequence of ideas occurs here as in verses 1-4: a vivid experience of God (v. 5) leads to a particular hope (v. 6). Though some suggest the banquet may be yet another allusion to the exodus (the feeding in the wilderness as in Ps 78:19), it is more likely that verse 5 introduces a fresh scene. The guest is invited into the tent of the great sheikh, and fellowship is established by that gracious gesture of welcome. A similar scene is Exod 24, where God hosts Moses, Aaron, and the seventy elders at a banquet, establishing a covenant bond with them. The phrase "in the presence of my enemies" would be difficult to explain if the context were feeding in the wilderness, but it makes sense in a context of establishing a covenant with one group rather than another. The phrase "dwell in the house of the LORD" is best interpreted as yet another reversal of the common covenant curse condemning one to the netherworld. May one always dwell in the land of the living, the Temple (cf. Ps 27:13)!

Theological and Ethical Analysis

Few prayers express life with God with such an economy of imagery as Ps 23. It draws on Israel's traditions of the exodus—the march through the wilderness, the covenant, and the settlement in the land—deftly adapting them to the experience of an individual. The psalm is not an idyll of the soul alone with God. The meal is a joyous banquet, not an intimate dinner for two; the house of the Lord is crowded with worshipers. The poem is realistic, reckoning with human need and danger, and traditional, portraying God in the traditional images of shepherd, host, and covenant-maker.

A poem that at first sight seems serene and consoling turns out to be imaginative and challenging. It takes traditions of Israel's national identity and unerringly transposes them to the personal experience of every person. The exodus and the covenant are national matters, to be sure, but also touch individuals. It is fitting that a psalm translate that experience for individuals.

For the Christian, the exodus is not simply a historical event but a present reality. Christians believe that Jesus' death and resurrection is "the paschal mystery" in which the power of sin is defeated and a people is formed for God. Easter is experienced in the ritual of the eucharist. Psalm 23 is a perfect expression of the ancient exodus because it fosters the hope of a new exodus and new covenant.

PSALM 24

The theme of Ps 24—the people worshiping the Divine King returning to the Temple—is related to the previous psalm. Psalm 23:5-6 spoke of the Lord as Shepherd (meaning King) and also mentioned the house of the Lord.

Literary Analysis

Psalm 24 has been classed as an entrance liturgy (like Ps 15; see also Isa 33:13-16; Mic 6:6-8) and as an enthronement psalm (like

Pss 29, 47, 93, 95–99). Indeed, it has elements of both genres, for it sets forth the stipulations (vv. 3-6) imposed upon those who worship the victorious Lord (vv. 7-10).

The unity and progression of the psalm are determined by the liturgical ceremony it reflects. The first stage is the proclamation of the victory of Yahweh (vv. 1-2), which naturally attracts worshipers to assemble to greet the Divine Warrior. The next stage, the entrance dialogue, makes clear that only the loyal (i.e., who have worshiped no other god) can be admitted and obtain a share of the fruits of the victory ("blessing," "vindication," vv. 3-6). The last stage is the liturgical welcome of the Lord in antiphonal question and answer. Psalm 24 in its present form is too brief to have been the script of an enthronement liturgy, but it may have been abstracted from such a liturgy to serve the needs of prayer outside the Temple.

The psalm presumes that readers know the combat myth, which is attested in Mesopotamia, Canaan (Ugaritic texts), and the Old Testament. According to the myth, a warrior god battles a monster threatening the world, wins the battle, and returns to the assembly to be crowned as supreme deity. In some versions, the triumphant return is accompanied by the building of a palace and the bestowal upon the deity of universal sovereignty. The combat myth is in the background of this psalm, for universal sovereignty is attributed to the Lord returning from victory. The Lord is given titles ("strong and mighty," "mighty in battle") and the people acclaim the Lord as king.

Exegetical Analysis

The proclamation that God has created the world (vv. 1-2)

How does a god in a polytheistic world become king over the other gods? By doing the one necessary thing for the survival of the universe, which no other god can do. The defeat of chaos (usually imagined as formless Sea) was such an act, for it removed the great obstacle to an orderly universe. To tame Sea was regarded as the central act of creation in Pss 89:11; 93; 95;

102:25; and Isa 48:13. The first two verses proclaim the stupendous event.

Who can enter to welcome the triumphant Lord? (vv. 3-6)

Not everyone can be admitted to the sacred precincts to celebrate. Only the one whose previous conduct shows commitment to the returning deity may enter. This is the purpose of the questions in verse 3, which may reflect an actual scrutiny at the gate, though it may simply be the words of an entrance hymn. The demand is not for cultic purity befitting a shrine (like Exod 19:21-25), but for fundamental loyalty of the kind represented by the Ten Commandments. Indeed, "not swear deceitfully" (v. 4c) is the third commandment against the wrong use of the divine name in oaths. (It is the second in Lutheran and Roman Catholic numerations.) The phrase "lift up their souls to what is false" (v. 4b) is a variant of the first commandment, "you shall have no other gods before me" (Exod 20:3, Deut 5:7). "What is false" (Ps 24:4b) refers to idol worship as in Ps 31:6; Isa 1:13; and Jer 18:15. "Clean hands and pure hearts" (Ps 24:4a) is a unique phrase, referring, it seems, to the inner (heart) and the outer (hands) person. Similar uncompromising demands for pure worship are found in prophetic texts like Isa 1:10-20 and Amos 5:21-24.

One reason for the insistence on loyalty is that the deity returning from victory shares the fruits of that victory with loyal followers; only the faithful ought to benefit. "The God of their salvation" (v. 5b) is a Hebraism meaning "the God who saved them" (by establishing or reestablishing the cosmos). "Receive blessing" and "vindication" (v. 5) mean sharing the benefits of the Lord's victory. Given that the psalm reflects the Lord's enthronement after defeating the forces of chaos, "blessing" and "vindication" are the fruits of an orderly world. Such a world would mean, negatively, freedom from the rule of other deities; positively, it would mean fertility that comes from rain in due season and justice that comes from restraining the wicked and upholding the righteous. Most important, it means the absolute supremacy of Yahweh who protects and supports Israel. "Such is the company" (v. 6) characterizes the group that has entered. Similarly, "those who seek" are those taking part in worship.

Let the assembly welcome the victorious King (vv. 7-10)

"Lift up your heads, O gates!" The Septuagint translated "Lift up your gates, O princes." The meaning of the phrase has been clarified by an Ugaritic text (*CTU* 2.i.21-28) in which the assembly of the gods sees the messengers of Prince Sea approaching and, terrified at the sight, "lower their heads on top of their knees, onto their royal thrones." The storm god, Baal, rebukes the gods for their craven submission and tells them to stand up proudly to the messengers: "Lift up your heads, O gods, from the tops of your knees, from your royal thrones." Later in the story, Baal will defeat Sea and, presumably, will return to the assembly and use the phrase "Lift up your heads"—in a positive sense—to announce his triumphant return. Some scholars believe "Be lifted up, O ancient doors!" (Ps 24:7, 9) is addressed to a portcullis gate (which moves up and down), but the portcullis was unknown in the ancient Near East. There is thus no doubt that the biblical poet has reimagined the traditional assembly setting and personified the gates of the Temple as courtiers awaiting the return of the Divine Warrior. The speaker commands them to rise in respectful welcome.

The question and answer antiphons in verses 7-10 presumably involved two choruses (or perhaps a cantor and the people). One may speculate that the question "Who is this King of glory?" reflects a convention by which the people asked what news the approaching messengers brought: good news or bad news, victory or defeat? At any rate, the answer in the psalm leaves no doubt: It is Yahweh who comes, who has been proved superior in battle.

Theological and Ethical Analysis

Though the original context was specific, the psalm itself decontextualizes the situation for a much broader audience. It can now be sung at times other than the enthronement festival and can be used to celebrate the sovereignty of the Lord, creator of the harmonious and secure world. The poem begins by observing that the beautiful and safe world we live in is the result of the Lord's victory over chaotic forces. That victory poses a challenge to the Lord's own people, however, for only the loyal can enjoy its full fruits. Hence there is need of a scrutiny of those who would celebrate the victory of the Lord. A beautiful gift calls for open-hearted reception. The poem directs our attention to "God laboring for us," defeating evil and arranging the world. As always, the Bible avoids utopianism, for it recognizes evil and the need to combat it.

In the Liturgy of the Hours (official morning and evening prayer in many Christian churches), Ps 24 serves as a psalm of invitation. It acknowledges the Lord as Creator of the world. It invites humans to acknowledge the Lord as they live in this world. The poet singles out one action as representative: the return of the Lord to the Temple and the people. For Christians, the poem is suitable for Easter, which is ultimately a victory over sin and death and the ushering in of a new age.

PSALM 25

Literary Analysis

Psalm 25 can be classed as an individual lament, for it contains a petition—to be delivered from danger—integrated with a complaint and statements of trust. It is something more, however. The middle (vv. 8-14 with the exception of v. 11) is a hymnlike description of the reliable and saving God. The acrostic nature of the poem may account for its distinctiveness. Acrostic psalms tend to rely on an alphabetic sequence of letters for their structure rather than on their internal logic. In an acrostic poem, each line begins with a successive letter of the twenty-two letter Hebrew alphabet, verse 1 beginning with *aleph* ("a") and so on. The final line (v. 22) opens with redeem (initial p) with the result that the first, middle, and last lines of the poem spell out *aleph*.

Though the structure is partly determined by the sequence of the letters beginning each line, there is another unmistakable grouping into three virtually equal parts (vv. 1-7, 8-14, and 15-22; cf. NRSV, which proposes a different structure). The first and third parts are extended petitions in which the psalmist's "I" addresses God as "you"; the middle part (with the exception of the petition in v. 11) is a hymn-lesson and speaks of God in the third person. Part 1 can be subdivided into three sections according to key concepts in each: verses 1-3, trust and shame; verses 4-5, teaching and path; verses 6-7, remembrance and steadfast love. The end of the poem (vv. 19-22) echoes several words from the beginning (vv. 1-3) ("enemies/foes," "shame," "my soul," "wait for you," "God"), to bring a sense of closure. The divine name Yahweh ("the Lord") occurs ten times, though only once in part 3.

Exegetical Analysis

Petitions: I take refuge in you. Teach me your ways.
Remember your mercy not my sins (vv. 1-7)

Profound sentiments are expressed simply and artfully. In this section, the art consists of repetition of key words, alternation of public and private spheres (see below on vv. 8-14), and skilled employment of the comparatively rare three-line verse (vv. 2, 5, 7) to expand the thought.

The prayer opens with a raising of the "soul" toward God, a more concrete gesture than the English translation suggests. Hebrew "soul" *(nepeš)* in its basic meaning refers to the throat area, the center of the body where vital signs such as breathing, moisture, and heartbeat are most palpable. By metonymy, *nepeš* means life, self, soul. To lift up the soul, therefore, is to raise one's center upward and outward. Such a gesture involves risk, however, for it relies on someone other than oneself. Hence the psalmist immediately prays not to be "put to shame," to lose face, which in that culture would result from the failure of what one trusted. The same hope is extended in verse 3 to all "who wait for you." The psalmist prays that "my enemies" (v. 2) will lose face as everyone sees their plans thwarted. Michael Barré (1990, 46-54) suggests that the Hebrew phrase "to lift up one's soul" to God in Pss 25:1, 86:4, 143:8 has a special meaning derived from similar idioms in the Sumerian and Akkadian languages: "to betake oneself to," "to flee for protection to." The three biblical psalms depict someone fleeing from enemies and finding refuge in God. This interpretation makes the opening verses more vivid.

The singer next asks to learn the Lord's paths (vv. 4-5). The theme of humans as learners and the Lord as teacher occurs even beyond these verses, in verses 8, 9, 12, and 14. In verse 14, God uniquely teaches humans about the covenant. Walking on a path is a common biblical metaphor for living as a moral being. The reference to "truth" in verse 5 is to be understood in relational terms as something stable and firm that can be relied on; in this case truth refers to God's reliability and faithfulness toward "me." The word is explicated in the next two phrases, which are in parallel (v. 5bc). The Gospel of John speaks of "truth" in this sense, for example, in John 16:13, "When the Spirit of truth comes, he will guide you into all the truth" (see also John 14:6 and 18:37).

"Be mindful/remember" in verses 6-7 means to keep a person or thing uppermost in one's mind when acting, in this case God's affectionate commitment ("steadfast love") and compassion ("mercy") in dealing with the psalmist. The only reason given for God not remembering the psalmist's sins is "your goodness' sake" (v. 7c).

Statement: God the good teacher will guide people
along the right way (vv. 8-14)

Apart from the special verse 11, the first five verses (8-12) are about the Lord keeping people on the right "paths" or "way." The other verses (13-14) continue the theme of divine guidance, if one takes the entire section to be an allusion to the exodus. The reference to "paths/way" evokes the journey through the wilderness (vv. 8-10, 12), "possess the land" (v. 13) evokes the conquest (as in Numbers, Deuteronomy, and Joshua), and "covenant" and "decrees" (vv. 10b, 14) evoke the Sinai covenant. The exodus thus provides the background, correlating national and private experience of God: being led on the right path // the ancestors being led through the wilderness; learning God's will // the ancestors receiving the covenant at Sinai; and receiving a blessing // the ancestors receiving Canaan. As already noted, the psalm views the covenant primarily as the giving of Torah, authoritative narrative and teaching.

What about verse 11, the petition that is seemingly out of place in the "hymnic" part 2? Formally, it is the middle verse of the poem, linking part 2 to the petition-dominated parts 1 and 3. Semantically, it too has an exodus undertone, recalling the time when Moses went up to Sinai and the people apostatized and would have been rejected had Moses not interceded for them (Exodus 32–34). Psalm 25:11b quotes Moses' intercession in Exod 34:9: "*Pardon our iniquity* and our sin, and take us for your inheritance" (identical words are italicized). Without verse 11, part 2 might be regarded simply as doctrine about God; with verse 11, part 2 can be regarded as the experience of someone whose hope is "your name's sake," that is, the character of God.

Petitions: I trust in you. Forgive my sins.
Redeem Israel (vv. 15-22)

Verse 15 serves as a transition, shifting in its first line to the first person ("*my* eyes"), and using for the last time the third person for God in its second line ("*he*"). First-person and second-person pronouns continue until the final verse. In verse 15, the metaphor of "the way" continues implicitly in the claim that "[God] will pluck my feet out of the net." As "my eyes" are on you (v. 15), so "turn to me" (v. 16) in friendly acceptance; verses 18 and 19 also urge God to *see* "my affliction" (NRSV: "consider"). The face or front part of oneself is important in the poem (cf. v. 1).

The sole motive for God to act is that "I am lonely [that is, have no other resource] and afflicted" (v. 16); the psalmist does not mention innocence or past devotion as incentives for God to act. The request, "relieve the troubles of my heart" (v. 17) is, literally, "widen the constrictions on my mind." The phrase is unique and dense, meaning something like "my sufferings have come into myself and disturb me." The psalmist refers several times to mental and emotional suffering (vv. 7, 11, 16, 18, 20) in addition to the fear of being shamed in verses 2-3, 20.

Theological and Ethical Analysis

Though the danger from enemies is real, the psalmist regards as an even greater danger the closed heart and mind that result from sinful actions. The opening and closing sections seek protection from enemies. In the middle section, the psalmist desires to be in right relationship to God and to link the present crisis to the national drama of salvation. The anxiety that drives this prayer arises not only from fear of enemies but also from fear of an unredeemed heart and unforgiven sin. Though the prayer might appear conventional and uninspired at first reading, it is in fact remarkably deft, the production of an ardent and articulate person.

PSALM 26

Literary Analysis

The genre and life-setting of the poem have proved difficult to classify. Hermann Gunkel, the great commentator on the psalms, classed it as an individual lament of someone seriously ill. Later scholars agreed it was a lament but, since illness is not mentioned, suggested its life-setting was a Temple procedure in which an accused person sought divine vindication (as in 1 Kgs 8:31-32). There have been other proposals: an entrance liturgy for pilgrims to the Temple like Pss 15 and 24; a national lament uttered *prior to* rather than after a disaster; and a protestation of innocence uttered by the king. None of these proposals are satisfactory. The psalm cannot be a lament because genuine lament is lacking; it is not a judicial procedure like that in 1 Kgs 8, for no oath is sworn; a pilgrim feast is ruled out because laity would not be admitted to the altar (v. 6); it is not a royal poem, for the king is not mentioned. Though kings in early times did offer sacrifice, it was not a defining duty.

The best clue to the genre of the poem and its situation in life is its central section, verses 6-8, which describe the concrete actions of washing one's hands, going around the altar, and joining in liturgical song. These actions can be used as evidence for the setting even if they are metaphors, for the metaphors would have had to be based on observable Temple realities in order to be understood. Biblical evidence is clear that the only people who could "go around your altar" were priests, for only they were allowed beyond the forecourt of the Temple and entered the area between the altar and the Temple porch. Two further details in the psalm suggest the singer was a priest. According to Exod 30:17-21 (paralleled in Exod 40:30-32), Aaronid priests washed their hands and feet in a bronze laver between the Tabernacle and altar "so that they may not die" by violating the holiness of the sanctuary. Priestly law matches Ps 26: the association of washing and going around the altar, hand washing as a symbolic act of purification, the threat of death to the Aaronid priests and to the singer of the psalm if they neglect their duty.

Two objections to this life-setting must be answered: (1) Why would a priest pray to be vindicated, proved, and tested (vv. 1-2) when, according to the rituals in Exod 30 and 40, he was in no danger provided he washed his hands, which he did (Ps 26:6); (2) how could such a class-specific prayer find its way into a psalter for all Israel? The answer to the first objection is that entering a holy place is always dangerous, for one enters the dwelling of the holy God who searches the heart and insists on proper sentiments to accompany sacred actions. The answer to the second objection is that the priest is a representative figure—

since Israel is a priestly people (Exod 19:5-6, Isa 61:6)—and the priest literally carries the names of the twelve tribes on his breastplate as he enters the sanctuary (Exod 28:29-30). With the life-setting established, one can be more specific about the genre. It seems to be prayer originating in priestly circles, which was transposed for any visitor to the Temple who felt awed by the demands of the all-holy God dwelling within.

The structure of the poem is partly determined by repetition of key words in the opening and closing lines: "I walk in my integrity" occurs in verses 1 and 11; the imperative verbs in verse 11b, "redeem me, and be gracious to me," balance the imperative verbs of verse 2a, "Prove me . . . and try me." Subsections are similarly marked off: "walk" in verses 1b and 3b; "sit" in verses 4a and 5b; "hate" in verse 5a, contrasted with "love" in verse 8a; three occurrences of "with" in verses 4-5, and two occurrences in verse 9. The only section of the poem not linked to any other by such repetition is the center, verses 6-7, which describes the physical act of washing one's hands, walking around the altar, and singing hymns.

There is considerable divergence among commentators on the strophic division. The chiastic outline below is based on the observations noted above and also reflects the views of several recent commentaries. Similarities to Ps 25 suggest either common authorship or editing. Both poems testify to the singer's trust in God (25:2 and 26:1) and use the imperative verbs "redeem" (25:22 and 26:11) and "be gracious to me" (25:16 and 26:11).

Exegetical Analysis

I walk in my integrity. Probe me (vv. 1-3)

On the basis of the other verbs in the section ("prove," "try," "test"), NRSV's "vindicate me" *(šāpat)* in verse 1a has the nuance "to decide, make a finding" that the psalmist is indeed innocent. It is not enough to declare oneself innocent; God must ratify that judgment. Innocence or integrity is necessary lest one be struck down for polluting the sanctuary. Since no human witness can speak authoritatively about anyone's inner integrity, the psalmist must turn to the all-seeing God for a decision. The imperatives "prove me" and "test my heart and mind" (v. 2) are pleas to be assessed. The verbs can refer to testing the genuineness of gold and silver by heating with fire. Such probing, it is hoped, will reveal that the psalmist was always loyal to God. There is always a risk, however, for who can know whether one has transgressed?

I do not consort with the wicked (vv. 4-5)

The expression "sit with" means to be partner in a group's projects, as in 1 Sam 2:8; Pss 101:6, 113:8; and Prov 31:23. The psalmist refuses to join in the projects of the wicked, indeed resolves to oppose them. The four characterizations of the wicked have a cumulative effect, that is, they are *profoundly* wicked. It is possible that the phrase "the worthless" (*mětê šāw'*, lit. "men of worthlessness") refers to false worship, since "*šāw'*" ("worthlessness") sometimes means false gods. "Hate" in verse 5a has the sense of "reject." The psalmist is using "either-or" language like that in Pss 1 and 101, according to which there are ultimately only two decisions: for good or for evil, for God or against God. The poet does not conceive evil abstractly, but imagines it embodied in people doing evil things.

I walk in your Temple and sing your praises (vv. 6-7)

Washing one's hands is commanded by rituals (Exod 30:21, paralleled in 40:31). It is also a general gesture of innocence, as in Deut 21:6 and Ps 73:13. Having asserted his or her innocence in verses 1-3 and separateness from sinners in verses 4-5, the psalmist now performs the requisite priestly acts that would be dangerous if improperly done.

I choose to be in your dwelling; do not sweep me away with evildoers (vv. 8-10)

Though one could perhaps assign verse 8 to the preceding section, "love" in verse 8a contrasts with "hate" in verse 5a. It seems best therefore to preserve the chiasm between verses 4-5 and verses 8-10. Because the psalmist "loves" God's dwelling, he or she hates associating with sinners and their schemes. The wicked are fated to die prematurely ("swept away") and the psalmist wants nothing to do with that doomed group.

I walk in my integrity. Be gracious to me (vv. 11-12)

Verse 11*a* repeats verse 1*b*, signaling a conclusion. The repeated verse has a significant change, however. The present/future sense of "I [will] walk in my integrity" contrasts with "I have walked" in verse 1, where the psalmist asked God to validate the claim of past integrity. The psalmist faces the future and resolves to be faithful. There is always need for divine grace, however, hence the prayer "redeem me, and be gracious to me."

Theological and Literary Analysis

The sacred loomed over biblical people more dramatically than over modern believers. God was Totally Other and the Temple stood on holy ground where one had to tread carefully according to ritual laws. God graciously "drew near" to people in the Temple. The psalmist is acutely conscious of walking in a sacred space charged with the grandeur and energy of God. Though the proper rituals have been carried out, the psalmist is unsatisfied with a self-declaration of innocence, for God is the only one who can truly judge past conduct and present disposition. The caution and boldness of the singer, so memorably expressed in this poem, is suitable for any person approaching God. The poem expresses profound reverence for the holy and transcendent God, while recognizing God's passion for the people and desire to draw near and bless them in the Temple.

PSALM 27

This poem is linked to the preceding by the desire it expresses "to live in the house of the LORD all the days of my life" (Ps 27:4), which echoes Ps 26:8, "O LORD, I love the house in which you dwell." The desire is reinforced by the use in both poems of the rare word *mîšôr*, rendered "level ground" in Ps 26:12 and "level path" in Ps 27:11. As in other psalms of longing for the Temple, the psalmist's desire for God above all other things is ultimately obedience to the first commandment, "You shall have no other gods before me."

Literary Analysis

Looked at exclusively from the perspective of the genres in the Psalter, Ps 27 is two psalms—a song of trust (vv. 1-6) and a lament (vv. 7-14). The first ends on a confident note (vv. 5-6), which, unexpectedly, is followed by a lament petition (v. 7). Psalm 27 is not the only "split personality" in the Psalter. Psalm 40:1-10 has all the marks of a thanksgiving, and 40:11-17, all those of a lament. Commentators today are inclined to accept the view that the two parts of Ps 27 (and Ps 40 for that matter) belong together. There are several reasons for so judging. The first is the distribution of key words throughout the entire psalm: The divine name ("the LORD" or "God") occurs fourteen times (two times seven, the sacred number); "my salvation" occurs in verses 1 and 9; "heart" in verses 3, 8, 14; "hide" in verses 5 and 9; "seek" in verses 4 and 8; "foes/enemies" in verses 2 and 6. The second reason for assuming unity is the persistent theme of the desire to see God's face in the Temple in spite of obstacles. The desire is first stated in verses 4-5 and reasserted in verses 7-9, 13 ("the land of living" being the Temple).

Exegetical Analysis

I will not fear because the Lord supports me (vv. 1-3)

The bold assertion that opens the poem is as much hope as triumph, for fear cannot be banished by a mere resolve. "Light" is associated with the sanctuary in Pss 36:9; 43:3; and 56:13, for

God who dwells there banishes the darkness that symbolizes death and chaos. Similarly, God is a refuge ("stronghold") for loyal clients who flee to the sanctuary. The images of enemies who "devour my flesh" refers to wild animals ready to tear their prey to pieces, as in Pss 7:2; 17:12; 22:13. "Stumble and fall" (v. 2d) refers to enemies falling into the traps they themselves set (see Pss 7:15 and 35:8); self-inflicted punishment is a sign of divine justice. Even systematic evils—an army (v. 3)—cannot succeed in paralyzing the sufferer with fear because God is a saving light and stronghold.

I desire to be with the protecting Lord in the Temple (vv. 4-5)

Being with God in the Temple is expressed by various metaphors, including living in a house, beholding beauty, and inquiring. The phrase "to live in a house" usually implies living in one's own house, as in Judg 8:29; Pss 68:6, 101:7. Only occasionally does it refer to someone enjoying the hospitality of God's house (cf. Pss 27:4c and 84:4). "Behold" is a metaphor for experiencing God, as in the appearance of Exod 24:11, when Moses and the chief men of Israel "beheld God, and they ate and drank." Reference to seeing God in the Temple is also found in Ps 42:2c, "When shall I come and behold the face of God?" The metaphor is also implied in the phrase "to seek God's face" in 2 Chron 7:14; Ps 24:6; 27:8; Hos 5:15. The expression "inquire" *(biqqēr)* puzzles commentators, for it has the sense of investigate rather than ask for an oracle. Another Hebrew word *(biqqēš)* would be more suitable, for it means "inquire for an oracle," hence seek God's face or word, and it occurs in verses 8-9. The sense of the verb in this psalm, however, is clearly to ask for divine guidance at the shrine.

Corresponding to the three metaphors for desire in verse 4 are three metaphors for hope in verse 5, "shelter," "tent," and "rock." The hope is practical and everyday: protection from enemies in the Temple. All three metaphors refer to the Temple. The word "shelter" *(sukkāh)* can refer to a lion's lair, a temporary sun shield erected for field workers, and the booths used during the Feast of Tabernacles. It also can designate a tentlike dwelling for

God, as in Amos 9:11; Pss 18:11 (= 2 Sam 22:12); and 31:20. In ancient Canaanite tradition, the high god El was conceived as living in a splendid tent, and that tradition shows up occasionally in the Bible. Here, "shelter" is synonymous with "tent" (v. 5a). "Rock" (v. 5d) refers to the Temple, as it does in Ps 61:2c.

I will offer thanksgiving when I find safety in the Temple (v. 6)

The phrase "[and] now" usually marks a new stage in Hebrew rhetoric. In this psalm, it marks the point where the psalmist can look down from a secure place upon the enemies who once posed a threat. God's protection is a judgment that the enemies were in the wrong. The rescued person's only response is praise, telling others what God has done and offering sacrifices of thanks in the Temple ("tent," v. 6). As the context shows, verse 6 is an expression of hope rather than a report. The psalmist regards the rescue as already done. The next section of the poem will show how difficult it can sometimes be to come into God's presence.

Hear my cry, for you have turned away your
face in anger (vv. 7-10)

Having expressed the desire to be in the sanctuary (vv. 4-5), even promising thanks in anticipation of deliverance, the psalmist suddenly shifts into the lament mode, evidently realizing that the enemy still threatens, and protection is far away. The unique phrase "my heart says" (v. 8a), a variant of the more familiar "to say in one's heart," indicates sincerity; the desire to seek God's face comes from the core of the singer's being. In three negative verbs ("do not," v. 9), the singer begs not to be abandoned, expressing the hope that God will do better than a parent ever could in this hour of need (v. 10).

Teach me your way that I may find you in the
land of life (vv. 11-14)

The metaphor of way (v. 11) is part of the theme of sanctuary, which has dominated the poem so far. Other psalms of longing for the sanctuary also mention the road to the sanctuary, (e.g., Pss 43:3-4; 61:1-4; 84:6-7). The psalmist prays to be led on "a level path" (v. 11b), that is, led safely to the sanctuary, though enemies block the journey. "The land of the living" (v. 13c) is better rendered "the land of life." In Pss 52:5c; 56:13; 116:9 the phrase refers to the Temple, and it does here as well. The phrase is an apt designation for the dwelling of the Creator of all living things. The final line (v. 14) is especially appropriate in light of the psalmist's experience of seeking, almost finding, and seeking again. The message: "Wait . . . and let your heart take courage!"

Theological and Ethical Analysis

Few psalms celebrate so eloquently the human hunger for God amid dangers and delays. It is a long journey from the opening "whom shall I fear?" to the final "wait for the LORD!" Between beginning and end there is desire, (anticipated) joyous thanks, anguish, and pleas not to be abandoned and to be guided home. These are the emotions of the great Christian saints, and they are also the emotions of ordinary people trying to remain faithful to God. Life does not move in a straight line from desire to fulfillment and neither does this psalm. It guides people through the turns and delays of life before God, teaching people to honor and nurture their desire for God.

PSALM 28

Literary Analysis

Most scholars judge the poem to be an individual lament, citing as evidence its anxious request to be heard (vv. 1-2), its life-or-death petition (vv. 3-5), anticipated thanksgiving (vv. 6-8), and final prayer. Several details of the poem do not fit the genre, however, as a few dissenting voices have pointed out. The psalmist seeks a decision (the prayer is that God not remain silent) that will set him or her apart from malefactors who are doomed (v. 3*ab*). Unusual attention is directed to seeking retribution for the same malefactors (vv. 3*c*-5). The statement "Blessed be the LORD" (v. 6) does not occur elsewhere as an anticipated thanksgiving, and the statements associated with the thanksgiving are so confident that it is difficult to regard them merely as anticipated. The concern with the welfare of the people (vv. 8-9) also does not fit individual laments. Classifying Ps 28 as lament, therefore, raises more problems than it solves. A fresh examination is called for.

The central request is that God not remain silent and allow the psalmist to be classed as a wicked person, for such people are doomed (vv. 1-3). Nothing is said about the wicked attacking the psalmist, which one would expect in an ordinary lament; the sole threat is being classed as wicked. It is reasonable to conclude, therefore, that the psalmist is undergoing a legal ordeal and asking for a divine judgment as to innocence or guilt. Ordeals were used when there were no witnesses to a crime, and suspects were subjected to a physical test by which God was believed to indicate guilt or innocence. A biblical example is Num 5:11-31 where a pregnant wife suspected of adultery was forced to drink a potion. If she were guilty, the water would cause pain, and her womb would discharge. Such a life-setting is the likely origin of the poem and the distinctive genre—thanksgiving for a declaration of innocence in an ordeal. As in Ps 41:4-10, the original petition (Ps 28:1-5) was incorporated into the thanksgiving.

Though an ordeal is the likely origin of the psalm, it must be said that the present poem reflects only remotely such a specific origin. Like many other psalms, it transposes rituals into prayers for ordinary people. The present prayer combines elements of ordeal prayer and thanksgiving to create a poem that gives thanks for a divine word that puts the singer back among the holy people of God. The psalmist makes no claim of virtue, praying only to be judged among the friends of God. The final verses give a hint of the possible speaker. The reference to the "anointed" in verse 8 and the prayer for the nation in verses 8-9 raise the question of whether the original singer was the king.

The structure is partly shaped by the answering of the petition in verse 2*a*, "hear the voice of my supplication" in verse 6*b*, literally, "he has heard the voice of my supplication." The NRSV paragraph division is widely used, though some translations do not make a break between verses 2 and 3.

Exegetical Analysis

Do not place me with sinners whose wickedness will be punished by death (vv. 1-5)

The psalmist complains of the silence of God rather than the attacks of the wicked, as would be expected in a regular lament. "The Pit" (v. 1*d*) is a synonym for Sheol, the place where the dead descended to live a shadow existence. Ancient depictions of pray-ers often show their hands outstretched to God. "Most holy sanctuary" *(debîr)* is used only here in the Psalter for the Holy of Holies; the term otherwise appears only in Kings and Chronicles. "Drag away" (v. 3*a*) is conjectural for an uncertain word, which may also mean "count, reckon." Verse 3 uses three phrases for the wicked; the third group (v. 3*cd*) is guilty of lying about others, a point that anyone falsely accused would want to make. The passionate prayer in verses 4-5 that the wicked be repaid for their malicious deeds is actually an argument for the innocence of the psalmist. The psalmist wants to be known as someone fully committed to divine justice, that is, punishment for sinners and reward for the righteous. Wordplay characterizes the prayer in verse 5 that the wicked be broken down. For those who "do not regard [*lō' yābînû*] the works of the LORD" (v. 5*a*), the Lord will "build them up no more" (*lō' yibnēm*, v. 5*c*).

Blessed be God who helped me (vv. 6-7)

As noted, "Blessed be the Lord," is a strong affirmation that is found normally in thanksgivings or hymns (e.g., Pss 41:13; 135:21). The affirmation is followed immediately in verse 6*b* by a citation of the prayer in verse 2*a* in the form of a thanksgiving: "he *has heard* the sound of my supplication."

Prayer for the people (vv. 8-9)

This extensive concluding prayer for the people is unusual in an individual lament. It continues the exaltation of the Lord begun in verse 6, going beyond personal benefits for the singer to benefits for the people and his "anointed" *(māšîaḥ)*. "People" and "anointed" are also in parallel in Hab 3:13. The expression "your heritage" (v. 9*a*) means the sacred land inherited from the ancestors. Some scholars believe that the concern for the people and the land indicates the singer is actually the king, a plausible though unprovable suggestion. Even if the king were the original speaker, it is noteworthy that his prayer is that *God* shepherd the people rather than himself. The image of God carrying the people belongs to two metaphorical systems. God "carries" the people in Deut 32:11, as an eagle carries them "aloft on its pinions." In Isa 40:11 the image is that of the shepherd who "will feed his flock . . . ; he will gather the lambs in his arms, and *carry* them in his bosom, and gently lead the mother sheep."

Theological and Ethical Analysis

It was necessary to speculate about the original situation in life of the psalm to criticize the majority opinion that Ps 28 is an ordinary individual lament. The view proposed here is that its inspiration was the Temple ceremony of an ordeal where an accused person who had no other means of establishing innocence, turned to God for adjudication. The moment of the psalmist's appeal to God for justification is nicely caught in this poem. The poem can be used by a broad spectrum of people. Any person who relies on God for ultimate justification can pray this psalm, any person who wants to join those loyal to God and be liberated from malefactors and liars. Such people can bless God for justification, and they can go on to make earnest petition for all the people.

PSALM 29

Literary Analysis

Though there is no doubt that the poem is a hymn praising God for having done a wondrous act, the congregation being invited to give praise is highly unusual. It is not Israel or a group within it, as in other hymns such as Pss 33:1; 113:1; 118:2-4. Rather, it is members of the heavenly court whom Jewish and Christian tradition know as angels. Throughout the ancient Near East and in Israel as well, people believed that heaven and earth were inhabited by intelligent beings. In the Bible, heavenly beings are loyal servants of the Most High, who presides over them as a potentate presides over a court. Israel, in contrast to its neighbors, seldom wrote about or invoked such creatures, though there are notable exceptions such as Deut 32:8 (Septuagint and 4QDeut), Pss 82 and 89:7; and Job 1:6 and 2:1. When a poem like Ps 29 does call on them to give praise to Yahweh, it is usually because the poet wants heaven as well as earth to acknowledge the *one* God who is supreme in power and authority.

Modern readers need to be reminded of the narrative implied in this hymn: the combat myth telling of the origin of religio-political authority in the universe. According to the myth, there was a threat to the stability of the world, which the gods could not defeat. An outsider god was selected to go out to battle, and he defeated the monster, restored order, and was given ultimate authority by the divine assembly. The myth is attested in Mesopotamian and Canaanite literature and in the Bible. This psalm concentrates on only one moment of the story: the acclamation by the heavenly beings of Yahweh's sole divinity. It presumes that readers are familiar with the story. The acclamation could be repeated annually, probably in connection with the early fall rains that signaled the end of the old year and the beginning of the new (see introduction).

On the basis of his pioneering work on the Ugaritic myths, which were recovered beginning in 1929, the distinguished

Semitist H. L. Ginsberg proposed that Ps 29 is an Israelite adaptation of a Canaanite hymn to the Storm God. The majority of scholars recognize the correctness of his observation, which explains so well the details in the poem. The speaker in the psalm is an official in the heavenly court who sees the victorious Lord returning from battle and commands the assembly to bow down and recognize the supremacy of the returning victor. (Kingship is understood concretely as supremacy over others achieved by victory.) "The voice *(qôl)* of the LORD" is understood very specifically as thunder, as in Exod 9:28; 19:16; 20:18; Pss 18:13; and 77:18. Analogously, the coming of the Lord is conceived as a thunderstorm moving westward from the Mediterranean Sea, pounding the coastal Lebanon and Anti-Lebanon ranges. "Sirion" (v. 6), parallel to Lebanon here, designates Mount Hermon. The dark yet luminous thunderclouds, accompanied by claps of thunder, wind, rain, and lightning, are imagined as stripping the mountains of their vegetation and shaking them to their foundations. The "flood" over which the Lord sits enthroned (v. 10) refers to the once-threatening monster, now tamed and made the base of the throne. Revelation 4:6 has the same image of the sea of glass (that is, a tamed sea) before the throne. The final verse (Ps. 29:11) asks the victorious God to grant blessings to the people.

Exegetical Analysis

Invitation to acknowledge the authority of the Lord (vv. 1-2)

The number of Hebrew words in the introduction (sixteen, vv. 1-2) matches the number in the conclusion (vv. 10-11). In the attested combat myths, the assembly promised supremacy to the warrior if he were successful in defeating the chaos monster. In Ps 29, as the Storm God returns, the heavenly beings recognize the supremacy demonstrated by the victory and acknowledge it by their decree. The Mesopotamian combat myths *Anzu* and *Enuma elish* conclude with the conferral upon the victorious deity of names signifying his new authority and grandeur. In Ps 29:1-2, "Ascribe . . . the glory of his name" acknowledges Yahweh's name as supreme over all others. The Hebrew phrase rendered as "in holy splendor" is uncertain; it occurs also in Ps 96:9. "Worship" is literally "bow down," which more effectively conveys the Near Eastern background of the scene.

The awesome arrival of God in the storm (vv. 3-9)

Perhaps the best way to understand these verses is to imagine a massive storm and see it as symboling a cosmic political event. The storm follows the west-to-east pattern of Palestinian weather. Thunderclouds roll in from the vast sea, with deafening thunderclaps, driving rain, and lightning flashes as it moves over the Levantine coast. The luminous thundercloud is the chariot of the victorious Storm God, and the thunder, rain, and lightning are the soldiers of his army. The phrase "voice of the LORD" (the sound of thunder) is repeated seven times in the poem. Nature itself proclaims Yahweh supreme Lord. "Mighty waters" (v. 3c) describes the vast sea resounding with thunder as Yahweh comes; it also refers to the cosmic waters surrounding heaven and earth, as in Ps 93:4 and Isa 17:12. As God's thunders roiled the sea, so they have the same effect upon the land and the Lebanon and Anti-Lebanon mountain ranges (vv. 5-6). The thunder, the rain sweeping across the trees, and the lightning that lights up trees appear to shatter and shake the forested mountain. Kadesh (v. 8b) is the desert east of the city Kadesh on the Orontes River in (modern) Syria. The torrential rains continue beyond the coastal regions to the wilderness further to the east. The Lord is master of the normally arid steppe, as well as the normally fertile coastal mountains and plains. This arid territory in the Ugaritic texts was the domain of Mot ("Death"), who ruled over the arid steppe. The scene resembles Isa 41:18,

> I will open rivers on the bare heights,
> and fountains in the midst of the valleys;
> I will make the wilderness a pool of water,
> and the dry land springs of water.

The wilderness locale seems to have caused some textual confusion in the Masoretic Text of verse 9. The Masoretic Text of 9a

155

reads, literally, "the voice of Yahweh causes hinds to calve" (NRSV margin), but such a meaning is not parallel with the Masoretic Text of 9b, "and strips the forests bare." NRSV and NAB prefer the forest images and make a slight adjustment, whereas REB and NJPS prefer the animal images.

In the context of the command to the heavenly beings in verse 1 to give glory to the Lord, "his temple" in verse 9c can only refer to the heavenly palace. Given the splendor of the returning Storm God, it is no wonder that the assembly of heavenly beings cries "Glory!" The heavenly palace is reflected on earth in the Jerusalem Temple.

The enthroned Lord blesses the people (vv. 10-11)

"The flood" *(mabbûl)* has provoked much discussion. Elsewhere in the Bible, it occurs only in Genesis 6–11 for the flood in Noah's time, designating either the event or the epoch. It can therefore mean "from the time of the flood" or "at the time of the flood," and scholars have taken it in both senses. A third interpretation is more likely, however. In all the combat myths with only one exception, the adversary is a form of the sea or cosmic waters. In one influential combat myth from Mesopotamia *(Enuma elish)*, the body of vanquished Sea serves as the material from which the universe is created. Accordingly, NRSV translates the word "over the flood," which implies that the throne itself symbolizes defeated Sea. The Lord's unlimited reign means that threat will never be triumphant.

The final line prays that the unchallenged authority and glory will benefit the Lord's own people. "Strength" and "peace" in similar ancient blessings usually mean physical health and vigor. The context suggests that here they have a national meaning: Israel's prosperity and security will advertise to the world their God's sovereignty.

Theological and Ethical Analysis

Can the originally mythic worldview of this prayer serve as a prayer for modern people? The answer is yes, for the poem essentially prays that the Lord's sovereignty be acknowledged in heaven and on earth. The aim is essentially the same as that expressed by the opening lines of the Lord's Prayer, "Hallowed be thy name . . . in earth as it is in heaven" (Matt 6:9-10 KJV). "Ascribe the glory of his name" means "may all peoples on earth join with the inhabitants of heaven in acknowledging the unique sovereignty of the Lord!" The goal is not to describe the ceremonies of heaven but to summon heaven and earth to acknowledge the supremacy of the Lord. Normally, the Bible hesitates out of reverence to speak about the heavens and the glory there celebrated. In fact, if one compares the Bible to the literature of its neighbors, one is struck by how seldom it speaks of the heavenly world and, in the few times that it does, how full of qualifications is its speech (e.g., Ezek 1). It simply accepts the ancient Near Eastern view that there are inhabitants of heaven and that they devote themselves entirely to serving the Most High.

The psalm does two things for modern prayers that are important and necessary. First, it invites the whole world to join the praising of the one God. Though obviously the whole world does *not* believe in the same God, the psalm, by inviting them, expresses the hope that all people will unite in giving praise. Thus the prayer expresses as a hope the biblical doctrine that one God created one human family. Second, it associates praise with a particular act of God—the act that created the world as orderly and beautiful.

PSALM 30

According to the superscription, Ps 30 is "a song at the dedication of the temple." Though the poem is much older than the second century BCE and the superscription is secondary, the psalm was used at the Feast of Dedication (Hanukkah), which celebrated the cleansing of the Temple by Judas Maccabeus in 164 BCE.

Literary Analysis

The poem is an individual thanksgiving with four parts: praise and thanks for deliverance and restoration (vv. 1-3), an invitation for others to join (vv. 4-5), narrative of the crisis, including the original prayer (vv. 6-10), and repetition of praise and thanks (vv. 11-12). Two metaphorical systems are at work: (1) going down, death, silence, and (2) rising up, life, praise. It is God who moves the psalmist from one state to the other. The number of divine names ("the LORD," "God") add up to twelve, which is the number of the tribes of Israel. Perhaps the psalm suggests that this healing of an individual is a type of what God does for all the tribes.

Teaching others about the Lord (vv. 4-5) is a standard way of giving thanks (as in 32:8; 34:11; 51:13). Such teaching has the same ultimate effect as public praise, for it increases the number of loyal worshipers of the Lord. The lengthy description of the psalmist's past overconfidence (v. 6), sudden crisis (v. 7), and prayer (vv. 8-10) is paralleled in other thanksgivings (41:4-10; 73:2-3).

Exegetical Analysis

I praise you, for you have drawn me up (vv. 1-3)

One of the two metaphor systems in the poem is directional: "down" and "up," signifying, respectively, disintegration and wholeness. "Down" is Sheol and the Pit (v. 3), the underworld where the dead exist in an attenuated shadow existence, and "up" is the earth, home of the living. God has "drawn up" (v. 1a) and "brought up" (v. 3a) the psalmist from those going down to Sheol or the Pit. Another way of expressing being raised up is not letting enemies "rejoice over me" (v. 1b), that is, keeping me from shame, healing me (v. 2b), and preserving me alive (v. 3b). The rich and varied imagery makes it difficult to discern exactly what the singer's experience really was. The poet supplies the varied images so the pray-er might appreciate more readily the breadth and depth of God's rescue.

Appreciate the nature and purpose of divine wrath! (vv. 4-5)

The rescued person invites the faithful to give praise for the rescue and at the same time to see its significance for their own lives. Divine wrath refers primarily to God's withdrawal from the people rather than to God's emotions. The rescue of the psalmist shows that divine "anger" (v. 5a) and human "weeping" (v. 5c) are not intended to be a permanent state but an "exception" ("for a moment," v. 5a), leading to the normal state of divine "favor" (v. 5b) and human "joy" (v. 5d). There is no disjunction between such learning and praising, for both actions acknowledge the true nature of God.

An ancient Jewish interpretation of verse 5b, discernible in the Septuagint, the Vulgate, and Jewish commentators, puts the opposition between God's being angry and being pleased: "For He is angry but a moment, / and when He is pleased there is life" (NJPS [6a], similarly, REB). NRSV posits a second opposition, between moment and lifetime. Though Hebrew "life" does not ordinarily mean duration of a lifetime, NRSV must be deemed a possible translation. The psalmist's main point is that the crisis, reflecting God's wrath, is part of a process leading to life.

The crisis and the prayer (vv. 6-10)

"As for me" (v. 6a) signals a shift back to the singer's story and to the complacency preceding the crisis, "I said . . . 'I shall never be moved' " (v. 6). When divine support was removed, the self-confident psalmist collapsed, like the creatures in Ps 104:27-30 who were dismayed when God hid his face. The psalmist managed nonetheless to present the eloquent argument preserved in verses 9-10: My death will bring no profit to you. The argument is not simply that God will lose my services as chorister of your glory. The prayer is also a protest against the silence and inertia of death. What profit is there generally if my voice is silenced prematurely? The psalmist quotes the prayer now as a kind of votive offering, put on display to show the seriousness of the danger from which the sufferer was saved.

I praise you, for you turned my despair into joy (vv. 11-12)

The poem ends as it began, with praise of God. The order of presentation in these verses, however, reverses verses 1-3 in that the act of rescue (in the past tense, v. 11) is described before the praise (in the present/future tense, v. 12). The verbs are specific. NRSV "mourning" (lit. "wailing") turns into joyous dancing. Grim garments, rent perhaps and with dirt rubbed into them, are exchanged for clothes fit for "joy," that is, outward expressions of joy such as songs and shouts. The sufferings of the psalmist, had they not been alleviated, would have brought joy to enemies (v. 1). Now the sufferer has been vindicated and it is the enemies who withdraw in confusion and shame.

Theological and Ethical Analysis

Giving thanks is not always easy. "Thank you" is often a conversation stopper. This psalm offers a model for responding to God's favor, by telling others what God has done for the psalmist, helping them to see a meaningful thread in the senseless destruction that might appall them, incorporating the painful past into a new narrative rather than forgetting or glossing it over. The poet offers an unusual wealth of images and metaphors to describe God's bringing a person to life once more: drawing up (from a pit), healing, snatching one back from falling into the underworld, making one survive a deadly peril. The profusion of metaphors teaches that experiences of peril and exaltation are part of life, especially part of a life of faithfulness to God's word. Christians cannot fail to see a prefiguring of the resurrection in the raising to life of the just person described here. Indeed, it is an experience of anyone who cries out in hope to the God of life and justice.

PSALM 31

Literary Analysis

The genre of the psalm is difficult to pinpoint. At first reading, the poem seems to be an individual lament (vv. 1-4, 9-18) combined with a thanksgiving (vv. 5-8, 19-24). Some scholars suggest that scribes expanded a lament by adding expressions of trust, and that a thanksgiving promised in view of rescue was developed into a thanksgiving for a past event. Such suggestions are highly conjectural, however, for it is questionable whether sacred texts were so casually expanded. It is best to accept the text as it is and assume that the author records a process too broad and complex to fit the conventions of a single genre. The structure of the present text is the best clue to its meaning.

That structure is marked off by themes and by word repetition. A consistent marker is the divine name, "the LORD" (ten occurrences), which appears in the first colon of each section. There are two sections, a lament (vv. 1-18) and a thanksgiving (vv. 19-24). The poet is writing about something more than deliverance from a specific crisis. The canvas is broader—life before God, which consists of multiple dangers, deliverances, and thanksgivings.

Exegetical Analysis

Lead me to your place of refuge (vv. 1-4)

The phrase "I seek refuge" also opens Pss 7, 11, 16, and 71. The petition establishes a bond so close as virtually to demand protection. The images for salvation are all spatial—rock, fortress (lit. safe house), crag, stronghold—symbolizing the strength of God. The images make their effect by accumulation. "Lead me and guide me" (v. 3*b*) continues the spatial imagery, for the psalmist wants to travel to a safe spot and be safe from traps along the way (v. 4). Other psalms, such as Pss 27, 42–43, and 63, ask to be led to the Temple, but the request here is more general: for a secure place.

I have always trusted you alone as my God (vv. 5-8)

The tenderness and ardor of the plea are extraordinary. Several words in the perfect tense, which NRSV translates as historical past ("have redeemed," "have seen," "have taken heed," "have delivered," "have set"), are best taken as expressing habitual activity describing the present relationship. Verse 5 expresses trust in both parts of the verse, for the second part of the verse should be rendered "you redeem me" or "you will redeem me." Verse 7 similarly describes an ongoing reciprocal relationship in which the psalmist responds with joyous shouts to God's noticing "my affliction." In short, the verses describe a relationship rather than discrete episodes. Verse 5 is quoted in Luke 23:46 as Jesus' last words on the cross.

Petition and complaint: personal distress and social ostracism (vv. 9-13)

The return to a verb in the imperative mood ("be gracious," cf. v. 2) signals a shift. The imperative is followed by a complaint about physical distress (vv. 9-10) and social exclusion (vv. 11-13). The symptoms are specific: Excessive weeping has weakened the psalmist's eyes; the throat area (NRSV: "my soul") and stomach have been damaged by grief and stress; the psalmist suffers from fatigue and perhaps severe arthritis ("my bones"). The sufferer does not hesitate to describe the symptoms to the divine physician (cf. Pss 103:3; 147:3).

The ancients took for granted that a good reputation is necessary for living well. Illness could damage one's reputation, for it could elicit the question, "What have you done wrong to deserve divine punishment?" Like Job, the psalmist knows the hostility and suspicion of friends. Ostracism, especially when combined with serious illness, can take away hope and crush one beneath unsupportable burdens. It is possible also that the symptoms are simply those of old age, when vitality wanes and neighbors and friends no longer visit. Such pain can be as hard to bear as a major illness.

I repeat: I trust you (vv. 14-16)

Verse 14*a* repeats verse 6*b* in striking fashion, as noted in the outline above. The repetitions affirm the act of trust made prior to the complaint, despite the suffering described in verses 9-13. "Let your face shine" means, as it does in Num 6:25 and Pss 4:6; 80:3, 7, 19; 119:135, an open countenance that looks directly at the other, not a face turned away in anger.

Petition that defamers be proved wrong (vv. 17-18)

This section prays that those who defamed the psalmist (vv. 11-14) themselves suffer shame. There is no corresponding prayer for healing of the infirmaries described in verses 9-10. Perhaps a petition for healing is included by implication.

Wonder at God's rescue of the imperiled (vv. 19-20)

The change of syntax in "how abundant" (v. 19) signals a major change in mood. The poem leaves behind complaints and protestations of trust to express thanks for specific favors received. The experience of salvation enables the psalmist to teach about the goodness of God. The benefits have been done "in the sight of everyone" (v. 19*d*) and thus add to God's glory, because all who see it will give praise. God hides the loyal in a shelter, which recalls the plea for a safe place that opened the poem (vv. 1-4). "Shelter" *(sukkāh)* can designate a tent dwelling for God as in Amos 9:11; Pss 18:11 (// 2 Sam 22:12); 27:5. In ancient Canaanite lore, the high god lived in a splendid tent. Here, the reference is most probably to the Temple at Jerusalem. Hence, the quest for a "safe house" in the opening verses is answered by God granting admission to the Temple.

Blessed be the Lord (vv. 21-22)

To bless the Lord is to acknowledge divine blessings publicly, in this case the "steadfast love" *(ḥesed)* responsible for the rescue.

The singer cites a past sentiment (cf. Pss 30:6; 73:1-3; 116:11) to illustrate growth in trust.

Be loyal to the Lord, all you saints (vv. 23-24)

Part of the thanksgiving is exhorting others to be loyal, in this case "the faithful" who have not had the psalmist's unforgettable experience of deliverance. Ordinary people who soldier away in the service of God can easily lose their enthusiasm and freshness. Such people need the exhortation of an individual who has personally experienced despair turned into hope. Such an experience this singer had and had as well the art to turn the experience into a psalm that edifies the community.

Theological and Ethical Analysis

Psalm 31 is a poem recording the ups and downs of a relationship with God. One might expect that being right with God ensures a serene and peaceful life. The reality is that fidelity to God practiced in the actual world can be anything but serene. This psalm records the afflictions, the moments of trust, the attacks of the wicked, and ultimately the triumph of a faithful person. The psalmist knows that the Lord rules justly (v. 23) despite the sufferings of the faithful.

PSALM 32

Literary Analysis

This poem is an individual song of thanksgiving and the second of the church's seven penitential psalms (Pss 6, 38, 51, 102, 130, 143). It places great emphasis on announcing to others the blessing that has been received. Such announcements are equivalently praise of God's fidelity and are a form of praise.

Repeated words guide the reader through the poem and demarcate its two sections. Section 1 (vv. 1-5) is defined by the repetition in verse 5 of words from verses 1-2. The repeated words are: to forgive, "transgression," "cover/hide" *(kisseh)*, "the LORD," and the Hebrew root *ht'* ("sin"). Verse 5 also completes the sentiments first mentioned in verse 1. Section 2 (vv. 6-11) is introduced by "therefore" in verse 6 and marks a shift from addressing God directly to addressing onlookers. Section 2 translates a personal experience of the merciful God into teaching to the onlookers. Verse 7 explicitly refers back to the original experience, ensuring that the teaching is not "doctrine," but the fruit of a profound experience of God.

There are three metaphors for sin and three metaphors of forgiveness. In the first, "transgression" (vv. 1, 5) is a burden that one has to carry *(nāśā')*. Wrongdoing is regarded not as an event or an action but as an object. As one carries that object about, one may suffer the evil consequences attached to it. The object can, however, be carried *away (nāśā')* by another. It no longer weighs on one's shoulders. One has been relieved of a heavy and (potentially) dangerous burden. Normally, God is the one who carries away the burden. Though many scholars assign to the verb *nāśā'* two separate figurative meanings: "to suffer, endure," and "to forgive," it actually has only one meaning, "to carry." The verb has two *uses*, however: to carry a burden ("suffer") and to carry away a burden ("forgive").

In the second metaphor, sin is something that God sees (it is "in God's face") and that angers God. Psalm 90:8 is a good example of the metaphor: "You have set our iniquities before you, / our secret sins in the light of your countenance." Forgiveness consists in covering the sin so God no longer looks on it and stays away. The third metaphor is similar to the second. God "imputes iniquity," that is, passes judgment that someone is a sinner and hence withholds blessing from the person. Forgiveness consists in abandoning that judgment, no longer imputing iniquity. In Gen 15:6, God judges that Abram's act of belief is righteous. In this psalm, God judges that the psalmist is no longer a sinner.

Verses 3-4 do not make the modern distinction between emotional and physical illness. The psalmist's health as a whole has been devastated. "Your hand was heavy upon me" (v. 4a). Verse 5 marks the point of conversion. The psalmist gives up carrying the burden and allows God to carry it away and gives up trying to cover the sin and allows God to cover it. As long as the psalmist tried to manage the sin with personal resources, it was a destructive load. One must respect the metaphors in the psalm. Sin is a powerful reality with many dimensions.

Exegetical Analysis

I acknowledged my sin to you, and you granted me forgiveness (vv. 1-5)

The section narrates the rescue for which thanks will be given in the form of a proclamation to others (vv. 6-11). Many psalms describe the rescue variously as healing of a sickness, delivering from accusations, or negating the effects of ostracism. Here, however, the evil did not arise from others. It was the psalmist who committed the sin; no denials or excuses are offered. The effects in this case were personal rather than social. The health of the sinner failed. Paradoxically, the psalmist's covering kept God from covering. Forgiveness of sin is God's work; it is not a human work. Despite the sinner's feverish efforts, God still looked at the sin and remained at a distance. The act of forgiveness has already taken place when the psalm begins. The poem uses the "divine passive," describing the work of God in passive rather than active verbs out of reverence.

Verses 3-4 describe the psalmist's sufferings. No distinction is drawn between physical and emotional pain. The joy and prosperity that make up ordinary happiness have disappeared. The psalmist feels vitality waning, is bothered and anxious (v. 3), senses God's enmity, and feels unable to do anything about it (v. 4). God's "heavy hand" suffocates rather than supports human efforts, as in Job 23:2 and 1 Sam 5:6, 11. Perhaps the ailment is depression, perhaps physical illness, perhaps the weakness of old age. The psalmist, however, interprets it as divine withdrawal because of sin. When God withdraws, human beings die, as in Ps 104:29: "When you hide your face, they are dismayed; / when you take away their breath, they die and return to their dust."

Deliverance comes when the afflicted sinner resolves to end the cover-up, allowing God to do a cover-up in the sense of no longer regarding the sin. God carries it away (NRSV: "forgave the guilt"). With the sin gone, physical deterioration ends and bodily wholeness returns.

The forgiven sinner teaches with authority about the forgiveness of God (vv. 6-11)

Profoundly moved by an experience of God's mercy, the singer in a sense "speaks the gospel." Addressed to the surrounding world, it is a message of salvation; addressed to God, it is praise. The words are not addressed to other sinners to convert them, but are addressed to the "faithful," God's loyal friends, to tell them something they do not sufficiently realize about the One they serve. Only the psalmist, who has had a unique experience of God, can tell them: Sin need not destroy you or separate you from God. Entrust the sin to God to carry away, to cease counting it against you. NRSV "at a time of distress" is a guess for a very obscure phrase. As if to reassure hearers the teaching is not a cliché but the result of an experience, the singer cries out to God, "You!" *You* (God) is the subject of the following three clauses (v. 7).

What gives the psalmist the authority to teach? Is it the experience of being forgiven, or is it rather the encounter with the God who forgives? Having been touched by God's mercy, the psalmist can make the extraordinary claim, "I will . . . teach you the way you should go" (v. 8). Hearers can of course turn away like work animals who do not heed words and require bridle and whip to move (v. 9). The essence of the singer's teaching is the general phrase contained in verse 8: "walking the right path." Verse 10 makes that general exhortation precise: The wicked person suffers "torments," whereas the person who trusts in God is surrounded by steadfast love. The verse states exactly the psalmist's own experience. Openness and trust led to the restoration of the relationship with God. The psalmist is trying to put that paradigmatic experience into a concise sentence. The psalm concludes by inviting God's friends to shout for joy (v. 11*b*).

Theological and Ethical Analysis

It is widely recognized that acting from shame and repressing negative thoughts can lead to depression and even physical deterioration. Though this truth is partly the topic of the psalm, it is not its central concern. The psalm is ultimately about the divine hand that lies heavy on a person who "lives in sin," that is, who is not on the right path and makes no effort to move on to it. Such a person misses the blessings of vitality and protection. Relying exclusively on one's own resources, one wastes away until one allows God to do what one insisted on doing oneself. When God covers it and carries it away, one is truly freed of the burden. One meets the merciful God. One lives again. The power of sin to separate is ended.

The drama of the psalm is enacted over and over in the healing stories of the Gospels. The sentiments are grandly expressed in Rom 8:35: "Who will separate us from the love of Christ? Will hardship, or distress, or persecution, or famine, or nakedness, or peril, or sword?"

PSALM 33

Literary Analysis

Psalm 33 is one of the few hymns in Book 1 of the Psalter. A special feature is its comprehensive outlook, for it explicitly includes the heavens, the sea, and the earth. Perhaps to underline comprehensiveness, the poet opts for an acrostic structure of twenty-two lines, the number of *all* the letters of the Hebrew alphabet.

As a hymn, Ps 33 has the expected invitation to praise, the naming of those invited to praise ("you righteous" and "the upright," v. 1), the mention of song and musical instruments (vv.

2-3), and the conjunction "for" (vv. 4 and 9) that introduces the reason for giving praise. In this hymn, the object of praise is God's powerful and just word that creates the three-tiered universe of heaven, sea, and earth (vv. 6-9). Against such a divine word (NRSV: "counsel" and "thoughts," v. 11), human words cannot prevail (vv. 10-11). On the basis of these hymn conventions, one would expect the poem to conclude by a reprise of the opening invitation to praise, but it does not. One reason for its unique turn is that the poem is also a twenty-two line acrostic poem (though without the customary feature that each line begin with a successive letter of the Hebrew alphabet). The first half of the acrostic poem (vv. 1-11) is constructed as a perfect hymn (invitation, the conjunction "for," the reason for praise). The second half (vv. 12-22) concentrates on one tier of the three-tiered universe—earth—in order to explore how its inhabitants respond to the God who brought it into existence.

The second half (vv. 12-22) develops two themes only hinted at in the first half: God's judgment of the inhabitants of earth (vv. 13-15, 18-19; cf. v. 10) and humans' response (vv. 12, 16-17, 20-22; cf. v. 8). The poem sees only two possible responses: (1) to accept being chosen as God's own people and respond by waiting, trusting, and hoping (vv. 12, 20-22), or (2) to rely on human resources alone—in particular weapons of war—for salvation and victory (vv. 16-17). By alluding back to verse 10, which mentions "the nations" and "the peoples," verses 16-17 suggest the contrast is not simply between two types of response (trust in God versus self-reliance) but also between Israel and the nations.

The acrostic convention explains much of the structure. The poem divides neatly into the two halves of the alphabet, verses 1-11 (80 Hebrew words) and verses 12-22 (81 Hebrew words). The first half is, as noted, a conventional hymn (minus the concluding invitation to praise) concerned with the hymnic topic of creation; the second half focuses on Israel. Hymns such as Pss 135 and 136 proceed similarly, from creation of the world to formation of Israel. The name of God is a formal feature unifying the poem; it occurs fourteen times (two times seven; "the LORD" 13 times and "God" once). Psalm 27 has the identical count. Many words occur several times, unifying the poem and spurring the reader to notice the slightly different uses of the word according to context, for example, "upright" in verses 1 and 4; "fear" in verses 8 and 18; "all the inhabitants of the world/earth" in verses 8 and 14; "peoples/people" and "nations/nation" in verses 10 and 12; "steadfast love" in verses 5, 18, 22.

The logic of the poem is implicit and must be made clear through restatement: Praise God whose powerful word created and now rules the universe of heaven-sea-earth and whose eye scrutinizes the inhabitants of earth. Accept the God who has chosen you as his people.

Exegetical Analysis

Praise God whose word created and governs the three-tiered universe (vv. 1-11)

"Rejoice" (v. 1) implies a community gathered to celebrate its joy. "You righteous" and "the upright" refer to Israelites made holy by God's choosing them and bringing them into the sanctuary; their righteousness derives from the holiness of the place on which they stand. As God is righteous and upright (vv. 4-5; cf. Ps 119:137), so are those invited into the Temple precincts. To sing a "new song" (v. 3) elsewhere is a response to God's creation of the world or the nation Israel (Pss 96:1; 98:1; 144:9; 149:1; Isa 42:10). The hymnic conjunction in verse 4, "for" *(kî)*, introduces that act for which praise is due, in this case, "the word of the LORD is upright." Though one might expect a clause such as "the LORD created the world," the poet focuses on the divine word itself as more revealing of God's self. This God "loves," in the sense of being committed to "righteousness and justice" (v. 5), and the world is praiseworthy because it is filled with these divine qualities. Because of God, the people now standing within the sanctuary are "righteous" and "upright."

Contrary to most, this commentary regards verses 6-11 as a subunit describing the three spheres of heaven (v. 6), sea (v. 7) and earth (vv. 8-10). Significantly, heaven is inhabited by "all their host" (v. 6b), who owe their being to the breath of God's mouth. Nothing is said about them beyond this phrase, suggesting that they accept obediently their role as God's creation. At any rate, the mention of the heavenly host prepares for the inhabitants of earth, the topic of the second half of the poem. The sphere of sea (v. 7) is without inhabitants but is mentioned in order to illustrate the Lord's power to gather the limitless primordial waters into a particular area (lit. "heap"). NRSV has "in a bottle"; the Hebrew word is unclear. Earth, in third and climactic place, also has inhabitants, but they are not automatically genuine worshipers of the Creator. The hymnic conjunction "for" in verse 9 affirms again the power of the divine word to create and rule ("he spoke, and it came to be"), and verses 10-11 continue the theme of divine governance of the earth. These verses are not, as one might be tempted to think, a condemnation of human striving as such, but an assertion that divine rather than human plans govern the world. Despite appearances to the contrary, God's "intent" ('ēṣāh, NRSV: "counsel") and "plans" (maḥšebôt, NRSV: "plans/thoughts") prevail over human intents and plans.

Respond to God whose eye judges the conduct of human beings (vv. 12-22)

For the first time, Israel is mentioned as "the nation" and "the people" (v. 12) whose God is the Lord. Israel is deliberately contrasted with the "the nations" and "the peoples" of verse 10, whose plans allow no place for the true governor of the world. Israel is not portrayed as doing anything; it is declared "happy" simply for being God's special people. In verse 13 this God, who graciously chooses one people, rigidly scrutinizes the entire human race. Nothing can be hidden from the One who watches from the heights and who also made the human heart (vv. 13-15). As already hinted in verses 10-11, human resources alone do not bring victory. There is perhaps a subtle reference to Gentile kings whose vast armies terrified Israel and sometimes caused them to desert their Lord. Those same divine eyes (v. 13) ultimately look for only one thing, "those who fear him, . . . who hope in his steadfast love" (v. 18).

The poem ends appropriately with a kind of invitation to praise in verses 20-22, transposed to a personal scale. Having accepted that we are the Lord's people, we wait for him, rejoice in trusting in his name, and pray for his steadfast love upon us.

Theological and Ethical Analysis

Though not mentioned explicitly, the face of God dominates the hymn. God's mouth speaks, and the universe comes into being. God's eye sweeps the earth in judgment and governs its inhabitants. Instead of saying "God created the world," the psalm prefers to hymn the divine word (vv. 4 and 9). Instead of saying "God is ruler of the world," the psalm points upward to God looking majestically upon the inhabitants of earth (vv. 13-15, 18-19). The reality of God thrusts itself upon the world. Divine power is especially clear in the creation of heaven and sea (vv. 6-7). Divine grace and desire to be in relationship is especially shown in the creation and rule of earth. In this sphere, the divine eye has a dual significance. On the one hand, it judges human pretense and grandiosity; on the other, it graciously bestows blessings and invites humans into a relationship like that of servant to lord—attending, receiving help and protection (v. 20)—and yet something more, gladdening the heart, trusting in his name, receiving the blessings that flow from God's steadfast love (vv. 21-22).

PSALM 34

Literary Analysis

The poem is distinguished by its concentration on the pray-er's relationship to the Lord and its serene confidence that nothing can happen to one who trusts in the Lord. The psalmist assumes the mantle of a teacher who can help others to the same special relationship. Faithful hearers will be protected from the wicked, and their own afflictions will in no way keep them from the Lord. The psalm is an individual thanksgiving that publicizes the psalmist as an encouragement for all who struggle to remain loyal to their God. It is in acrostic form in which every line begins with a successive letter of the twenty-two letter Hebrew alphabet. In this poem, there is no verse beginning with the letter *wāw*, and the final verse is out of the series. The acrostic form perhaps explains why the specificity one expects in a thanksgiving is diluted. A thanksgiving resembles a hymn, for in Hebrew thinking giving thanks meant declaring what God has done for the speaker. A thanksgiving can be didactic as it is here, for one way of giving thanks is to instruct others about how to serve God. Thus it is not necessary to describe the didactic element as "wisdom" style and language.

The structure: verses 1-4, invitation to praise; verses 5-11, narrative of the rescue interspersed with admonitions; verses 12-22, the instruction. Verse 23 is the closing line, lying outside the acrostic scheme. The exact middle of the acrostic poem (v. 11), signals a clear change, "Come, O children" (lit. "sons," meaning adult disciples).

Exegetical Analysis

The superscription attributes the poem to a particular moment in David's life, when he pretended to be mad before Achish (not Abimelech as the superscription mistakenly has it) in 1 Sam 21:10-15. Scribes were perhaps led to this passage because two Hebrew words in Ps 34 also appear in the Samuel passage: "So he changed his *behavior* (*ṭ'm*, cf. "taste" in Ps 34:8) before them; *he pretended to be mad* (*hthll*, cf. "boast" in Ps 34:2) when in their presence."

Praise the Lord with me (vv. 1-3)

Though the psalm is a thanksgiving, it begins by inviting others to join the song. The psalmist wants to widen the circle of those praising God (vv. 1-3) and living in accord with divine teaching (vv. 11-22). The praise that is invited is not, however, limited to a once-for-all response to a specific rescue, for it is to be done "continually" (v. 1). The psalmist calls for a praising style. "Makes its boast" (v. 2) means to acknowledge triumphing with God's help and to attribute victory to God. Verse 2*b* can be paraphrased: Let those in need as I was sing jubilantly!

Report of the rescue and exhortations to be
faithful to the Lord (vv. 4-10)

Every thanksgiving is at bottom a report of a rescue. The rescue reported in verses 4 and 6 is, exceptionally, couched in the most general terms: seeking and being heard (v. 4), being delivered "from all my fears" (understood objectively as "what makes me afraid"). Report, reflection, and exhortations alternate: report (v. 4), exhortation (v. 5), report and reflection (vv. 6-7), exhortation (vv. 8-9), reflection (v. 10). The phrase "be radiant" (v. 5) occurs also in Isa 60:5 where the people of Zion see the nations bringing their treasures in homage: "Then you shall see and be radiant; / your heart shall thrill and rejoice." It means to have a bright and smiling countenance (Jer 31:12). "Never be ashamed" (v. 5*b*) means that what one trusted always proves reliable. Verse 4*b*, literally, "from all that he fears he delivers him," is echoed with only slight changes (in the Hebrew) in verses 6*b* and 17*b*, forming a thread through the whole. The repetition underlines the fact that one may attain intimacy with God, but never equality; before God one is always in need and a beggar.

"The angel of the LORD" (v. 7) is a member of the heavenly entourage of the Most High, eager to do the sovereign's will. Such "angels" sometimes have a military function (as in Judg 2:1-4; 6:11-22). Here they are a military escort for those who fear the Lord. The figure is a concrete way of expressing divine protection. Later Jewish and Christian belief in guardian angels comes from such passages as this. In verse 8 the invitation to "taste" is a metaphor for experience. In Ezek 3:3, God tells the prophet, "eat this scroll that I give you and fill your stomach with it. Then I ate it; and in my mouth it was as sweet as honey." The psalmist exclaims in Ps 119:103, "How sweet are your words to my taste, / sweeter than honey to my mouth!" Experience is the best teacher that God is a refuge. God will protect the loyal, though mighty lions go hungry.

The psalmist as teacher of wisdom (vv. 11-22)

From verse 11 to the end of the poem, the psalmist assumes the mantle of a teacher, even assuming certain traits of personified Wisdom (cf. Prov 9) with the goal of teaching others how to gain life. The resemblances to Prov 9:4-6, 11 are striking (identical words are italicized):

> *Whoever* [Ps 34:12*a*] is simple, turn aside here. . . .
> *Come,* eat my food,
>   drink the wine I have mixed.
> Leave behind simpleness and live,
>   walk on the path of understanding. . . .
> For by me will your *days* be made many,
>   and years of *life* will be added for you.

"Life" here is long life resulting from righteous conduct opposed to the brief life of the wicked, who are cut off prematurely. In addition to shared vocabulary, Proverbs' exhortation to "leave behind (simpleness)" (meaning "convert from evildoing") is equivalent to Ps 34:14, "depart from evil." As in Prov 9:1-9, "children" (lit. "sons, disciples," v. 11) are the recipients of instruction. Psalm 34:11-14, perhaps even the whole block of verses 11-22, could be inserted into Prov 9:1-9 without seeming out of place. The difference between Proverbs and Psalms is the location of the teacher's authority. In Proverbs, it is the social position of the father (or the father and mother in Prov 1:8 and 6:20). In Ps 34, the teacher has authority as someone rescued by a special intervention of God and thus endowed with divine wisdom.

"Fear of the LORD" (v. 11) is the traditional, though unsatisfactory, translation of a Hebrew phrase better rendered "revering

Yahweh." The title "LORD" is the traditional surrogate in both Judaism and Christianity for the proper name "Yahweh." The phrase "fear of [divine name]" is widely attested in the ancient Near East. Not primarily an emotion or general attitude, it means being loyal to a particular deity by carrying out that god's rituals and commands. Doing so invites the god's blessing: healthy and long life, children, wealth, standing in the community, and protection from enemies. The relationship between divine patron and human client is not simply a *quid pro quo*, a quasicommercial agreement. It is heartfelt and deep, for the individual is characterized as "humble" (v. 2), "righteous" (v. 15), and "brokenhearted" (v. 18), that is, one who is loyal and in need of divine protection. The psalmist does not come to God as an equal, but with hands outstretched in need. The Lord is portrayed in verses 15-22 as just, that is, as intervening on the side of the righteous and poor against their oppressors. The Lord's friends are dramatically portrayed as beset by enemies.

Theological and Ethical Analysis

Many thanksgivings are poems of spontaneous delight, relief, and gratitude toward God. The rescued person "cannot keep from singing." Other acts of deliverance, like this one, are recollected in tranquillity and recast as a thanksgiving plus teaching. The psalmist, highly aware of being "poor" (v. 6), that is, in need of divine protection and blessings, was led thereby to seek the Lord who hears and answers (v. 4). For the psalmist, life with God is dialectical, human weakness encountering divine power, as in 2 Cor 4:7-9: "But we have this treasure in clay jars, so that it may be made clear that this extraordinary power belongs to God and does not come from us. We are afflicted in every way, but not crushed; perplexed, but not driven to despair; persecuted, but not forsaken; struck down, but not destroyed." Though vulnerable, the psalmist found protection and can witness that a faithful life, though full of struggle, will be victorious. This prayer is particularly suitable for those who have experienced God's power in their weakness and wish to show their appreciation by encouraging others.

PSALM 35

Literary Analysis

This psalm is an individual lament. Verses 11-16 seem highly specific about the identity of the enemies: They are legal adversaries who used to be friends, people whose troubles the psalmist once openheartedly shared. One should be wary about taking the detail as genuine autobiography, however, for the enemies are elsewhere described under the metaphors of soldiers (vv. 1-3), hunters (v. 7), and lions (v. 17). The poem uses the imagery of war, lawsuit, and conspiracy to show how the whole world is arrayed against a lone individual. Verses 11-16 constitute the main complaint, however, for its details make clear that the opposition was undeserved and doubly painful in that it involved close friends. As usual, the poem's references are broad enough to serve as a text for almost any sufferer yet concrete enough to provide memorable images and phrases.

Modern readers may find themselves confused by rapid alternation of positive pleas (vv. 1-3, 17, 22-24, 27), imprecations (vv. 4-6, 8, 19, 25-26), promises of thanksgiving (vv. 9-10, 18, 28), and complaints (vv. 7, 11-16). It may help to realize that petitions and imprecations are two sides of the same coin, appeals to "save me" and "fend off my enemies." The psalmist's promise of thanksgiving is at the same time a statement of trust in the present distress ("I still have faith in you") and a motive for God to act. The complaint is the description of the pain or injustice designed to stir up divine pity and justice. Though I am innocent, says the psalmist, I suffer the bitter wound of betrayal by friends.

The poem structure has been analyzed by scholars with quite different results. NRSV has eleven paragraphs, which reflects the alternations noted previously. Alternative analyses with fewer stanzas are also possible:

1. Plea to repel my enemies, complaint, and promise of praise (vv. 1-10)
2. Complaint, plea, and promise of praise (vv. 11-18)
3. Imprecation, plea, imprecation, and promise of praise (vv. 19-28).

The above outline presumes that the promises of praise (vv. 9-10, 18, and 28) conclude each section. The alternation of prayer/imprecation, complaint, and promise of praise is not unusual in long individual laments such as Pss 22, 31, 69, and 102.

Exegetical Analysis

Plea to repel my enemies, complaint, and promise of praise (vv. 1-10)

The metaphor of Divine Warrior is a common one in the Bible (e.g., Exod 15:1-18; Ps 18:6-19; Isa 63:1-3; Jer 20:11) and will be repeated toward the end of the psalm in verse 23, for the appeal, "bestir yourself for my defense," seeks to wake the sleeping warrior god. The psalmist is beset by enemies and problems—outnumbered and discouraged. The psalmist longs for the assurance, "I am your salvation" (v. 3). The sufferer would take the assurance as the word of God and live by it. In verse 2, "shield" (large) and "buckler" (small shield, sometimes attached to the arm) would not have been worn at the same time, nor would "spear" and "javelin" be wielded by the same warrior. The accumulation of details lends urgency to the appeal.

There are two aspects of the plea: Help me, and put down my enemies. The imprecation against enemies (vv. 4-8) is therefore the inverse of the plea for help. Shame and dishonor were highly significant in the culture, for defeat advertised to all that one had backed the wrong cause. Victory, on the other hand, showed one to be in the right. Honor was, moreover, regarded as a limited commodity, so that in a dispute the honor given to one person was denied to the other. The most profound issue of the psalm is transcultural, however, and it is that the one whom God upholds is in the right. In the dispute, the psalmist wants to be judged righteous and be *seen* so by others. Modern readers may be offended by the psalmist's apparent self-righteous tone. It is worth noting, however, that the psalmist allows God to judge and to punish.

The enemies' flight "like chaff before the wind" (v. 5) is flight from the Storm God. According to Isa 17:13, "[God] will rebuke them, and [the nations] will flee far away, / chased like chaff on the mountains before the wind / and whirling dust before the storm." "The angel of the LORD" (see Ps 34:7) is in the heavenly army of the Most High and leads the army against God's enemies (cf. Judg 2:1-4; 6:11-22). "Net" (v. 7) is a common metaphor for trap (Pss 9:15; 31:4; 140:5). It was stretched over a concealed pit to catch an animal's foot so it would fall into the pit. Poetic justice demands a similar fate for those who set a trap for others.

The psalmist looks forward to "deliverance" (v. 9) and thus to giving thanks to the Lord. The prospect of praise is an incentive for God to act. Rehearsing the thanksgiving in verse 10, the psalmist acclaims the Lord's incomparability. "LORD, who is like you," is a response to a mighty act of God (e.g., Exod 15:11; Pss 71:19; 89:8). "Rejoice" and "exulting" (v. 9) imply verbal expression. Notable in the poem are the many references to words acknowledging God's actions (e.g., vv. 3d, 10, 18, 27-28) and to words attacking the psalmist (e.g., vv. 11, 16, 20-21, 25-26).

Complaint, plea, and promise of praise (vv. 11-18)

The complaint is designed to make the psalmist look pitiable and unjustly treated so the God of mercy and justice will be moved to act. The stress is on the sorry condition of one deceived by cold and calculating friends. Few pains are more bitter than to have friends whose sorrows one has shared turn into assailants. The description serves to demonstrate the psalmist's purity of motives, for the attack was wholly undeserved. When they stumbled, I mourned with them. When I stumbled, they attacked! Though complaint predominates in this part, the sufferer manages to make a brief plea (v. 17) and promises to give thanks in the public assembly (v. 18).

Imprecation, plea, imprecation, and promise of praise (vv. 19-28)

Reversing the order of plea-imprecation (vv. 1-3 and 4-7) in the opening section, this section begins with imprecation (vv. 19-21), in which the psalmist begs not to allow the enemies to speak as if their side had won. The enemies' words are deceitful and hostile (v. 20). They are happy to see with their own eyes the psalmist's downfall ("our eyes have seen it," v. 21). Such malice cannot be allowed to succeed.

Next comes the positive plea (vv. 22-24). "Wake up" is a common appeal in ancient Near Eastern prayers and the Bible (e.g., Pss 44:23; 59:5; Isa 51:9). People sometimes presumed the gods rested at night like human beings; they also believed a god might rest after performing some great deed (as in Gen 2:3). God has already been addressed as warrior in this psalm (Ps 35:1-3). This call arises from frustration at the silence of God as the enemies rampage. Another imprecation follows in verses 25-26. The enemies' success would give the inevitable impression that they were in the right and the psalmist in the wrong.

What the psalmist wants is that God's justice be publicly acknowledged (vv. 27-28) and "those who desire my vindication" (v. 27a) join in shouting for joy. Final vindication is left in God's hands. If it were not, the psalm would never have been uttered. The poem springs therefore from faith and desire for justice.

Theological and Ethical Analysis

The profusion of metaphors for God (warrior and judge), for the psalmist (a victim on the battlefield and in the law court), and for the enemies (soldiers, hunters, perjurers, ungrateful betrayers, competitors) shows that the imagination and thirst for justice of the sufferer have not been worn down by the present crisis. The psalmist pleads for justice in this case on the grounds that God's justice should prevail at all times. There is much less anger here than in comparable psalms. The chief emotions are deep hurt at betrayal and a focused desire to see God's will done on earth as it is in heaven. The psalm is for anyone who has had to battle alone for a just cause. The very struggle can increase one's loneliness and heighten the malice of enemies. At the end, however, allies will arise (v. 27) as God grants deliverance.

PSALM 36

Literary Analysis

The poem skillfully combines prayer and instruction. It begins with the portrayal of human wickedness and offers a model of how to react to such malice. The wickedness that frightens or depresses most people provokes the psalmist to think of God's grandeur and pray for peace.

The poem displays several conventions belonging to the genre of individual lament: portrayal of the wicked (vv. 1-4), expression of trust in God (vv. 5-9), and plea for divine help (vv. 10-12). The serene tone suggests, however, that the psalmist is not threatened by an immediate danger, making it unlike a lament. Though the psalm focuses on God's orderly universe and the Temple where its bounty is made available, it nevertheless shows a keen awareness of evil. The intense portrayal of the wicked is unparalleled in the Psalter. If one must classify the psalm, it is best taken as a song of trust in the Lord in the Temple, perhaps even a Song of Zion.

Instead of describing an urgent threat from the wicked, the psalmist presents a type (that is, one representing the whole, vv. 1-4), a person given over to wickedness. NRSV translates the masculine singular nouns and pronouns of the Hebrew as plural for the sake of inclusiveness. Such typical figures are common in Wisdom literature, especially Proverbs and Sirach, occurring usually in binary pairs such as the wise versus the foolish, the righteous versus the wicked. Of all the passages in Proverbs, Prov 6:12-15 bears the most striking resemblance to Ps 36:1-4, though it does not have a binary opposition. Like Ps 36:1-4, Prov 6:12-15 intensifies the traits of the wicked person, focusing on the organs of reflection and action (heart, eyes, mouth, feet [implied in "way" of v. 4b]) and the social damage the type does. The description of the type functions in Ps 36 like the threat from the wicked in individual laments.

The confession of awe at God's rule of the universe (vv. 5-9) functions analogously like the statement of trust in a lament, expressing confidence that human malice will not prevail against the world that is ruled by the Lord. The plea (vv. 10-12) is not for rescue from a particular danger (as in a normal lament), but for the continuance of the life and protection already experienced on Zion.

Accordingly, the structure has three parts: the wicked person as threat (vv. 1-4); statement that the Lord's steadfast love rules the whole world (vv. 5-9); prayer for continued steadfast love (vv. 10-12).

Exegetical Analysis

The superscription credits the psalm to David, who is further specified as "servant of the Lord" as in the superscription of Ps 18. "Servant of [a god, a king]" was a prestigious title, and seals with the name of the servant and king were worn proudly.

The wicked person as threat (vv. 1-4)

Pervading the poem is an implicit contrast between the "self-ruled" individual and the God-ruled cosmos. "Deep in their hearts" (v. 1) shows that all the person's thoughts and designs come entirely from within. There is no hint of the "listening heart" (1 Kgs 3:9; NRSV: "understanding mind") of the wise Solomon; this individual is self-enclosed and autonomous, accepting no moral code and unmoved by others' example. The "transgression speaks to the wicked" (v. 1) is, literally, "an oracle of rebellion in his heart." This expression may parody genuine oracles such as that in Ps 110:1 in order to show the pomposity and delusion of the wicked person. In a true oracle, God speaks, not a human. The Hebrew word for "transgression" connotes political rebellion, for the individual rebels against the rule of God expressed in verses 5-9. "Fear of God" (v. 1) is not the usual Hebrew phrase for "revering Yahweh." It rather means being struck with awe and rendered submissive by an action of God. Such obedience is completely beyond this individual; delusion prevents any recognition that human actions lie open to divine scrutiny and assessment (v. 2).

Wisdom literature emphasizes words to be extraordinarily expressive, for they reveal the heart where decisions are made. This individual's words are lies because they disguise the malice within (v. 3). "On their beds" (v. 4) is a phrase that means true intent (cf. Pss 4:4; 149:5; and Hos 7:14), for it connotes private moments when one is alone and uninfluenced by others.

The accumulation of details in verses 1-4 is meant to intensify the malice. The individual, a type, is completely the servant of evil. The psalmist refuses to pretend evil does not exist.

God's steadfast love rules the whole world (vv. 5-9)

The shift in the poem from self-enclosed individual to open cosmos is abrupt and stunning. Praise replaces horrified description. As in Pss 8, 19, and 33, the universe itself reveals its maker. All lost in wonder, the psalmist sees God's "steadfast love," "faithfulness," "righteousness," and "judgments" symbolized by the mass and beauty of the cosmos. These qualities bespeak God's acts; they are not attributes of God in a modern sense. Vast and limitless, they are completely unlike the ridiculously limited life of the sinner. One thinks of the Pauline metaphor of space for the divine presence, "the breadth and length and height and depth" of the love of God (Eph 3:18-19). "The mighty mountains" (v. 6) are the great mountains holding up the disk of earth upon the "great deep." God's judgments are as measureless as that deep.

The unimaginably vast space of creation is full of God's goodness. All living creatures, "humans and animals alike" (v. 6)—not just all Israelites or even all humans—are the objects of God's care. God's care is described by the verb "save" (v. 6), for the inhabitants of the world must be preserved from the chaos that presents itself in the form of sin and instead be given life. "Saving" is what a king does. Hellenistic kings took pride in their title "savior"; sceptics of Saul's ability to be king did so by asking, "How can this man save us?" The center of the poem therefore hymns the cosmic reigning of God.

At verse 7 the psalm turns explicitly to the Jerusalem Temple. It is not, however, a turn away from the universe, for the Temple, like any ancient Near Eastern temple, had cosmic significance. The temple represents the god's heavenly palace (as in Isa 6), and the river that fertilizes the world arises within the temple precincts (as in Ps 46:4 and Ezek 47). The Temple is the place where the Lord's steadfast love is experienced directly, where life is lived most intensely, for one finds there food and drink as well as divine protection. It is the place of life (cf. Ps 63:3).

People are "saved" by taking "refuge in the shadow of your wings" (Ps 36:7). "Taking refuge" is associated with the Temple in Pss 5:11; 57:1; 61:4, though there is some doubt about its exact meaning. Most scholars believe that "your wings" are the wings of the cherubim (animal guardians) overshadowing and protecting the throne of God in the Holy of Holies (as in 1 Kgs 6:27; 8:6). Others point out, however, that the wings of the cherubim are not identical with "your [the Lord's] wings," for the cherubim carry the throne rather than represent the Lord, and ancient depictions show them guarding with their paws rather than their wings. They suggest, therefore, that "your wings" is a metaphor for God as a bird keeping predators from its nestlings by fluttering its wings (see comment to Ps 57:1). An Egyptian influence may be present as well, for the wing motif was used of solar deities or the sun itself; the winged sun represented the sun's daily course across the heavens, repelling evil (by casting its light) and bestowing life.

In the Temple, the bounty of the universe becomes available to humans, as Ps 65:4 declares: "Happy are those whom you choose and bring near / to live in your courts. / We shall be satisfied with the goodness of your house, / your holy temple." "The river of your delights" (v. 8, *'ēden*) refers to the fertilizing waters flowing from the cosmic center, as in Gen 2:10 (cf. "Eden"), Ps 46:4, and Ezek 47. "With you" in verse 9 has the nuance of "in your house."

The phrase "in your light we see light" (v. 9) is a long-standing puzzle. Some suggest "in your light" is short for "in the light of your face" (cf. Pss 4:6; 44:3; 89:15), which yields the meaning, "your favoring gaze enables us to live." Another suggestion is that darkness characterizes the underworld, the place of the dead (Ps 49:19), so that seeing light is equivalent to avoiding death. The latter suggestion makes a good parallel to "fountain of life." Possibly, there is an implicit reference to the sun, which, in neighboring cultures at least, was the divine judge who brought all matters to light through his brilliant rays. If this is the reference, the Lord's judging makes it possible for human beings to live in safety.

Prayer for continued steadfast love (vv. 10-12)

The psalmist never doubts that God's love and justice fill the world or that they can be found in the Temple. Hence the prayer is to "continue your steadfast love" (v. 10*a*) rather than to initiate what has been interrupted. "Those who know you" (v. 10*a*) means "those who have entered into covenant with you," for "know" expresses here a legally defined relationship. God has already promised protection, argues the psalmist, and will follow through on the promise. Verse 10*a* has the third occurrence of "steadfast love" in the poem. The prayer asks that "the wicked" (v. 11, reprising v. 1) not be allowed to drive the psalmist away from the Temple. The singer's belief in the inviolability of Zion prompts an expression of hope (v. 12). The impregnability of the mountain of God is part and parcel of the Zion tradition. Psalms 46, 48, and 76 declare that those who attack Zion will be defeated there: "His abode has been established in Salem, his dwelling place in Zion. There he broke the flashing arrows, the shield, the sword, and the weapons of war" (Ps 76:2-3).

The word "there" *(šām)* in verse 12 has puzzled commentators. Some take "there" as a euphemism for the underworld (cf. Job 1:21; 3:17; and Ezek 32:22-30), and others make it an adverb of time rather than place. The simplest solution, however, is to take "there" as referring to Mount Zion. In poems about Zion, "there" occurs often, always in reference to the holy mountain, for example, Pss 48:6; 76:3 (*"There* he broke the flashing arrows"); 87:4, 6; 122:5; 132:17; Isa 33:21. Verse 12, therefore, continues the prayer of verses 10-11: Keep protecting me (v. 10), prevent the wicked from driving me off (v. 11), finish off the wicked on your holy mountain (v. 12). The verbs in verse 12 are best taken as petitions with NAB: Make them lie prostrate, and thrust them down!

Theological and Ethical Analysis

The poem begins with a hard look at a subject most people would rather turn from (especially in prayer): the malice of human beings. The poet uses the literary device called a type, which was common in Wisdom literature. The reader is forced to acknowledge how much human activity is utterly self-regarding and destructive. How can one continue to believe that the world is beautiful and created by God? The poem gives no answer, instead shifting to another image, the vast universe, which symbolizes the governance of the just and loving Creator, and to yet another image, the Temple (vv. 7-9), where the Creator's goodness is dispensed to human beings. The final prayer in verses 10-12 is that the gracious order continue always and that the wicked not succeed in cutting off humans from their source. May Zion remain the place where the righteous are fed and the wicked punished!

The sequence of images is memorable: malicious people, the vast and orderly cosmos, the Temple where people come to find life. First there is human evil, then divine rule and the feeding of all creation. The poet gives the symbol first, then draws out the inference.

PSALM 37

Literary Analysis

This poem, like Pss 49 and 73, is provoked by the problem of evil, which, in good biblical style, is personified as evil people triumphing over the righteous. How can a just and loving God permit this? The poet's "solution" to the delay of justice is practical rather than theoretical: to encourage the righteous to overcome evildoers by trusting in God alone. The encouragement is done through exhortations based on divine promises (vv. 1-8, 27, 34, 37), aphorisms about divine justice in the world (vv. 10-24, 28c-33, 39-40), and the personal testimony of the psalmist that such justice actually operates in daily life (vv. 25-26, 35-36). Many moderns do not use aphorisms and are unmoved by "old saws." But to ancients and to very many people today, the brevity and "rightness" of axioms are a guarantee of their divine origin.

Problem-oriented psalms like Ps 37 are hard to classify in a particular genre. Many scholars call them "Wisdom psalms" on the grounds that their theme of divine governance (i.e., God's dealing with the good and the wicked) and didactic style are derived from Wisdom literature such as Proverbs, Job, Ecclesiates, and Sirach. Though similarities in theme and style are obvious (especially with Proverbs and Sirach), the term "Wisdom psalm" tells us little. It is more enlightening to ask about the source of the teacher's authority in the various genres. In Proverbs, authority comes from the role the king, scribe, and parent or teacher play in the mediation of heavenly wisdom to human beings on earth. In psalms of thanksgiving, authority to teach comes from the intense knowledge of God that the rescued person has gained through the experience of rescue (see Pss 34:11-12; 40:1-3). In a problem psalm like Ps 37, the psalmist's authority comes both from experiencing God as vindicator, as in psalms of thanksgiving (see vv. 25-26, 35-36), and from playing the role of scribe in the mediation of heavenly wisdom, as in Wisdom literature.

In its format Ps 37 is an acrostic poem, each segment beginning with a successive letter of the twenty-two-letter Hebrew alphabet. Though Ps 37 relies on the acrostic frame for the progression of its thought, it has distinct sections. In verses 1-11 several words from the opening verses are reprised in the concluding verses, and the section is further unified by verbs urging or commanding trust in God. In contrast, verses 12-28 are characterized by the recurrent contrast between the righteous and the wicked regarding land possession. With verse 27, verbs in the imperative mood appear again (vv. 27a, 34a, 37a), and the theme of "wisdom" and "teaching" (vv. 30-31) is introduced, though themes and styles used earlier in the psalm continue.

Exegetical Analysis

Do not be disturbed when the wicked seem to prosper (vv. 1-11)

Repetitions clearly mark off the section as distinct: "do not fret" in verse 1 and in 7 and 8; "the wicked" in verses 1 and 9; the Hebrew participle *'ōśēh* (NRSV: "wrongdoers" and "carry out") in verses 1b and 7c; and "delight" in verses 4 and 11. The section is also united by verbs in the imperative mood that urge trust in God. The exhortations offer a motive for calm and hope (e.g., "for they will soon fade like the grass," v. 2a) with the exception of verse 7.

The theme of the section is retaining one's equanimity before the ongoing prosperity of the wicked. The singer's solution is practical and personal: Do not be disturbed, for retribution will not be long in coming. Retribution against the wicked is expressed in two metaphors of premature death: The wicked will fade like the grass (v. 2), a common comparison for short-lived and fragile humanity (Pss 90:5-6; 103:15-16; Isa 40:6-7); they will be cut off (i.e., from the land, implied by the parallel v. 9b). The verb "cut off" similarly means cut off from the land in Prov 2:22; Jer 11:19; and Ezek 14:17. Most of the motives for remaining calm are positive, however: The righteous will live securely in the land (vv. 3b, 9b, 11a); their cause will be upheld publicly (v.

6); they will enjoy prosperity (v. 11*b*) and will see the downfall of their enemies (v. 10). The last benefit, seeing the downfall of their enemies, is important because it demonstrates to the faithful that their way was the right way. The wicked are shamed because everyone now sees that everything they pinned their hopes on turned out to be worthless. The most persistent metaphor of retribution is the land. The righteous live safely upon it and enjoy its fruits, whereas the wicked are cut off from it. The land was a primal symbol of life and the source of anxieties and hopes.

The wealthy set the tone in any society. People inevitably look up to them as models of dress, manners, and morals. Verses 1-11 advise something different. Standards have already been set by God (divine justice), and these standards have inevitable and certain consequences. The psalmist dethrones trendsetters who rebel against God no matter how prestigious and powerful. They are doomed. It invites those loyal to the Lord to be serenely confident in the hidden rule of God.

The wicked attack, but the Lord defends the righteous (vv. 12-20)

The theme of the first section was the destinies of the righteous and the wicked. The theme of this section is the attacks of the wicked on the righteous and the Lord's defense of them. In the first two subsections (vv. 12-13, 14-15), the wicked "plot" and draw their swords to kill but to no avail. The actions are foiled. "Their day" (v. 13*b*, i.e., the inevitable consequences of evil) will come upon the plotters, and the sword will pierce their own hearts (v. 15). Their arms are broken (v. 17), so they cannot steal the portion of the righteous (v. 16). The wicked ultimately vanish like smoke (v. 20*c*), though they once seemed substantial and solid. Though the righteous person may have "little" now, it is greater than the "abundance" of the wicked because "the Lord upholds the righteous" (v. 17). In verse 13, the scornful laughter of the Lord recalls the divine laughter at the rebellious kings (Ps 2:4), "He who sits in the heavens laughs; / the LORD has them in derision." As in the first section, the land of Israel is a symbol of blessing. "Their heritage" (v. 18*b*) refers to the land. Verse 19*b* also refers to the land that produces food for the just when there is famine elsewhere.

The righteous lend but always have enough (vv. 21-26)

This subsection is marked off verbally by the inclusion of the root *lwh* (NRSV: "borrow" [v. 21*a*] and "lending" [v. 26*a*]) and of the verb *ḥānan* (NRSV: "are generous" [v. 21*b*] and "giving liberally" [v. 26*a*]). Its theme is the paradox that the very generosity of the righteous is what keeps them prosperous. Once again, land is one instance of wealth (v. 22). Verses 25-26 are the first of two places where the singer witnesses, the other being verses 35-36. The singer's claim never to have seen the righteous forsaken or their children begging bread may seem startling to modern readers. Such claims in Wisdom literature are typical rather than exhaustively empirical. They tell one how the universe *ordinarily* works, not how it always does.

Depart from evil, wait for the Lord, and mark the blameless (vv. 27-40)

The last section of the poem is marked by three verbs in the imperative mood, singular in number, addressed to the pray-er. The imperatives introducing each subsection are quoted in the above title (vv. 27, 34, 37). The bold exhortation to "depart from evil, and do good" (v. 27) is based on a remarkable trust in the reliability of the world. In two verses, the Lord is depicted acting as a vindicator directly (vv. 28, 33). In the other verses, the verbs are impersonal or passive ("the divine passive").

In the second subsection (vv. 34-36), the author witnesses again to the inherent justice of the universe (vv. 35-36). The statement has strong affinities to Prov 24:30-34. The present towering stature of the Lebanon cedar is no indication of its ultimate fate. In Wisdom literature, the final state (*'aḥarît*) of anything is the determinant of its value. The third subsection, introduced by "mark the blameless," makes another appeal to look at the righteous. Their prosperity, measured over a long period of time (note the reference to their children), proves the validity of their way. The author speaks typically rather than empirically.

Theological and Ethical Analysis

This psalm deals with the problem of evil as it presents itself in the life of one who believes in the Lord. It avoids all theory. Recognizing that the continuing prosperity of the wicked and the lack of success of the faithful can lead to discouragement and even despair, the poem tries to foster courage and endurance. Do not be disturbed, it urges. The way of fidelity and virtue is the only way, and it will eventually confer its reward and consolations. The poet knows the importance of redundancy in communicating an important message. One must say the same thing in many arresting ways so that the hearer will take in at least some of the metaphors and examples.

Modern readers usually read Ps 37 as a series of timeless exhortations to trust in God. Such a reading was not that of many early readers. The Qumran community read it as predicting the reversal of status in the new age when the land would revert to the true children of Israel (4Q171, 4QpPs[a]). The early church had a similar preoccupation with the dawning new age, one mark of which was a renewal of communal life and dissolution of the gulf between the (wicked) rich and (oppressed) poor. This preoccupation is reflected in Matt 5:5, "Blessed are the meek, for they will inherit the earth" (cf. Ps 37:9). How did the psalm become bound up with historical hope as to speak of the new age among many in Judaism and Christianity?

One reason is the psalm's extraordinary concern with the land, which is shown by its vocabulary: "land" occurs six times and "heritage" once; the related verb "to inherit" occurs four times and "to live/dwell" three times. Though land possession would be important in any agricultural society, it had added significance for Israel, for at the nation's origins the land was distributed in perpetuity by sacred lot to tribes and families in egalitarian fashion (Joshua 13–21). Each Israelite family felt its land was a gift of the

Lord and therefore inalienable. Seizure of property, as might happen in hard economic times, called into question the Lord's fidelity and justice.

Another factor made the topic of land highly important in the centuries just before the rise of Christianity. Many Jews, at least in Palestine, believed that the predicted return of Israel to its land after the sixth-century exile was not yet complete and therefore waited eagerly for its completion through repossession of the land from the Roman occupiers. As late as the turn of the era, some circles in Israel looked for a new exodus in which the land would be finally possessed by true Israel (such as the Qumran covenanters). It is easy to understand, therefore, why this psalm was important at Qumran and among early Jewish Christians. One of the signs of the Messiah was to restore the land to its rightful owners, the meek, that is, those who waited for the Lord for justice.

For the psalmist teacher the greatest metaphor of divine blessing is the land, for it provides food and a place to live. The land is all the more precious because it always seems threatened by many forms of malice: land grabbers and foreign powers as well as drought and famine. It is the great blessing.

PSALM 38

Like most of the poems in Book 1, this psalm is ascribed to David. It stands in the middle of personal laments (Pss 35–36, 39), and expressions and ideas from these laments recur in Ps 38: "those who seek my life" in 35:4 and 38:12; "[my enemies] repay me evil for good" in 35:12 and 38:20; "do not let my . . . enemies rejoice over me" in 35:19, 24 and 38:16. Like Ps 37, it has twenty-two verses although, unlike that psalm, its lines do not begin with successive letters of the alphabet. The sufferer in Ps 39:1-3 resolves to remain silent before enemies who will misuse what they hear, and the sufferer in Ps 38:16 is too exhausted to refute enemies (v. 15); both are almost forced to address God. Psalm 41 is also concerned with enemies using the occasion of illness and physical weakness to attack. Grouping similar psalms together helps readers to interpret Pss 38 and 39, for, as we shall see, both have a dense logic that is hard to grasp on a first reading.

Literary Analysis

The genre is individual lament. There is the opening unadorned cry to the Lord and the self-portrayal of the pray-er as miserable and worthy of divine pity. Enemies put the worst possible construction on the psalmist's illness: It is a sign of divine rejection, and people should withdraw from such an accursed wretch. Expressions of hope are hidden in the petitions (vv. 9, 15).

Dramatic movement is marked by the occurrence or nonoccurrence of the divine titles LORD, God, and Lord (*'adōnāi*) that begin certain lines, and the predominance of first, second, or third person pronouns in various sections. Verses 1-2 open with "LORD" and contain four instances of "your" referring to the Lord. Verses 3-8, in contrast, make no reference to God (beyond one "your" in v. 3), being rather entirely concerned with the sufferer in the third person. Verse 9 begins with "Lord" and has two occurrences of "you" referring to God. Verses 10-14, in contrast, are exclusively in the first or third person without any address to God. Verse 15 contains three names of God and two second-person pronouns. Verses 17-20 exclusively employ first and third person references without any address to God. The last two verses address God in three divine titles and bring the titles in intense relationship to "me," the sufferer. The *first-person* pronoun occurs five times in the two verses.

Expressions of pain alternate with pleading. The opening and closing petitions (vv. 1-2, 21-22) are syntactically similar and refer to all the suffering, both personal and social. Verses 9-10 are based on the anguish described in verses 3-8; similarly verses 15-16 are based on the anguish in verses 11-14. Verses 17-20 comprehend both the bodily pain of the first description and the social scorn of the second, provoking the climactic plea of verses 21-22.

Exegetical Analysis

Opening plea to God (vv. 1-2)

Verse 1 is the same as Ps 6:1, suggesting that poets borrowed from each other or used a common stock of expressions. "Rebuke" and "discipline" are also a fixed pair in Jer 2:19 (NRSV: "punish" and "convict") and Prov 9:7 (NRSV: "corrects" and "rebukes"). Divine wrath is a metaphor for the withdrawal of God's presence and power from sinful human beings; it is not a literal description of a volatile and furious deity. God is imagined as a hostile archer shooting arrows at the poor sufferer. Similarly, Job does not hesitate to accuse God, saying that "the arrows of the Almighty are in me" (6:4). See also Deut 32:23; Ps 7:12-13; Lam 3:12.

Physical collapse (vv. 3-8)

The psalmist moves from plea to description of physical and emotional disintegration. "Your" in verse 3a is transitional. Unlike Job, the sufferer fully accepts the suffering as punishment for sin, owning up to "my sin," "my iniquities," and "my foolishness" (vv. 3-5). The suffering is both bodily sickness ("flesh," "bones," "wounds") and its mental and emotional effects. An example of emotional effects is the line "all day long I go around mourning" (v. 6b), which apparently refers to the incessant walking characteristic of agitated depression. Other examples are references to bending over (v. 6a) and involuntary groaning (v. 8b). The psalmist mourns the loss of health and social standing.

The second plea to the Lord (vv. 9-10)

The placement of "Lord" at the very beginning of the verse and the change of grammatical person from first and third to the second signal a new stage. The sufferer acknowledges that God already knows his or her wretchedness, for God well knows the suffering behind the groaning, which is like the groaning of the Hebrews in Exod 2:23-25. In this psalm the groaning indicates the psalmist's confused mind ("heart") and fading vitality (v. 10).

"The light of my eyes" can mean a welcoming glance (as in Prov 15:30), but here it refers to the life-force itself, as in Ps 13:3, "Give light to my eyes, or I will sleep the sleep of death." The needy psalmist wants to be transparent before God.

Exposure to enemies (vv. 11-14)

The illness has a social effect: ostracism. Friends fail to visit; enemies spread calumnies (vv. 11-12). Friend and foe are a merism, a figure of speech in which the extremes of the spectrum signify its whole range: *all* people have abandoned me. The calumnies, probably interpretations of the illness as punishment for horrible sin, go unanswered, for the psalmist, who can neither hear nor speak, is in no position to respond to them. Such complete passivity is a sign of depression and grief over loss of status in the community. The person's senses are shutting down. The mention of "no retort" in verse 14 prepares for the next section in which God is asked to give the answer the psalmist cannot.

Third plea to the Lord (vv. 15-16)

The three divine titles plus the pronoun *you* mark a fresh section. Just as verse 10 summarizes verses 3-8, so verse 16 summarizes the preceding verses 11-14. NJPS, "For I fear they will rejoice over me," catches the Hebrew of verse 16 (lit. "For I said") better than NRSV. The sufferer alternates between pain-filled despair and hope in God.

Physical collapse and exposure to enemies (vv. 17-20)

The section sums up both kinds of suffering, physical-emotional distress (vv. 17-18) and malicious enemies (vv. 19-20). In verse 19, the NRSV emendation "without cause" for "living" finds support in the Qumran scroll 4QPs[a].

Closing plea to the Lord (vv. 21-22)

There are three divine titles, three verbs with second-person singular subjects (God), and five instances of the pronominal suffix "my," all of which lend an intense and intimate tone to the finale. In contrast to the friends and companions who abandoned the sufferer (v. 11 "stand aloof"), the psalmist begs God not to "forsake me . . . not be far from me." The syntax in verses 21-22 imitates the opening prayer ("O Lord, do not . . .") and brings the prayer to a close.

Theological and Ethical Analysis

One of the effects of modern medicine has been to objectify disease, to enable people to describe its symptoms accurately so a physician can diagnose it and prescribe remedies. Such an approach has brought immense gains to the human race. At the same time, viewing illness exclusively in terms of germs and medicines can have the unfortunate consequence of reducing sickness to bodily malfunction. The emotional, spiritual, and social aspects of sickness must be addressed as well. A sick person can experience healing even if the physical sickness remains. This psalm vividly records the experience of illness as a force that destroys the self in society. The illness has brought on a crisis with friends and family and driven them away. Bereft of human supports, the sick individual is vulnerable before gossipers who view the illness or weakness as a moral failure. They do not want to be around a diminished person. This psalm allows modern pray-ers to experience their illness as something more than germs and remedies. It enables them to grieve in depth and to express their hope amid enormous distress.

Should modern sufferers regard their illness as a heaven-sent punishment for their sins as this psalmist unquestionably does? Three times the sufferer mentions personal sin as the source of the illness (vv. 3-5). Does God send sickness to punish us for our sins? The ways of divine justice are mysterious, and human beings are not privy to its workings. It is generally unwise as well as impertinent to interpret anyone's illness (including one's own) as divine punishment.

One solution to the problem of illness as punishment is to

interpret illness as a metaphor of the muddle resulting from our own folly. One might think a self-inflicted wound would make anyone too embarrassed to go to God for help. This psalmist, on the contrary, is shameless, never making excuses or making claims on the Almighty. The psalmist simply lays everything out before God—the appalling physical and emotional devastation, the social isolation, the loss of standing in the community. Reduced almost to being a nonperson, the psalmist keeps turning to God, never giving in to discouragement.

PSALM 39

Psalm 39 resembles the immediately preceding psalm in genre (individual lament), phraseology, and themes. The Hebrew verbs translated "rebuke" and "discipline" in Ps 38:1 (NRSV) recur as "chastise" and "punishment" in 39:11; the topic of 38:13-14 (remaining silent) is also a topic in Ps 39. Psalm 38:15 speaks of waiting for the Lord alone, as does 39:7; Pss 38:16 and 39:1 use the verb 'amartî, "I said/prayed"; "affliction" in 38:11 is the same Hebrew word as "stroke" in 39:10.

Literary Analysis

In Ps 39, the sufferer tries to remain completely silent lest an enemy use any utterance maliciously (vv. 1-3). The psalmist can at least talk to God, praying in verse 4 to know how much longer the suffering will last (for this interpretation see below) and arguing that human life is too short to be spent in suffering (vv. 5-6). Verses 7-11 take the prayer one step further: Since my affliction is entirely from you, O God, only you can take it away. Verses 12-13 are a final plea to be heard.

The fourfold dramatic structure is supported by the Hebrew word count: verses 1-3 (24 words); verses 4-6 (36 words); verses 7-11 (37 words); verses 12-13 (22 words). Parts 1 and 4 have approximately the same number of words, as do parts 2 and 3.

The parts are tied together thematically: The themes of silence and suffering that dominate part 1 are repeated in part 3 (v. 9); and the theme of transience of human life in part 2 is repeated in part 4 (v. 12*cd*). Such devices give unity and shape to the highly passionate plea.

Exegetical Analysis

The struggle to submit in silence (vv. 1-3)

The psalmist initially resolves to be silently submissive. The nature of the suffering is not identified, though some scholars assume it is sickness. The fact that the nature of the suffering is unspecified enables any sufferer to use the psalm. As in other laments, there is a wicked person who in this case is all too ready to interpret maliciously whatever words the psalmist may utter (v. 1*d*). The psalmist's feelings are too intense to be contained, however, like those of Jeremiah (Jer 20:9) and Elihu (Job 32:19-20); they must come forth in prayer to God (vv. 4-13).

NRSV "sin *(ḥāṭā')* with my tongue" (v. 1*b*) is less satisfactory than NJPS "offend by my speech." Hebrew *ḥāṭā'* does not always mean to sin against God but can have a more general meaning of falling short or offending. An angry outburst by the psalmist would be judged by enemies as rebellion against God and grounds for ostracism. Such a judgment the psalmist seeks to avoid. Reining in deep emotions is painful, however. The suffering is thus twofold: the affliction itself and not being able to speak about it freely to a sympathetic listener. The rest of the poem is directed exclusively to God and is, one presumes, heard by no one else.

How long will my affliction last? (vv. 4-6)

The thought of part 2 can be paraphrased: Let me know exactly when my suffering will end (v. 4), for human life is so short and insubstantial that you, O God, cannot allow the whole of it to pass in pain (vv. 5-6).

Our interpretation of verse 4 differs from virtually every commentator and translator (including NRSV) and requires demonstration. For virtually all commentators the prayer in verse 4, to know "the measure of my days," means to realize the brevity and fragility of life so that one can accept one's mortality. Such acceptance makes one truly wise, able to bear the absurdities and pains of life. This interpretation, despite its well-nigh universal acceptance, runs into major logical and linguistic problems. The logical problems: (1) The psalmist is already aware of the transience of life (vv. 5-6, 11c) and does not need to ask for further awareness; (2) it is not clear how knowing one's life span makes it easier to bear suffering. The lexical problems: (1) "End" means a definite term, not shortness of time; (2) "measure of my days" means merely a predetermined number, not a few days (as is shown by the related phrase "number of days" in Exod 23:26; Eccl 2:3); (3) NRSV "fleeting" is not an accurate translation of the Hebrew adjective ḥādēl.

This commentary takes verse 4 as a request to know the term of the psalmist's *affliction* rather than the term of the psalmist's *life*. In antiquity, people commonly assumed that the gods (or God) sent afflictions on human beings for a set period of time. Biblical examples of set times of affliction are the seventy years of Babylonian rule predicted by Jeremiah (25:11, 12; 29:10); the prophet Gad forcing David to choose as punishment three years of famine or three months of fleeing from enemies or three days of pestilence (2 Sam 24:13); and the complaint in Ps 74:9, "and there is no one among who knows how long [the affliction will last]." Mesopotamian literature has even more examples of specified times of affliction or divine absence; sufferers expect diviners to tell them the time limit for their illnesses. Some Mesopotamian medical omens end with a prognosis for the patient's recovery such as "within seven days" or "within three days." The common question in biblical laments "How long, O Lord?" is thus a genuine question. These factors therefore suggest that the best translation of Ps 39:4 is (paraphrasing for the sake of clarity): Lord, let me know my term (of affliction), / what the measure of my days is (that is, the predetermined length of my affliction). / May I know how I will cease (from my affliction).

This interpretation of verse 4 restores rhetorical force to part 2: Let me know how much longer I have to bear my suffering! Life is so short and human beings have so few resources!

*You alone are responsible for my suffering, and
you alone can relieve it (vv. 7-11)*

The phrase "and now" (v. 7a) in prayers often signals a shift from complaint to petition (as in Pss 2:10; 27:6; Dan 9:15, 17). Here, the complaint has already been made in verses 1-3, and the petition to know its duration has been made in verse 4. The phrase "and now" brings the complaint and the initial petition to their completion: It states that the whole problem comes from God and demands its full removal now.

In verse 7, the psalmist claims to have no other source of help than God. Such a claim puts God on the spot, imposing an obligation to act. "My transgressions" in verse 8 are the consequences of transgressions rather than the acts; they refer to the trouble that the transgressions have brought on the psalmist. Some Hebrew words for sin can refer both to the act and its effects upon the agent. Such troubles bring "the scorn of the fool" (v. 8b). The psalmist makes no claim of innocence (unlike Job) nor a confession of specific sin, accepting, it seems, his or her own sinfulness, along with its necessary consequences, as a manifestation of human frailty. Verse 11a, "you chastise mortals in punishment for sin," states this submissive attitude. Verse 9 refers back to the original resolve to be silent in the presence of fools (v. 1). Unlike the self-conscious and grim resolve to be silent toward others in verse 1, the psalmist instinctively here bows in silence ("I am silent," v. 9a) before the all-powerful God ("for it is you who have done it," v. 9b). Verse 10 describes the affliction as "your stroke" and "the blows of your hand." What do the terms mean? It is impossible to say concretely, for the psalmist interprets the suffering radically, as totally from God. This view differs from modern interpretations of sin and retribution according to which

God allows bad things to happen to good people but does not directly cause them. The psalm, on the contrary, imagines God acting directly and immediately upon the world. The final phrase in verse 11, "surely everyone is a mere breath," reprises verse 5. The phrase is a way of asking God, the only savior, to act.

Final plea to be heard (vv. 12-13)

Having made the detailed petition for forgiveness in verses 7-11, the psalmist now begs that God attend to the prayer and show compassion. There is another allusion to the fragility of life in the comparison of "passing guest" and "alien": God is, as it were, obligated to protect the sojourner, for Israelite law mandated protection for the resident alien (e.g., Exod 22:21; 23:9, 12; Deut 24:17). The psalmist almost glories in powerlessness, laying aside all claims of righteousness, making an appeal to the divine character. The last petition is to be left alone, free from God's severe scrutiny, like Job's petition (7:16-21).

Theological and Ethical Analysis

Like Job, the psalmist desires to cry out to friends for understanding and sympathy but cannot, for enemies are eager to misinterpret the words and use them maliciously. The psalmist would be written off as a sinner and forced to endure the community's rejection. To the original affliction is thus added the pain of isolation and frustration. Alone and unable to speak from the heart to other people, the sufferer has only God as confidant and patron.

Many people today endure alone painful matters that they cannot easily speak about to others. Sometimes the matter is an illness considered shameful by many people, sometimes it is a family unhappiness that is difficult to share (a wayward child, an incompatible spouse), and sometimes it is a failure that cannot be talked out. Right or wrong, the sufferings are borne alone. Psalm 39 provides a model for such people. One may not be able to "speak with the tongue" to others but can surely speak to God without fear of offending. This poet is bold, speaking almost rudely to God ("it is you who have done it"), demanding to know the exact time when relief will come, and insisting on being taken seriously.

PSALM 40

Psalms 38–41 share several features: Each contains a statement of the psalmist's intent—"I pray/said" (*'āmartî*, Pss 38:16; 39:1; 40:7; 41:4); "my cry" in 40:1 links back to "my cry" in 39:12; the phrase "make haste to help me" in 40:13 hearkens back to the same phrase in 38:22.

Literary Analysis

The genre of this psalm is not easy to determine, for verses 1-10 have all the marks of a thanksgiving and verses 11-17 all the marks of a lament. The thanksgiving recounts a rescue from death (vv. 1-3*b*), which provokes the grateful psalmist to glorify God with a song (vv. 3*c*-10). The joyous thanksgiving tone, however, changes abruptly in verse 11 to an anxious petition for deliverance from enemies (vv. 11-17).

What is the meaning of this strange juxtaposition of genres that are elsewhere distinct? Some scholars assume that two separate psalms have been mistakenly transmitted as a single piece, as happened, they say, with Ps 27, which combines a song of trust (27:1-6) and a lament (27:7-14). To support their case that the lament of Ps 40 is an addition, these scholars point out that verses 40:13-17 are duplicated in Ps 70. This solution is unsatisfactory, however, for only a part of the lament section (Ps 40:13-17) is duplicated in Ps 70. Moreover, though 40:11-12 are part of the lament, the verses reuse words from the first section: *kālā'* ("withhold") in verse 11*a* reuses *kālā'* ("restrained") in verse 9*c*; the word pair "steadfast love" and "faithfulness" in verse 10*c* occurs again in verse 11b. Verses 11-17 are therefore intrinsic to Ps 40.

The linking of thanksgiving and lament was intended by the poet. The psalmist has had a profound experience of salvation and now must face further adversity. After all, praise and petition make up the rhythm of human life. One no sooner gets through thanking God than a fresh crisis presents itself and a petition becomes necessary.

Verses 1-3b are a standard thanksgiving—the report of a divine rescue from death. Yahweh graciously swept up the sufferer from the miry pit symbolizing death (as in Pss 28:1; 30:3; 88:4, 6) onto firm ground (as in Ps 26:12) and even supplied the song of thanksgiving, "a new song" (v. 3ab).

"New song" is an important clue to the meaning of the poem. Typically, a new song contains an invitation to others, sometimes the nations, to behold the wondrous actions of Yahweh and respond with appropriate worship (Isa 42:10-12; cf. Ps 40:3). To worship Yahweh as the sole powerful deity unmasks other gods as powerless (Ps 96:5; cf. Ps 40:4). The new song urges people to proclaim Yahweh victorious over enemies (Pss 96:10-13; 98:7-9; cf. Ps 40:9-10) and bring offerings to the temple (Ps 96:8; cf. Ps 40:7, a substitute for offerings). All these elements are found in 40:3-10. The "new song" is sung in response to the divine salvation narrated in verses 1-3b. This "new song" has a novel twist, however. The psalmist declares that in place of the customary sacrifice offering (v. 6) God asks for a self-offering in obedience (vv. 7-8), "Here I am." The task the psalmist undertakes in obedience is to proclaim the story of God's rescue (vv. 1-3b) to the "great congregation" (vv. 9-10).

The joyous thankful tone changes abruptly and unexpectedly in verse 11 when the poet, beset with a fresh threat, asks God not to "withhold (kālā') your mercy from me" just as "I have not restrained (kālā') my lips" from giving you praise (v. 9). What is the fresh threat in verses 12-17? Though certainty on the point is not possible, the best answer is that the acceptance of the task of proclaiming the divine deeds (vv. 7-10) has put the psalmist in danger from the enemies of God. The psalmist appeals to God: It is in your own interest to protect anyone who proclaims your power and mercy (vv. 11-17). Though the singer admits in verse 12*b* that "my iniquities have overtaken me," such avowals in time of trouble were well-nigh universal in laments and is no indication that the psalmist is unwilling to be God's herald.

In summary, the singer is to lead others in responding to God's wondrous actions. The response displaces the sacrifice that normally accompanied such songs. In the face of the opposition that such proclamation will incur, the psalmist cries out insistently for further protection.

Exegetical Analysis

Report of the rescue (vv. 1-3b)

Report of the rescue is a feature of thanksgivings. When danger threatened, the psalmist waited expectantly. God heard the cry and took the sufferer from the miry pit to level ground. "Pit" *(bôr)* is sometimes in parallel with Sheol, the realm of the dead (Ps 30:3; Isa 14:15; 38:18). The actual peril here is left unspecified, but it was deadly. Solid ground symbolizes stability and security (Pss 27:5; 61:2). Verse 3*a* acknowledges God as the ultimate source of the thanksgiving: "[God] put a new song in my mouth." God not only effects the rescues but provides the text for the song sung in response.

The new song (vv. 3c-10)

The song begins in verses 3*c*-4 with the hope that "many" (a Hebrew idiom for "all" or "a large crowd" in contrast to an individual) will see Yahweh's great deed and respond. They will respond with obedience and will refuse to join worshipers of other "gods." The six lines of verses 3*c*-4 make a single statement. Verse 4*ab* makes the same point as verse 3*cd*, employing the singular number in stylistic contrast to the plural number of the previous verse (lit. "happy is the person who"). Verses 4*cd* extend the statement through negation: To turn to Yahweh means to turn away from worshipers of other gods. In short, verses 3c-4 express the hope that all who see the saving act of Yahweh will choose Yahweh as their God. Ancient people judged gods worthy of allegiance on the basis of their power to benefit their clients. Rescuing someone from death (symbolized by "desolate pit") is the act of ultimate power. A saving god is worthy of one's allegiance.

The fact that the new song is a response to a mighty act of God explains two distinctive features in this psalm: its statement of the incomparability of Yahweh (v. 5) and its transposition of the traditional summons to offer sacrifice to obedience (vv. 6-8). Other new songs assert that Yahweh acted alone, implying that other gods are without power and are therefore "false gods" (v. 4d).

Another feature of Ps 40 that is explained by the conventions of the new song is the change in the thanksgiving response: Instead of offering sacrifice, one proclaims Yahweh's rescue of the client from death (vv. 7-10). Though substituting praise for sacrifice is mentioned in the Psalter (e.g., Pss 50:8-15; 51:16; 141:2), Ps 40 gives it extraordinary emphasis.

Verse 5 changes from third to second person, addressing God directly. God's "wondrous deeds" *(niplĕ'ōt)* are elsewhere acts of national redemption (Josh 3:5; Pss 98:1; 106:22) or creation (Ps 96:5). Psalm 40 reckons the rescue of the individual in verses 1-2 as an instance of the divine power that saved all Israel in the past. NRSV "your thoughts" (v. 5) is better rendered "your intentions," referring to what God intends to do. God has acted innumerable times in the past and will do so again, preparing for the petition in verses 13-17.

Verses 6-8 have provoked puzzlement. As noted, in new songs, sacrifice and other liturgical responses are a way of responding to a divine deed (Pss 96:8; 98:4-6). Psalm 40:6-8 transpose the expected oblation of animals and grains into an oblation of the psalmist's very self. The words used to describe sacrifice in verse 6 are cumulative, describing the range of offerings a person giving thanks would likely provide. "Sacrifice" is a general term, and "offering" can designate a grain or animal offering. In a "burnt offering" the animal was entirely burned at the altar except for the hide which went to the priest (Lev 7:8). The "sin offering" cleansed the sanctuary of the impurity that had been attracted there. Psalm 40 transposes God's desire for sacrifice to desire for public praise. Most modern commentators agree that verses 6-8 do not condemn animal and grain sacrifices as such. Rather, the verses use the Hebrew figure of dialectic negation, which is characterized by exaggeration in the negative member. Contrast-by-negation is a literary device to express emphasis.

The traditional translation of verse 6b, "but you have given me an open ear" (NRSV) is not quite accurate, for there is no "but" *(wāw)* in Hebrew. Christian translations have been influenced by the very free rendering of the Septuagint. NJPS, not dependent on the Septuagint and Christian interpretive tradition, renders with some tentativeness as "You gave me to understand that / You do not desire sacrifice and meal offering." Though the phrase in the Hebrew text is possibly out of place (it would fit better immediately before v. 7a), it makes sense in the context: God has made the person ready to do the divine will, as in Isa 50:5: "The LORD GOD has opened my ear, / and I was not rebellious, / I did not turn backward."

Verses 7 and 8 continue the transposition of sacrifice language: "Then I said, 'Here I am' " (*hinnēh bā'tî*, lit. "behold I have come"). The closest biblical parallel is Num 22:38, where Balaam uses the same Hebrew phrase to express subordination to another's will. Another relevant passage is Isa 6:8, "Then I heard the voice of the LORD saying, 'Whom shall I send, and who will go for us?' And I said, 'Here am I; send me!' " In these quotations, the speakers make themselves completely available to carry out God's task.

The reference to "the scroll of the book" (v. 7b) means that which is decreed from on high and immutable, as in Isa 65:6, "See, it is written before me," and Ps 139:16b, "In your book were written / all the days that were formed for me." Verses 8-10 accept the divine task. "I have told the glad news of deliverance" (v. 9a) is a single Hebrew verb, *biśśēr*, which is often used for reporting good news such as victory or deliverance. Isaiah uses it in chapters 40–55 to report the restoration of Israel. Here the glad news is the deliverance of the psalmist from death (vv. 1-3*b*), which is interpreted as an instance of God's favor toward Israel through the ages. The deed is told to "the great congregation," which in Pss 22:25 and 35:18 is a liturgical assembly.

A plea for a new deliverance (11-17)

As noted, the section contains a complaint (vv. 13-17), which is nearly identical to Ps 70. Verses 9-10 repeat three times that the psalmist has not kept silent about the divine deliverance ("not restrained" *[kālā']*; "have not hidden"; "have not concealed your steadfast love and your faithfulness") and now can rightly ask God not to withhold *(kālā')* mercy and steadfast love and faithfulness in the psalmist's hour of need (v. 11*a*). Why does the tone change at this point from joyous proclamation of God's merciful intervention to anxious pleading for protection? Why does the poet complain of troubles so numerous and so dire as to devastate sight ("I cannot see," v. 12*d*) and mind ("heart," v. 12*f*). Scholars' various answers are given under the Literary Analysis above. The fact that the psalmist admits that "my iniquities" caused the sufferings (v. 12) should not be interpreted as if the suffering is purely the result of personal sin. Almost any ancient pray-er would own up to limits and sins.

The best answer to the question of where the fresh danger comes from is that acceptance of the task of proclamation has placed the psalmist in danger. The poem sets up a stark contrast between those "who *seek* to snatch away my life" and "all who *seek* you," and between the enemies "*who say* to me, 'Aha, Aha!' " (v. 15*b*) and the friends "*who . . . say* continually, 'Great is the LORD!' " (v. 16*d*). The psalmist dramatizes the danger through the metaphor of the two ways, which sees human life in either-or terms. Those on the straight road are protected, and those on the crooked road are punished. The psalmist prays that one group will be exposed for what it is, and the other will be acknowledged by God as righteous. In verse 17, the psalmist wants to stand in the circle of the righteous who can count on God's protection. The self-designation "I am poor and needy" immediately puts one in relationship with the God who has promised to be close to such people. The final plea not to delay (v. 17d) links back to the same plea in verse 13b to form an *inclusio* rounding out the final prayer.

Theological and Ethical Analysis

The psalm focuses consistently on God as life-giver before whom death loses its sting. The rescue from death, described in verses 1-2, could have been a seemingly ordinary incident. To the eyes of faith, however, the living God is as surely working in that event as in the great deeds of Israel's history. To the rescued person, the traditional framework for giving thanks—sacrifice—is inadequate because it does not make known to the world how great the God of Israel is. So the person is allowed to give praise rather than sacrifice, to proclaim that all other gods and powers are nothing. Our God acted even in my own small life!

The stance of praise puts the psalmist in danger, however, for there are many adherents of other gods and systems who look upon such proclamation with hatred and move to suppress it. The paradoxical result is that the individual rescued from death (vv. 1-2) steps into fresh danger. Such is the common experience of those who are loyal to God: They always require divine protection (cf. 2 Cor 6:1-10). This psalm is for grateful and generous souls.

The Letter to the Hebrews uses the Septuagint text of Ps 40:6-8 to argue that Christ's once-for-all sacrifice of himself is superior to the old system of animal sacrifice (Septuagint reading italicized): "Sacrifices and offerings you have not desired, but *a body* you have prepared for me" (Heb 10:5b). The speaker is Christ and the "body" is Christ's body offered once and for all in sacrifice for sins and memorialized forever in heaven.

PSALM 41

Psalm 41 is the final poem in Book 1. Psalm 41:13 is the concluding benediction of the first book of the Psalter, not the final line of the psalm. Psalm 41 points back to Ps 40 in its vocabulary: "Happy are those" in 41:1 links back to 40:4; the infinitive "to see" in 41:6 links back to the same Hebrew form in 40:12*b*; "I said" appears in 41:4 and 40:7; "trust" appears in 41:9 and 40:3, 4; and "be pleased/desire/delight" appears in 41:11 and 40:6, 8.

Literary Analysis

Scholars are divided on the genre. For some, the psalm is a thanksgiving, the grateful report of someone who has been healed of a serious illness and vindicated as righteous in the sight of enemies. Verses 1-3, in the form of a beatitude (Lat. *beatus,* "happy"), are a declaration over the psalmist who has experienced healing and vindication: Those who are merciful to the poor and sick will themselves receive mercy when they are sick and ostracized. Verses 4-10 record the prayer uttered in the illness that is past (evident from the perfect tense in v. 4, "I said"). Verses 11-12 tell how it was that the psalmist came to know that he or she was vindicated.

Other scholars classify the psalm as a lament because they interpret verses 4-10 as a petition; statements that imply the sufferer is already healed (vv. 1-3 and 11-12) are rather statements of hope. It is more likely, however, that the poem is a thanksgiving because of verse 4 ("As for me, I said"), which indicates the psalmist spoke the prayer in the past. In either interpretation (lament or thanksgiving), the psalm clearly has an instructional aim: to teach people how to be faithful to God in the midst of serious illness and rejection.

The poem has three sections: verses 1-3, 4-10, and 11-12. Verse 1*a* is a beatitude originating in the psalmist's experience (illness, ostracism, rescue); it declares happy everyone who is merciful to the "poor" (i.e., those similarly suffering illness and rejection). What "happy" means is explained in verses 1*b*-3: divine healing (vv. 1*b*-2*b*, 3) and protection from malicious talk (v. 2*c*). The second part, verses 4-10, is a citation, the complaint and petition uttered at the time of affliction. It is a "heard prayer," a kind of verbal votive offering of past suffering comparable in a sense to the images of the healed organ or body part hung up in ancient shrines and found even today in some churches. The citation of the prayer functions as report of rescue, for it communicates to readers the wonder of the healing. The last part, verses 11-12, is the report of the rescue ("my enemy has not triumphed over me. . . . you have upheld me").

Exegetical Analysis

Blessed are the merciful for they shall obtain mercy (vv. 1-3)

Other psalms also begin with "happy is/are" (*'ašrê*), for example, 1:1 and 32:1. The opening declaration is actually the *conclusion* derived from the profound experiences described in the psalm. In Ps 32:1, for example, the psalmist begins by declaring happy anyone "whose transgression is forgiven" and then describes how miserable it was to hold back from confessing one's sin and receiving forgiveness (v. 3). Psalm 41:1 is similar; anyone who (like this psalmist) has kept faith in God and been rescued is declared "happy."

It must be admitted that the beatitude in 41:1, "who consider the poor," is somewhat odd. One would expect something closer to the psalmist's experience, for example, "blessed are they who keep praying in their affliction." The beatitude "who consider the poor" ought therefore to be taken in a broad sense, for acting compassionately toward the poor is a way of stating that one is being faithful to God (cf. Pss 15:3; 37:11; Tob 14:9; Sir 40:17; 1 Macc 2:57). "Consider the poor" implies action as well as thought. The only parallel to the Hebrew phrase "who considers" is Prov 16:20, "those *who are attentive to* a matter." This verse also suggests that the phrase means to pay *active* attention to something. "Poor" in Ps 41:1*a* refers to those who are weak (Gen 41:19, NRSV: "poor") and sick (2 Sam 13:4, NRSV: "haggard"). The psalmist's suffering consisted of enduring sickness and ostracism (vv. 4-10), and these are the evils mentioned in the beatitude. The following verses expand the beatitude: The Lord will keep the faithful alive in mortal danger (so the connotation of the verb in v. 2*a*); they will not lose their good name (v. 2*b*, "they are *called* happy"); they will not be given up to the will of their enemies (v. 2*c*); their sickness will be healed (v. 3). Drawing on a vivid experience of the saving God, the psalmist can declare happy all those who similarly endure illness and ostracism with faith. The beatitude is also a praise of God, ever faithful to needy clients.

This was my constant prayer (vv. 4-10)

In verse 4*a*, "I said" makes clear that the complaint and petition in verses 4-10 took place in the past. The petition "be gracious to me" in verses 4*a* and 10*a* frames the prayer and alerts the reader that the section is a citation. In verse 4*b*, the psalmist admits the illness was the result of personal sin. Unexpected suffering in that age would commonly elicit an admission of personal sin. Individuals assumed that God is in heaven and that we, poor creatures of a moment, are on earth. How can I help from all offense? Such admission of fault does not necessarily mean that the psalmist has a low self-regard, for verse 12*a* speaks of "my integrity" in the face of the malicious attacks of enemies.

The prayer framed by verses 4*a* and 10*a* is a complaint about the malicious speech of enemies. The petition to be healed from illness occupies only the framing verses 4*b* ("heal me") and 10*b* ("raise me up"). Why does the psalmist fear the enemies? Because they want the psalmist to die and leave no issue so that his or her name perish (v. 5). "Name" in a broad sense means everything that presents the person to others even after death. In Deut 7:24; 9:14; 25:6; 2 Sam 18:18; Ps 109:13, "name" means a person plus all descendants. "Name" can also refer to the memory others hold of us after we die, as in Prov 10:7, "The memory of the righteous is a blessing, but the *name* of the wicked will rot." By wishing the sufferer's name to perish, the enemies wish the annihilation of all that the psalmist was, is, and could be. They deprive the sufferer of any future by denying the possibility of recovery and divine vindication.

The enemies, like Job's friends, seem to have concluded that the sufferer has gravely sinned, has become God's enemy, and fully deserves pain and anguish. What is hard for the psalmist to bear are the honeyed words of concern that mask hostility (v. 6). The weak sufferer is powerless to stop the campaign of negative publicity that begins as soon as the enemies leave the sickroom (v. 7). Verse 8 suggests that one aspect of their malice is that they take away hope: The sickness will lead to death. In a word, they wish sickness and death to triumph. Verse 9 informs us that even a close and trusted friend has behaved like an enemy, "has lifted the heel against me." Though the exact meaning of the idiom is unknown, it no doubt means to betray, perhaps by agreeing with the judgment of the enemies.

As already stated, verse 10 is an *inclusio* of the beginning of the prayer in verse 4, letting the reader know the prayer has been fully cited. The psalmist prays to be raised up *(qûm)*, a verb that is sometimes used in parallel to the verb "to live" and can refer to healing from mortal illness (e.g., 2 Kgs 13:21; Isa 26:19*a*). Once healed, the invalid intends to "repay" *(šallēm)* the tormentors (v. 10*b*). That a human being would undertake to repay enemies is unusual, for elsewhere in the Psalter God, not human beings, repays evil (31:23; 62:12; 137:8). It is probable, therefore, that the psalmist does not intend personally to inflict punishment on the enemies. Rather, being raised up from the sickbed is a form of judgment, letting the enemies know that God has declared the psalmist innocent or righteous and declared them guilty or unrighteous. The recovery of the patient shows that God is on the side of the sick person; the sickness was not a sign of a grievous sin. The wicked were wrong. Their malicious ignorance is revealed by God's upholding of the sick person.

You have upheld me (vv. 11-12)

The psalmist interprets the healing as personal vindication: "By this I know that you are pleased with me; because my enemy has not triumphed over me." Rather, God has "upheld me because of my integrity." "My integrity" has a legal sense; it means my innocence as to the charge leveled against me by the enemies. In verse

12 the psalmist is confident that being rescued from the power of death means at the same time to rest content in the presence of the Lord without any limit of time.

The blessing at the end of book 1 (v. 13)

Though the blessing at the end of Book 1 might seem a cliché, it is a profound and apt conclusion. To wish that the Name be blessed is to wish that all peoples see what the Lord has done and respond with appreciative praise. God blesses or bestows gifts on human beings. How can human beings bless the God who has all things? By giving the one thing God lacks: honor freely bestowed by human beings on earth, who acknowledge all works as God's. This is what the benediction effects.

Theological and Ethical Analysis

As noted at the beginning, some scholars take the poem as a thanksgiving, whereas others take it as a lament. This commentary takes it as a thanksgiving on the grounds that verses 4-10 cite the petition the psalmist used while ill; it is now a votive offering of past suffering. In either interpretation (lament or thanksgiving), suffering and thanks are intimately related. One cannot give heartfelt thanks without a keen sense of "how bad things were," and one cannot plead for help without a hope that "things can be better." Without a memory of past suffering, thanksgiving gives way to short-lived euphoria. Without hope, there is only surrender and despair. As an instructional poem, the psalm urges prayers to keep thanksgiving and lament together.

BOOK TWO
(PSALMS 42–72)

PSALMS 42–43

Like Psalms 9–10, Psalms 42–43 have been handed down in the tradition as separate, though they actually form one poem. The Septuagint and the Vulgate, and even a few Hebrew manuscripts, put the superscription "A Psalm of David" at the beginning of Ps 43. As is shown below, however, there can be no doubt that Psalms 42–43 form one poem. The poems open the first series of Korahite psalms (42–49; 84–85, and 87–88). The Korahites were a guild of Temple singers (2 Chron 20:19) whose psalms have several features in common, such as the epithet "living God" (Pss 42:2; 84:2), the mention of "the face of God" (Pss 42:2; 44:24; 88:14); and God as "refuge" (43:2; 46:1, 7; 48:3).

Literary Analysis

The three refrains (42:5, 11, and 43:5) unite the poem and also mark out its tripartite structure: 42:1-5; 6-11; 43:1-5. Another indicator of unity is the lack of a superscription in the Hebrew manuscript tradition of Ps 43. The genre is individual lament, with a special affinity to other poems of longing for the Jerusalem Temple such as Pss 27, 63, and 84. Being away from the jubilant throngs celebrating in the Temple brings anguish and depression (42:4). The singer asks that the heavenly servants Light and Truth be sent to guide the journey back to "your holy hill" (43:3) and the "altar of God" (43:4a). The presence of God is conceived largely in terms of communal worship—walking in procession and joining in the glad songs of fellow worshipers.

As in other individual laments, there are three actors in the drama: the sufferer, the wicked, and God. Far from the protection of the Temple, the sufferer is taunted by unbelievers (the wicked) and pleads with God to send a guide for the journey back to the Temple. The psalm is unusual in highlighting so vividly an internal dialogue of discouragement and resolve, despair and hope.

Exegetical Analysis

Longing for God amid taunts and memories
of past worship (42:1-5)

Comparison of desire for God to thirst is also found in Pss 63:1 and 143:6. Comparison of desire to an animal's thirst is found in an Ugaritic text where the monster Mot's "throat is the throat of the lion in the wasteland . . . and it craves the pool (as do) the wild bulls." "Soul" *(nepeš)* is, literally, the throat area where thirst would be especially experienced. Experiencing God in the Temple can be expressed as "seeing" as in the phrase "Behold the face of God" (v. 2; cf. Ps 27:4). The phrase "to seek the face of God" occurs in 2 Chron 7:14; Pss 24:6; 27:8; and Hos 5:15. The symbol of water in "flowing streams" (v. 1) reappears in negative terms in "my tears" (v. 3) and the dangerous "deep" (v. 7). The derision that the psalmist experiences stirs up painful memories of past participation in Temple (v. 4). NRSV "How I went with the throng" (v. 4c) is textually uncertain. On the basis of parallelism and the Septuagint, it is possible to emend the Hebrew text to *běsōk ʾaddîrîm,* "How I entered the tent of the Glorious One."

Verse 5 displays a conflicted self: on the one hand depressed by mockery and loneliness, and on the other, buoyed by hopes of participating again in Temple worship. It is not by chance that the word "soul" *(nepeš)* occurs seven times in the poem.

Longing for a God in a far country (vv. 6-11)

Whereas the first section expressed taunts of enemies and painful memories of past worship, the second expresses something more—anger against God for callous disregard of a loyal worshiper (vv. 9-10). The section begins with a statement of depression and helplessness (v. 6b), unlike the more hopeful beginning of the next section (43:1). Verse 8 is best taken not as a statement of trust (so NRSV and REB), but as a prayer (so NJPS and NAB), "may the LORD bestow faithful love" (NAB). Otherwise, the anguish expressed in verses 9-10 would not fit the context. Walking about "mournfully" (cf. 43:2cd) seems to be what psychologists today call agitated depression; the depressed person cannot stop moving. Perhaps the isolated and disturbed walking is meant to contrast with the stately communal processions of the Temple liturgy for which the psalmist longs.

The geography of verses 6-7 is puzzling. The phrase "land of Jordan" occurs only here in the Bible; "Hermon" is in the southern part of the Anti-Lebanon mountain range, which extends eighteen miles into the northeast border of Israel. Its three peaks are the highest in the Levant. The Anti-Lebanon range is the principal source of the river Jordan, and "land of Jordan" may refer to this area. "Mount Mizar" is unknown; the Hebrew word means "few in number, a little," and an unfamiliar location may have been confused with a familiar Hebrew word. Though the geographical details are unclear, the psalmist seems near the headwaters of the Jordan, which is far distant from the Temple.

"Deep" in verse 7 refers to the subterranean cosmic waters that in the Bible symbolize chaos and death. Jonah 2:3-4 is a good example (the italicized words are identical to Ps 42:7cd): "You cast me into the deep, into the heart of the seas, and the flood surrounded me; *all your waves and your billows passed over me.* Then I said, 'I am driven away from your sight; how shall I look again upon your holy temple?' " In Ps 18:4-6, the king is similarly trapped: "The torrents of perdition assailed me. . . . In my distress I called upon the LORD. . . . From his temple he heard my voice." The psalmist, distant from the saving God, is compared to being in the power of Sea. In ancient Near Eastern myths, creation was often imagined as the Storm God vanquishing Sea and building a palace to commemorate creation-victory. It is no coincidence that the poets here contrast Sea and Temple.

A prayer that God will send messengers to bring the psalmist to the Temple (43:1-5)

In contrast to the anguished tone of 42:6a, part 3 (43:1) opens with hope for vindication. Though the same questions are asked as in part 2—why have you cast me off? why must I go about sad and disturbed?—the psalmist soon begins to pray in a positive tone. God is imagined as a grand sovereign surrounded by courtiers and servants, "angels" in modern parlance. In the Ugaritic texts, divine servants are sent out in pairs to do the work of the god, which seems to be the case with Light and Truth in this psalm. Psalm 43:3-4 asks that your Light and your Truth be sent forth as servants to lead the psalmist to the Lord's shrine. The psalm ends with an inner dialogue of discouragement and hope, offering a way out of the loneliness and immobility that suffering induces. The sufferer can move back and forth between pain and hope.

Theological and Ethical Analysis

The poem expresses intense desire to be with God though the psalmist is trapped in a place where people reject the God of Israel. There is a huge gap between aspiration and present reality. The poem forges an inner dialogue between depression and loneliness on the one hand, and, on the other, memories of past worship and hope of fulfilling worship. The poem, in short, expresses the situation of serious believers who live in a land where God is mocked.

The psalm offers no intellectual solution to the problem of God's absence. It provides instead a dialectical framework for respecting one's feelings both of alienation and of longing. Longing for God is simply obeying the Great Commandment—loving the Lord above all else. The point is admirably made by the fourth-century church father John Chrysostom in speaking about the psalm as a responsorial verse in the liturgy:

> Do not think that you have come here only to say the words. Rather when you sing the response, be aware that the response is a covenant. For when you say, "As the hart desires the springs of water, so my soul desires you, O God," you make a covenant with God. You have signed a contract without paper or ink, confessing with your voice that you love him above all things, that you put nothing above him, and that you burn with love of him. (John Chrysostom, *Expositiones in Psalmos* 5 [PG 55:161a], AT)

Psalm 44

Literary Analysis

The poem is a lament of the community. The community has suffered military defeat though conscious of no sin that might have caused God to abandon them. Since God was on the side of the generation that conquered the land, the community cannot understand why God is not on their side now. A singer, possibly the king, speaks for all.

Commentators have long noted that community laments remember a glorious past that is set in contrast to the sorry present. As noted in the introduction, the glorious event remembered is particular, the flip side as it were of the present deprivation. Psalm 77, for example, narrates the cosmic victory that brought Israel into existence (Ps 77:11-20) as they complain that the people's existence is now threatened with extinction; Ps 89 narrates the divine victory and installation of the Davidic king as God's regent (Ps 89:1-37) before complaining of the king's defeat.

Similarly Ps 44 narrates the conquest of Canaan before complaining of Israel's loss of the land. The community remembers
before God the story of the conquest, posing to God the question:
*Will you allow the work you have begun to be destroyed? will
you fail to fulfill the terms of the covenant* (v. 17) *you entered into
with us?*

As L. D. Crow has seen, the poem has five parts arranged in a
loose chiastic frame (Crow 1992, 394-401).

A. Remembrance of the original act of God (vv. 1-3)
  B. The community's exemplary trust in God (vv. 4-8)
    C. Complaint: God's withdrawal from the community
       and their present shame (vv. 9-16)
  B'. The community's exemplary fidelity to God (vv. 17-22)
A'. Petition that God act again (vv. 23-26)

The time of composition cannot be determined. At least some
of the people have suffered exile (v. 11*b*), which would fit either
the period after the destruction of the kingdom of Israel in 722
BCE or the period of the destruction of Jerusalem in 586 BCE. The
insistence on the people's innocence in verses 17-22 makes an
exilic date unlikely, however, for the literature of the time was
highly conscious of the guilt of the people. The general situation
is clear enough, however: The people have suffered military
defeats of such proportions that their hold on the land is in peril,
and the ancient promises seem to have become invalid.

Exegetical Analysis

Remembrance of the original act of God (vv. 1-3)

The singer remembers the event (the conquest of Canaan) that
brought into being the state that is now threatened (loss of the
land and exile). NRSV "deeds" is singular in the Hebrew, "deed,"
which better describes the past event, for the conquest of Canaan
includes the exodus from Egypt. Literarily, they are two moments
of a single event: the transfer of the Hebrews from Pharaoh's

dominion in Egypt to the Lord's dominion in Canaan. The psalms presume the exodus-conquest is a single event, as in Pss 105, 106, 114, 135, and 136. The Pentateuch, for reasons peculiar to its exilic editing, tells only of the exodus from Egypt and the journey through the wilderness, ending the story with Israel poised for conquest on the other side of the Jordan rather than possessing the land. Psalm 44 focuses on the conquest, underscoring the divine role. It asserts that it was "your own hand" (v. 2), not Israelite swords, that gained the victory. Arguing in this fashion lays the rhetorical groundwork of the argument for God to act: Since it was entirely your victory, how can you allow an enemy to annul what you did?

"Light of your countenance" (v. 3d) seems to refer to the radiance of the conquering deity as in Ps 89:15. In Mesopotamian literature, deities radiated a brilliance (Akkadian *melemmu*) that terrified opponents.

The community's exemplary trust in God (vv. 4-8)

That ancient deed inspires the present community to the confession "my King and my God." "King" connotes sovereignty demonstrated in an act, in this case God's wondrous conquest of Canaan. The speaker asserts that the present community trusts in God as fully as did the first generation, not trusting in its own sword (v. 6) as did the first generation (v. 3) and giving full credit to God ("boasted," v. 8a).

God's withdrawal from the community and their present shame (vv. 9-16)

The tone changes. The vehement accusation against God is the center of the poem. The Hebrew particle rendered yet (v. 9a) marks an abrupt break with the preceding recital (vv. 1-3) and confession of faith (vv. 4-8). The poem now becomes a complaint. Each verse in verses 10-14 begins with a verb with the letter *tāw* (English *t*) as initial letter, creating a staccato effect: "you made us turn back," "you have made us like sheep," "you have sold your people," "you have made us the taunt," "you have made us a byword." God has abandoned the people to plunderers and made them refugees. The metaphor "sold your people" occurs in the Song of Moses in Deut 32:30 where Israel's Rock sold them like a slave dealer.

The community's exemplary fidelity to God (vv. 17-22)

The section balances part 2, both sections making it clear that God's withdrawal has not been caused by the people's infidelity. Crow points out that the section has two parallel subsections, verses 17-19 and 20-22. In each, the first two verses insist on the people's fidelity whereas the last verse (vv. 19 and 22) accuses God of betrayal. The latter verses (vv. 19 and 22) begin with the Hebrew particle kî in an adversative sense ("but"). NRSV obscures the symmetry by translating kî in verse 22 "because." The sin of which the community claims to be innocent is reducible to one: violation of the first commandment. All the phrases of human failure in the poem—being false to the covenant, the heart turning back, allowing one's steps to depart from the way (vv. 17-18), forgetting, worshiping other deities—describe apostasy. "Jackals" (v. 19) inhabit the no-man's-land of the desert, a place where chaos reigns. "We are being killed all day long" (v. 22) shows the community struggling with being the Lord's people and witness while the Lord remains silent before their pain. Romans 8:36 cites the verse to show the vulnerability of God's people, though it manages to highlight the hope contained in the psalm.

Petition that God act again (vv. 23-26)

Complementing the opening recital of God conquering the land for Israel, the final verses pray that God wake from the sleep that has caused the people to suffer. The motif of the sleeping warrior is found in Mesopotamian literature and also in the Bible as in Ps 59:4 and Isa 51:9. The singer wants God to wake up and do something! Verse 25 has perhaps a double meaning: We are brought very low, and we humble ourselves in the dust before you.

Theological and Ethical Analysis

The psalm focuses only on one moment—the conquest—of the founding deed of the exodus-conquest. That act liberated the Hebrews from the dominion of Pharaoh in Egypt and put them under the dominion of the Lord in Canaan. The singer, keenly aware of the significance of the ancient deed, is scandalized that God no longer seems to stand by it. The singer attempts to bring it to life by narrating it in the liturgy, holding it up so that God will renew the act.

Christians can make this psalm their own prayer as they too experience God's absence as they feel "accounted as sheep for the slaughter." They look for the power of the exodus-conquest, which for Christians has been renewed by the resurrection of Jesus. Alas, they can find its effects hidden from view. They therefore remember the ancient event in the hope that God will renew it.

PSALM 45

Literary Analysis

Psalm 45 is the only royal wedding song in the Psalter. It offers a precious glimpse into the day to day realities of the king.

Though it is impossible to determine which king is intended, the wedding might be that of Ahab and Jezebel in the 860s BCE, for Jezebel was from Tyre (v. 12). At any rate, it was composed during the monarchic period, for it reflects the concrete realities of a dynastic marriage. It was incorporated into the Psalter, however, because it was thought applicable to other kings and the messianic king.

Comparable marriage texts suggest that only the final part of the marriage ritual is the subject of Ps 45. The economic and diplomatic arrangements of a royal marriage have been concluded. The rites in the home of the bride, exchange of gifts, and groom's payment to the father of the bride, have taken place. The final and "personal" part can begin, the meeting of bride and groom and the consummation of their marriage. Rightly does the superscription call the poem a love song.

The poetic structure is determined by the successive topics of war and love as well as by the parallel syntax of verse 2 ("You are the most handsome of men . . . therefore God has blessed you forever") and verse 7 ("you love. . . . Therefore God, your God, has anointed you") that introduce the two major sections, verses 2-6 and 7-16.

Exegetical Analysis

The first line functions somewhat like the invocation of the muse in classical poetry. It can be paraphrased, "My heart is stirred to write words that give delight; / I will proclaim my poem to the king. / May my tongue be like the pen of a deft scribe."

The blessings of military might on the king (vv. 2-6)

Verse 2, which introduces the section, is parallel in syntax to verse 7a. Verses 2 and 7 are similar in meaning as well, for being beautiful and gracious in speech (v. 2) are equivalent to loving righteousness and hating wickedness (v. 7a). Though the equivalence might seem odd to modern readers, the Hebrew word for "beauty" marks someone as *chosen;* examples are Sarah (Gen 12:14), Joseph (Gen 39:6), David (1 Sam 16:12; 17:42), and Mount Zion (Ps 48:2). "Grace of lips" is more than superficial charm, for Prov 22:11 pairs the phrase with "pure of heart." "To speak graciously" is to utter decisions made by a wise heart, which, in the case of a king, means righteous decisions and decrees. Thus both verses 2 and 7 in different ways say that the king is a chosen instrument of divine justice. As divinely chosen, he will be given further blessings.

The blessing mentioned in verses 3-6 is military success, in the form of an oracle promising victory in war. NRSV "ride on victoriously" combines two Hebrew verbs, the first of which (ṣālaḥ) means "to advance; triumph" and the second (rākab), "to ride, mount." REB renders, literally, "advance . . . ride on." It is worth noting that ṣālaḥ, "to advance; triumph," occurs in another oracle of war (1 Kgs 22:15b): "[Micaiah the prophet] answered [the king of Israel], 'Go up and triumph; the LORD will give it into the hand of the king.' " The placement of the oracle in Ps 45 is appropriate, for the king is the instrument of God's justice, and his wars carried out the divine will.

"Your throne, O God" is a much controverted phrase. Some take "God" as the divine name, whereas others take it as the king (in the hyperbolic language of the court). The arguments in favor of interpreting God as king are that (1) the context is the king's power, not God's; (2) "son of God" is used of the king in 2 Sam 7:14; 14:17 ("angel of God"); Ps 2:7; and (3) in Exod 4:16, Moses is "God" for Aaron and in 7:1 is "God" to Pharaoh (similar usage is claimed for Exod 21:6 and 22:8-9). Three arguments against interpreting "God" as the king are that (1) the applications of "god" to Moses are clearly marked as metaphorical; (2) since "God" occurs in the psalm three times as the divine name, it would be strange if the fourth occurrence had an utterly different reference; and (3) the similar phrase "throne of the LORD" occurs in 1 Chron 29:23. This commentary prefers verse 6a NRSV "your throne, O God" or, alternately, "your divine throne."

The blessings of virility, a royal princess, and progeny on the king (vv. 7-16)

The second section of the poem, parallel to the first section, is introduced by verse 7a, which, as noted, matches verse 2 in syntax and sentiment. Because the king is dedicated to carrying out the divine will, God prepares him for marriage, anointing him with "the oil of gladness" and making his robes fragrant with aromatic spices. The equivalent to God blessing the king in verse 2c is anointing the king in verse 7b. Verses 2-6 strengthen the king to defend the land, and verses 7-16 enhance the beauty and virility of the king for marriage to beget an heir. Kings ancient and modern are ever concerned with defending their borders and begetting an heir.

"The oil of gladness" (v. 7c) does not, despite some commentators, refer to the anointing of the king at his installation. Anointing can take place outside of enthronements, for example, Pss 23:5; 133:2; Eccl 9:8; Cant 1:3. The only other occurrence of "oil of gladness" is in Isa 61:3 amid marriage metaphors. "Gladness" is associated with marriage (e.g., Jer 7:34; 16:9; 25:10; 33:11); the spices that make the royal robes fragrant in the next verse (Ps 45:8a) establish a sensuous and erotic mood just as they do in Prov 7:17-18 and Cant 1:13; 5:13. The oil contributes to the sensuous ambience for the consummation of the marriage that will soon take place.

Though the "queen" in verse 9b is thought by most commentators to be the bride, the queen-to-be, she is much more likely the queen mother. For one thing, verse 13 says the bride is "in her chamber" from where, according to verse 14, she will be led to the king. For another, the Hebrew word *šēgal* seems to be an alternate to the native Hebrew word for "queen mother," *gĕbîrāh*. Also *šēgal* is derived from the Akkadian phrase *ša ekalli*, "the one from the palace." Moreover, 1 Kgs 2:19, says the queen mother sat on the king's right, exactly where Ps 45:9b places her. Consequently, the queen mother is the one who addresses the bride in verses 10-12, not the court singer as is often assumed. The poem has the queen mother give a speech immediately after she is mentioned, before the procession that brings the one addressed by the speech, the bride, into the hall. NRSV "the people of Tyre" (v. 12a, lit. "the daughter of Tyre") is correct, though most translate mechanically "Daughter of Tyre" and presume the bride is meant. The phrase "daughter of [city name]" in the Old Testament means the city and its population (e.g., Daughter Zion) rather than an individual resident of a city. The queen mother tells the bride that her husband, the king, is so important that even a great city like Tyre will bring its wealth to her. She had better realize that she has married very well—exactly the sentiments a daughter-in-law might expect to hear from her mother-in-law!

Verses 13b-15 sketches a memorable picture: the young woman accompanied by her friends led in solemn procession to her new husband, the king. "Joy and gladness" characterize the procession, the very same sentiments of the young woman in the Song of Songs as she enters the chambers of her boyfriend ("king" in the conventions of the Song; Cant. 1:4). In verse 16, the singer addresses the king directly. NRSV inserts "O king" to make the shift clear. The singer gives an oracle assuring the king of "sons" to succeed him on the throne and share in the governance of the realm. This oracle balances the earlier oracle of victory in war (vv. 3-6). The court singer's two oracles—assurance of victory, assurance of sons—address the abiding concern of the Davidic king, indeed of any king.

Conclusion by the court singer (v. 17)

The singer's task is comparable to a modern-day publicist—to make the king's name known by such songs as these. They will echo down the ages, as indeed this song has. Because the Davidic king is the regent of the one powerful deity, all nations will bring tribute.

Theological and Ethical Analysis

The limits that an occasional piece like a marriage song imposes are transcended in this poem. Though it appreciates the sensuousness and pageantry of the royal marriage and celebrates the physical beauty of the bride and groom, it focuses on the king as regent and representative of the unique and just God of Israel. God embraces the human institution of kingship with its tasks of defending the land and continuing the dynasty.

Jewish tradition sees the singer as a model Torah scholar, and the king as the Messiah. Christianity sees a messianic reference; Heb 1:8 quotes Ps 45:6-7 and interprets "O God" as referring to the Son. The psalm is sometimes used to illustrate the parable of the ten bridesmaids, "Look! Here is the bridegroom! Come out to meet him" (Matt 25:6). The words praising the beauty of the king and his devotion to justice and the attractive picture of the bride brought to the royal groom have made a strong appeal to Christian imagination.

PSALM 46

The royal marriage song in Ps 45 is followed by three poems on the Lord reigning in Zion. Psalms 46 and 48 extol Zion where God reigns as king, and Ps 47 celebrates the enthronement. Like Pss 48, 76, 84, and 122, Ps 46 is a Song of Zion. It celebrates Zion (a sacred name for Jerusalem) as the unshakeable center of the world. Though the earth may quake and give way, Zion will be secure. Though the vast waters of the cosmos grow turbulent, in Zion the river of life, safely channeled, flows out to make the world fertile. The real subject of the poem is God; the word "God" occurs seven times, and "LORD" three times.

Literary Analysis

The poem has three refrains, verses 1, 7, and 11. The Hebrew rubric "selah" marks the end of each. Though verse 1 is slightly different from verses 7 and 11, it is no less of a refrain than the other two, for "refuge" *(mahăseh)* in verse 1*a* and "refuge" *(miśgab)* in verses 7*b* and 11*b* are a fixed pair (as in Ps 94:22), and "God" appears in all three verses. The structure is thus: verses 1-3; 4-7; and 8-11. The signal that verse 4 marks a new section is its images of calm and tamed water that contrast so sharply to the chaotic and dangerous waters of verses 2-3.

Exegetical Analysis

God reigns in Zion though the world appears to collapse (vv. 1-3)

The psalmist begins with an act of trust that God always offers shelter (v. 1), refusing to be paralyzed by fear. The greatest catastrophe that can be imagined—the collapse of the world back into watery chaos—will not affect God as ultimate shelter. Though it was God who floated the disk of earth on the cosmic sea and anchored it by massive mountains, the possibility always exists that the structure could give way and everything plunge into a watery morass. The images are unforgettable. It is hard to imagine anything more terrifying than to feel the ground giving way beneath one's feet and find oneself sliding into the depths. Undaunted before the prospect, the psalmist dares to hope in something stronger, Zion, the city of the God who offers a sure refuge.

Some scholars and NAB assume that a refrain identical to verses 7 and 11 originally followed verse 3 and dropped out in the course of textual transmission. NAB goes so far as to add the refrain after verse 3. The addition is not warranted without textual support. Ancient poems were not written with modern notions of symmetry; verse 1 serves satisfactorily as the opening refrain.

The waters in Zion are calm and life-giving,
while the nations rage (vv. 4-7)

A new section is signaled by the word "river" *(nāhār),* which appears at the beginning of verse 4, giving it unusual emphasis. The stately river in God's city is commonplace in Canaanite mythology. In the topography of Jerusalem, however, the only "river" in Zion is a spring in the Kidron Valley that was, and still is, the principal water supply of Jerusalem, the Gihon. Jerusalem is the Lord's own city, however, and its features are heightened in religious literature. Genesis 2:13 makes the Gihon one of the four world rivers branching off from the single water source in the garden of Eden (Gen 2:10). The Canaanite high god El, from whose literary portrait biblical poets borrowed to describe Yahweh, lived "at the sources of the Two Rivers, / in the midst of the pools of the Double-Deep" (*CTU* 1.3.v.13-16 and several other citations). So also Yahweh ("the LORD") lived at the sources of the cosmic waters, which arose in the holy city, the very center of the world. A sign of Yahweh's total mastery is that the cosmic waters, potentially so dangerous (as in vv. 2-3), flow calmly within the city, making the city rejoice at the fertility they represent.

Functioning as a complement to the "natural disasters" in verses 2-3 are the political attacks of the kings in verse 6. Despite their assaults, the city is not "moved" (v. 5*a*; the same Hebrew verb as "shake" in v. 2*b*); God will "help it" (v. 5*b*; the same Hebrew root as the noun "help" in v. 1*b*). Verse 6 depicts not just any political instability, but a world at war against the Lord. The war is ended abruptly by the thunderous weapons of the Storm God; when "he utters his voice, the earth melts" (v. 6*b*).

In the refrain (v. 7), "the LORD" is the head of the heavenly army ("hosts") of the denizens of heaven. Against such divine might, earthly kings cannot stand. The divine title implies the end of ancient Near Eastern polytheism as the former deities enter Yahweh's entourage as prisoners of war. The refrain is uttered in response to the divine victory.

See the victory of the Lord! (vv. 8-11)

Like the Zion Song, Ps 48:12-13 ("Walk about Zion . . . consider well its ramparts"), verse 8 issues a command to contemplate the result of the divine victory. Verse 9 is not a general statement about God but a description of the victory just won. The grim picture of the battlefield—broken bows, shattered spears, and burning shields—functions as an announcement of victory. The destruction of the weapons of war means peace in the future.

"Be still!" is a command to stop what one is currently doing, which here is giving way to fear about the battle and security of Zion. The battle is won, which elicits the confession "know that I am God," that is, I have proved to be supreme deity by the victory (v. 10*bc*). Zion is the place where God's victory is most visible and most appropriately praised. The refrain (v. 11) is a response to the victory.

Theological and Ethical Analysis

Though full of triumph, the psalm is keenly aware of horrific threats to life, ranging from natural disasters to violent assault.

The poem holds up to people of faith a center, a place where God dwells and has promised to protect those who take refuge in it. Martin Luther's famous hymn, "A Mighty Fortress Is Our God," excerpted below, translates the psalm for a sixteenth-century audience, transposing the enemy kings into the devil.

> A mighty fortress is our God,
> a bulwark never failing;
> our helper he amid the flood
> of mortal ills prevailing.
> For still our ancient foe
> Doth seek to work us woe;
> his craft and power are great,
> and armed with cruel hate,
> on earth is not his equal.
>
> Did we in our own strength confide,
> our striving would be losing,
> were not the right man on our side,
> the man of God's own choosing.
> Dost ask who that may be?
> Christ Jesus, it is he;
> Lord Sabaoth his name,
> From age to age the same,
> and he must win the battle.
> (*The United Methodist Hymnal*
> [Nashville: The United Methodist
> Publishing House, 1999], hymn 110.)

The psalm expresses the two sides of a life of faith. On the one hand, there are the dangers among which is the possibility of personal and cosmic collapse. And on the other hand, there is God who has promised "to be there for us." The poem invites people of faith to hold steady even before nameless and limitless dangers. It does not promise escape from disturbance, but only from their power to destroy. In Christian interpretation, the "place" where God dwells has been seen as the risen Christ and as the church.

PSALM 47

Literary Analysis

Psalm 47 is the second of three psalms concerning the Lord reigning in Zion. Psalms 46 and 48 extol Zion, where God reigns, and Ps 47 celebrates the enthronement of the Lord as king.

This enthronement psalm summons the nations to acclaim Yahweh the supreme deity in heaven and on earth. Examples are Pss 93, 95–99, as well as Pss 24 and 29. Enthronement psalms draw selectively on the combat myth. Several biblical psalms adapt the myth, alluding only to what serves their purpose. Some describe the rise of Yahweh to the head of the pantheon (for example, Pss 29, 96:4; 97:7), while others like Ps 47 focus on the recognition of universal kingship.

Psalm 47 has three parts (vv. 1-4, 5-7, 8-9). Part 1 (vv. 1-4) summons all peoples to acclaim Yahweh as supreme among the heavenly beings and to recognize Yahweh's own people, Israel, as supreme among the nations. Part 2 (vv. 5-7) invites all peoples to acclaim the Lord "going up" to sit on the throne. Part 3 (vv. 8-9) describes the nations and Israel assembled before the triumphant Lord.

Exegetical Analysis

Acclaim Yahweh supreme in the heavens and
recognize Israel's primacy on earth (vv. 1-4)

This psalm focuses only on the rise of the victorious deity to supreme rank and the acknowledgment of it in heaven and on earth. "Most High" was a title for the chief god in the assembly. Verse 2b should be rendered "the Great King," for it was a regular epithet of the suzerain in Mesopotamia, Egypt, and the Hittite kingdom. Verses 3-4 presuppose a kind of parity between the realms of heaven and earth. As Yahweh is the Most High in heaven, so Israel, Yahweh's own people, is "most high" on earth;

other nations are under them in principle if not in historical reality. "Heritage" refers to the land that the Lord assigned to Israel in primordial times when decrees were issued, as depicted in Deut 32:8-9: "When the Most High apportioned the nations, when he divided humankind, he fixed the boundaries of the peoples according to the number of the gods; the LORD's own portion was his people, Jacob his allotted share." "Heritage" or "land" is part of the establishment of the people. A striking claim of the enthronement psalms is that while God's sovereignty is universal, it is exercised in a particular place: Zion.

Join your voices to the sound of trumpets as
the Lord goes up to his throne (vv. 5-7)

The verb "has gone up" refers to ascending to a height, presumably the throne. For similar texts of ascending the throne, see 2 Sam 6:15 and Isa 14:13. It is possible that the ark, the throne of the invisible God, was carried in solemn procession into the Temple. The verb "sing" *(zimmēr)* is repeated five times in two verses. A symphony of sound arises as the ark, symbolizing the presence of the Lord, is borne into the Temple symbolizing the heavenly palace of Yahweh. The ark is carried into the Temple in Ps 132.

The nations and Israel assemble before their Lord (vv. 8-9)

The verb that NRSV translates "is king" *(mālak)* in 8a has provoked disagreement. Both the verb *mālak* and its parallel "sits" *(yāšab),* however, are best interpreted as verbs describing motion or change of state. Thus the best translations are "has become king" and "has sat on the throne" rather than NRSV's "is king" and "sits." The rendering "to become king" does not, of course, mean Yahweh was once not king. Rather, like the Christian Easter cry, "Christ is risen," it celebrates an original event made present in ritual. The community celebrates the enthronement of the Lord as king upon defeating the forces of chaos. The enthronement can be celebrated in ritual, as at the New Year festival. In Ps 47, the Lord takes a seat on the throne before a great assembly of the nations and Israel. In the extant combat myths, the scene takes place in heaven; this scene is the earthly reflection of the heavenly scene.

Verse 9*b* is puzzling in syntax and meaning; the Septuagint has "The princes of the peoples gather with (*'im*) the God of Abraham." Some scholars emend the Masoretic Text to "with the people (*'im 'am*) of the God of Abraham." When written without vowels in ancient manuscripts, the words *'m* ("with") and *'m* ("people") would be identical and hence could easily have been mistakenly written by a scribe. If this suggestion is correct, the original reading was: "The princes of the peoples assemble with the people of the God of Abraham." It is also possible that *'im* means "toward, in the direction of," which would yield the meaning "The princes of the peoples have assembled 'toward' [i.e., before] the God of Abraham." NRSV "shields" in verse 9*c* is metonymy for "rulers."

Theological and Ethical Analysis

In the thinking of ancient Near Eastern peoples, a politically insignificant people would have had as its heavenly patron a relatively minor deity. A people's fortunes reflected the heavenly influence of its patron deity. This psalm proclaims a different message. Though Israel played an independent international role only sporadically, its poets asserted its God was the supreme deity, the one who had created the world and decreed all destinies.

This psalm displays Israel's great faith in the Lord and its own fierce pride in being the Lord's special people. God's universal grandeur finds in Israel a local habitation and a name. The people of a politically insignificant nation stand shoulder to shoulder with the leaders of the world, both joining in praise of the Lord of the world (v. 9). Modern readers may perhaps be uneasy at the people's large claim for themselves, for it does not seem to be accompanied by any protestations of humility or awareness of the dangers of superiority. The absence of such sentiments does not mean the people are unaware of them, however. The focus is entirely on what is happening before the congregation's eyes. Yahweh the Lord ascends to the throne and is proclaimed Most High; the Lord's people Israel delight in standing with the nations of the world in common worship of this God (v. 9).

In Christian imagination, ascending to the throne evokes the resurrection by which Jesus begins to exercise sovereignty over the world. It could be applied to the ascension of Jesus as described in Acts 1:9: "When he had said this, as they were watching, he was lifted up, and a cloud took him out of their sight."

PSALM 48

Literary Analysis

This psalm is the last of the three on the Lord reigning in Zion. Psalms 46 and 48 extol the city where God reigns, and Ps 47 celebrates the enthronement and its effect on the nations.

The poem is a Song of Zion, like Pss 46, 76, 84, 87, and 122. Though it narrates a great battle, the city of which it sings is a symbol of peace as in Pss 46, 76, and Isa 2:1-4 (same as Mic 4:1-3). The poem might have been used by pilgrims celebrating one of the three pilgrimage feasts of the year. Zion, the city on the hill, would have made an unforgettable impression on pilgrims as they drew near it in the final part of their journey. The psalm authoritatively interprets the city as a symbol of God's steadfast love and power over chaos.

To understand the significance of Mount Zion for Israel, one needs to know the story in which it plays a role. The story is a version of the combat myth, which begins with a massive threat to the stability and peace of the cosmos. The Lord intervenes and, after defeating chaotic forces that threatened the world, returns triumphant to Mount Zion, there to be acclaimed king and to build a palace symbolizing the new peace. Hence, the Temple on Zion is not merely a large edifice but a symbol of the majestic authority that upholds the universe. It should be pointed out that chaos in the Bible can be represented by various images, for example, raging cosmic waters or a monster. In this case the image of chaos is the kings of the world attacking God's city. The same image is found elsewhere (e.g., Ps 76 and Ezekiel 38–39).

Psalm 48 is framed by two panels, verses 1-3 and 12-14 (each with 24 Hebrew words), which tell of the grandeur of the city and its palace. Between them are two panels: one on the victory (vv. 4-8) and the other on the joyous reaction to it (vv. 9-11).

Exegetical Analysis

The grandeur and beauty of the city of God (vv. 1-3)

Though Zion is spoken of at length, the real object of praise is Yahweh, who dwells therein; in typical ancient Near Eastern fashion, the deity is associated with the major cult center. "Greatly to be praised" (v. 1a) is taken by most, including NRSV, to mean "exceedingly praiseworthy." "Greatness," however, can also come from the fact of praise; the sign of a great god is the lavish praise offered in the god's own city. If it were to diminish, the god would appear diminished, so flourishing praise and a flourishing god are interrelated.

Seven epithets are applied to Zion in verses 1b-2; the word pair "city" ('îr) in verse 1b and "city" (qiryat) in verse 2d form an inclusion. Verses 1c-2d are a subunit of two clusters, each having three epithets of Zion and each beginning with the word "mountain." Each cluster moves from "local" to "universal" dominion in that the first begins with "his holy mountain" and ends with "all the earth," and the second begins with "Mount Zion" and ends with "the great King." "The great King" is a title with international scope, for it was an epithet for suzerains in the Hittite Kingdom, Mesopotamia, and Egypt. "In the far north," it is now widely recognized, should be rendered "the Heights of Zaphon," which is the storm god Baal's sacred mountain in the Ugaritic texts. People of the time identified Zaphon with modern Jebel el-Aqra', classical Mons Casius, a peak of 5660 feet on the coastal border between Syria and Turkey. The appearance of the phrase "in the far north" in the psalm suggests that Yahweh has taken over the domain of Baal, a sign of the worldwide dominion of Yahweh. Verse 3 is transitional to the account of war in the next section by its mention of "citadels" and "defense."

The basis of Zion's greatness: God's defeat of the hostile kings (vv. 4-8)

The assembling of the kings for battle does not refer to a historical battle, but, like the gathering of kings under Gog of Magog in Ezekiel 38–39, represents a chaotic assault on God's governance of the universe. The enemy vanquished by Yahweh can be portrayed in mythic terms as Sea (as in Pss 77:16-19; 89:9-10; 114) or in "historical" terms as here. At any rate, the battle described here took place in primordial times; it was over as soon as it started, the panic of holy war stunning the warriors and sending them pell-mell in retreat. The "east wind" (v. 7a) evokes the wind weapon of the Storm God.

Verse 8 is open to several interpretations. NRSV assumes worshipers have actually witnessed the battle and victory ("so have we seen"), which has confirmed the ancient traditions ("as we have heard") of Yahweh's absolute sovereignty. Another interpretation is that the beauty and size of the Temple symbolize to visitors the power of the God who dwells there.

Joyous reactions to the victory at Zion (vv. 9-11)

"Steadfast love" (ḥesed, v. 9) here means God's fidelity manifested in the victory defending creation. What better place to ponder divine love than in the Temple that symbolizes that victory. In verse 10, God's "name" (self-manifestation) extends the victory over the kings to the whole world. God's deed receives the worldwide acclamation it deserves; "your praise" means "the praise of you." Though God is celebrated as a victorious warrior in verses 9-11, the basic issue is right governance of the world, which is the fruit of the victory. Military power is a means to justice. When violence threatens the just order, God reacts as a warrior, to be sure, but only to disarm the threat and reaffirm the creation that is good and beneficial to all.

Invitation to view the buildings that show
forth God's victory (vv. 12-14)

Continuing the theme of divine authority symbolized by the house of God, the psalmist exhorts visitors to walk around and see the buildings with their own eyes. To people of an agricultural society with no large city except Jerusalem, buildings of fine materials and workmanship must have made an extraordinary impression. Though Mount Zion is not a high hill, it does overlook the immediately surrounding valley (steeper in antiquity than today) and stimulated the imagination and faith of visitors to regard it as towering over all else. The great buildings symbolize God's power over every threat and loving commitment to dwell with the holy community.

Theological and Ethical Analysis

In comparison with other capital cities, Jerusalem was one of the smallest and least imposing. Its mountain, Mount Zion, was dwarfed by mountain residences of other gods and even by the Mount of Olives nearby. The city and the Temple were destroyed by the Neo-Babylonian Empire in 586 BCE, and again by the Romans in 70 CE, after which it was never rebuilt. How does one respond to the seemingly huge gap between the vision of Ps 48 and historical reality?

First, the psalm itself makes clear that it is about God rather than about the Temple or the city as such. Though dwelling at the stable center of the world, God remains sovereignly free. In an act of supreme graciousness, God meets human beings at a particular place—Jerusalem—to receive worship and to teach. For Judaism, Jerusalem as the place of meeting and of teaching is especially sacred. For Christians, Jerusalem is perhaps less sacred, for God's dwelling is realized in different ways. The privileged "place" of encounter with God is Jesus Christ. In fact, as the Word of God was shared with Gentiles, the capital of Judaism was reinterpreted. One can hope that such reinterpretation does not lessen the perennial sacredness of Jerusalem. For Christians, therefore, this psalm celebrating God's self-presentation in a particular place and peace-bestowing victory remains one of the most arresting in the Psalter.

Saint Augustine shows a great Christian mind interpreting the psalm:

> "As we have heard, so too we have seen." O blessed Church, at one time you heard, and at another time you saw. The Church heard the promise and now sees the promises fulfilled; it heard in prophecy what it now sees made manifest in the gospel. Everything that is now being realized was prophesied beforehand. Lift up your eyes, let your gaze sweep round the world, look at the inheritance that stretches to the end of the earth. (Boulding 2000, 342)

PSALM 49

Psalms 46–48 have two themes in common: The Lord is Sovereign of the world, and Zion is the place for divine-human encounter. Though it seems at first to differ completely from these poems, Ps 49 actually develops their themes. It is, after all, last in a series of Korahite psalms. It proclaims to "all inhabitants of the world" that the Lord alone rules the world, that rich and powerful people do not and all hopes placed in them are vain. The poem brings together two concerns usually treated in different genres: the Lord's sole dominion (hymns) and the folly of relying on wealth to obtain life (Wisdom literature).

Literary Analysis

Psalm 49 is an instruction like those in Proverbs 1–9 and Ecclesiastes. In such instructions, the teacher, appealing to personal experience and tradition, makes use of a process ("discipline") so that the student will understand where true wisdom and life are to be found. The instruction does not simply impart information; it is a transaction between teacher and student. Didactic moments occur, of course, in the Psalter as when a vivid experience of salvation prompts the psalmist to teach, as in Ps 34:11-12, "Come, O children, listen to me; I will teach you the fear of the Lord" (cf. Ps 51:12-13). Psalm 73, the story of one individual's struggle to trust God, also becomes a lesson. Nothing in the Psalter, however, equals the explicitness of Ps 49 in teaching that God, not wealth, ransoms and "takes" one from death. Some have suggested that Ps 49 was written at a time when Israel was a poor and subject people occupied by a foreign power. The temptation to regard wealth as the solution to every problem would have been strong. The psalm dethrones wealth and upholds God as savior.

God rescuing an individual from death is a common metaphor in the psalms, for example, Pss 9:13; 18:16-17; 56:13. Psalm 49 brings the metaphorical use to a new stage by asserting that God will "take" (NRSV: "receive") an individual from the power of death (v. 15b). The verb "to take" *(lāqaḥ)* develops an ancient Near Eastern and biblical tradition of just individuals taken up to heaven. See commentary on Ps 18:16. Elijah was similarly taken by God to heaven in 2 Kgs 2:1-12 *(lāqaḥ* occurs in v. 10). In Ps 73:24, the psalmist declares, "You guide me with your counsel, and afterward you will receive [lit. "take," *lāqaḥ*] me with honor." The same verb is used in Ps 49:15, "[God] will receive me." Daniel 12:1-3 in the mid-160s BCE, applied the tradition of heroes going up to heaven to a group rather than an individual: to "those who are wise shall shine like the brightness of the sky, and those who lead many to righteousness, like the stars forever and ever." Though it is possible that "receive me" in Ps 49:15 is simply a variant of the common metaphor of God rescuing from death, it more likely marks a new stage. The individual is contrasted with the overconfident wealthy who die and never again see light (vv. 10-11, 14, 17-19), and the psalmist expects to be rescued from such a fate. The psalmist teaches that only God can provide a way out of mortal danger and employs the story of the hero taken to heaven to make the case. A bold faith uses bold narratives.

The opening verses (vv. 1-4) are clearly introductory, and verse 5 is the thesis (in the form of a rhetorical question) that the poet will seek to demonstrate. The remainder of the poem is organized by two interlocking sets of refrains, verses 7 and 15, and verses 12 and 20. The NAB, REB, and NJPS rightly divide the poem on the basis of the refrains and the themes: verses 1-4, 5-12, 13-15, 16-20. The first line of verses 7 and 15 echo each other in sound and sense, as can be seen in Hebrew transcription: verse 7a, *'aḥ lō' pādōh yipdeh 'îš* (lit. "alas, [riches] cannot ransom a person"); verse 15a, *'ak 'ĕlōhîm yipdeh napšî* (lit. "But God will ransom my life"). The second verse echoes and then reverses the sentiments of the first. This is also true of the first line of the second set of refrains. Verse 12 reads, literally, "A human being with wealth does not abide *(yālîn)*, / he is like the beasts that perish"; verse 20 reads, literally, "A human being with wealth if he is not wise *(wĕlō' yābîn)*, / is like the beasts that perish." Again, the second refrain reverses the sentiments of the first.

The twin themes of the poem—the folly of relying on wealth for rescue from death and the wisdom of relying on God—are asserted throughout the poem rather than developed sequentially, leaving it to the refrains to move the poem forward. The second half of the poem (vv. 13-15), for example, continues the theme of the folly of wealth until the refrain in verse 15, "But God will ransom my soul," abruptly switches to a new theme. The defiant tone is maintained to the end. The last part, verses 16-20, echoes verses 5-9 by repetition of words: "fear" (v. 5a) in "do not be afraid" (v. 16a); "life" *(nepeš,* v. 8a) in "themselves" *(napšô,* v. 18); and "never see the grave" (v. 9b) in "never again see the light" (v. 19b).

Exegetical Analysis

Introduction (vv. 1-4)

The introduction is unusually solemn, comparable to Deut 32:1-3 and Ps 78:1-4. Like the instructions of Proverbs, it addresses everyone. "Proverb" and "riddle" (v. 4) can have a broader sense than in English, here something like "theme" and "lesson" (so NJPS). "Incline my ear" means "give my attention to." The instruction is sung "to the music of the harp." Like the instructions in Proverbs 1–9, the teaching effectively uses contrast: Trust in wealth is folly; trust in God is wisdom.

The psalmist's faith and the threat to it (vv. 5-12)

The verb "I fear" is common in the psalms (e.g., Pss 3:6; 23:4; 27:1; 56:3, 11; 118:6), sometimes occurring in statements of *not* fearing enemies. "Why should I fear?" is a rhetorical question meaning "I will never fear!"

A group that holds a view opposite to the psalmist's is now introduced—"those who trust in their wealth" (v. 6a). As in Proverbs, there is a contrast between the wicked (always plural) and the righteous person (always singular). The arrogant wealthy in verse 5b do not assault the psalmist. "Surrounds" (v. 5b) means to stand in opposition to the psalmist, thereby presenting two "types" of people like the contrasted types of Proverbs, the wise person and the foolish, the righteous person and the wicked. The teacher exposes their folly in two arguments, positive and negative. The argument is presented negatively in verses 7-12: Wealth cannot stave off death. In verses 13-20, it is presented both negatively and positively: Wealth cannot save from death (vv. 13-14, 17-20), and God will rescue me from death (v. 15). The refrains in their first occurrence are negative (vv. 7 and 12); they will be positive in their second occurrence (vv. 15 and 20). "Ransom" (v. 7) can refer to someone "buying back" an animal or human being by a substitute sacrifice or money offering (e.g., Exod 13:13; 34:20). It can also refer to the people ransoming Jonathan from Saul's anger (1 Sam 14:45), to God redeeming the people out of Egypt (e.g., Deut 9:26), or to God ransoming an individual, as in Job 33:28: "He has redeemed my soul from going down to the Pit, and my life shall see the light."

A refrain in verse 12 ends the first section, and a variant will be repeated at the end of the next section (v. 20). Verse 12, literally reads, "A human being with wealth does not abide, / he is like the animals that perish." For the meaning of verse 20 and the inter-play of verses 12 and 20, see below.

God will ransom me from the power of Sheol (vv. 13-20)

Verses 13-14 continue the theme of the previous section. Verse 15, however, shifts from critique to triumphant assertion, "But God will ransom my soul." "Ransom" and "receive" *(lāqaḥ)* are metaphors of rescue, each of a different origin, as explained above. Continuing boldly, the psalmist urges "Do not be afraid" (v. 16a), which develops the boast of verse 5a "Why should I fear?" (the verb is *yārē'* in both verses). The exhortation in verses 16-20 is directed at those intimidated by wealthy people whose arrogant behavior appears to have won them privilege and fame. Such people, says the psalmist, cannot purchase what they most want, escape from death.

In verse 20, NRSV follows the Septuagint, which harmonizes verses 12 and 20. Like the other set of refrains (vv. 7 and 15), however, this set of refrains contains subtle variations. Verse 20 should be translated literally: "A human being with wealth if he is not wise, / he is like the beasts that perish." The wisdom the psalmist wants to impart is that one must place all one's trust in God in the face of death. True wisdom here, as in Proverbs, shows the way to life.

Theological and Ethical Analysis

The core of the poem is the singer's conviction that only God can give and sustain life. The psalmist unmasks the hidden moti-vation behind frenetic pursuit of wealth—anxiety about death. Confident of speaking for the Lord (vv. 1-4) and showing a holy boldness (v. 5), the singer analyzes obsession with wealth from different angles and finds them all foolish. Wealth has no value before death; death strips away the very riches one hoped would keep it away; death moves from dreaded specter to actual ruler ("shepherd," v. 14b), herding all to Sheol. There is one way out from death's hold, faith in the God of life. Such faith takes away fear and gives one the boldness to teach others.

Judaism and Christianity both affirm the goodness of the material world and the importance of having enough, indeed of "eating your fill," as in Deut 8:10, "You shall eat your fill and bless the LORD your God for the good land that he has given you." At the same time, they recognize what wealth cannot do: "Riches do not profit in the day of wrath, but righteousness delivers from death" (Prov 11:4). The only one who can give life is God. Judaism and Christianity affirm resurrection from the dead. In Christianity, it is the central message: "If there is no resurrection of the dead, then Christ has not been raised; and if Christ has not been raised, then our proclamation has been in vain and your faith has been in vain. We are even found to be misrepresenting God, because we testified of God that he raised Christ—whom he did not raise if it is true that the dead are not raised" (1 Cor 15:13-15). Psalm 49 leads one through a process by which one puts one's hope for life in God rather than in wealth.

The psalm brings to mind the parable of the rich fool in Luke 12:19-21, in which Jesus says: "I will say to my soul, 'Soul, you have ample goods laid up for many years; relax, eat, drink, be merry.' But God said to him, 'You fool! This very night your life is being demanded of you. And the things you have prepared, whose will they be?' So it is with those who store up treasures for themselves but are not rich toward God."

PSALM 50

Psalm 50 is the first of the psalms of Asaph; the others are Psalms 73–83. It may have been placed here because of its similarities to the preceding and following poems; Ps 50 opens with a universal appeal like Ps 49 and ends like Ps 51 with a hope for purified sacrifices. It now forms a bridge between the first collection of Korah psalms (42–49) and the second collection of David psalms (51–57).

Literary Analysis

Psalm 50 is one of three covenant renewal liturgies in the Psalter, the others being Pss 81 and 95. In this psalm, God brings a complaint against the people for breach of covenant and calls upon the witnesses of the original covenant—heaven and earth—to testify to the people's failure. Examples of such complaints are Deut 32 (see v. 1), Isa 1:1-9 (see v. 2), and Mic 6:1-8. Though Ps 50 is accusatory, its aim is positive: to help the people acknowledge their sins and renew their commitment. One can imagine an appropriate cultic situation—the people in the court of the Temple listening to an officiant speaking in God's name at one of the great pilgrimage feasts. The present poem perhaps draws on such a ceremony.

The liturgical origin may account for God appearing in a storm theophany, for the theophany at Mount Sinai is transposed to another holy mountain, Zion. A holy mountain could attract to itself traditions from other sacred mountains. Psalm 48:1, for example, calls Mount Zion "Zaphon" (NJPS), which is the name of the mountain of Baal the storm god known from the Ugaritic texts. According to Exod 19:16-19, when God appeared at Sinai, "there was thunder and lightning, as well as a thick cloud on the mountain, and a blast of a trumpet so loud that all the people who were in the camp trembled. Moses brought the people out of the camp to meet God. . . . As the blast of the trumpet grew louder and louder, Moses would speak and God would answer him in thunder." God's proclamation of the Ten Commandments so terrified the people that they asked Moses to mediate all future divine-human encounters (Exod 20:18-21; Deut 5:22-31). In the liturgy, an officiant taking the role of Moses presumably spoke the Ten Commandments. "The Decalogue," according to Moshe Weinfeld, "was solemnly uttered by every faithful Israelite as the God of Israel's fundamental claim on the congregation of Israel, and it became the epitome of Israelite moral and religious heritage" (Weinfeld 1991, 26). Adherence to the Commandments and participation in worship of the Lord gave Israel its identity as

God's people. A likely festival for covenant renewal was the Feast of Weeks (Pentecost), which was associated with the law in post-biblical times, probably as a continuation of an earlier tradition.

The psalm has three parts: theophany and summons to Israel (vv. 1-6); instruction on proper sacrifice and attitude toward God (vv. 7-15); rebuke of violations of the Decalogue and final exhortation (vv. 16-23).

Part 2 is an instruction (using animal sacrifice as an example) on the proper relationship to God. Verses 7-13 rebuke indiscriminate sin offerings on the grounds that multiplying such offerings without genuine conversion reduces God to just another deity needing food and ignores the universal dominion of Israel's God. The point at issue is not animal sacrifice, for the thanksgivings and fulfilling of vows in verse 14 involve such sacrifices. These latter have certain characteristics not shared by sin offerings, however: They are performed with rejoicing; the meat is shared with the offerers and others; and they give thanks for God's positive action in one's life. Why are these sacrifices acceptable but not sacrifices for sin? Because, it seems, they express the right relationship of God and people, a relationship that is spelled out in attitudinal terms in verse 15: the people cry out to God when in need, God graciously delivers them, and they glorify God with grateful hearts. Sin offerings, on the other hand, express only one aspect of the relationship to God, that of sin. Moreover, as will be shown in part 3, they had become a substitute for real conversion. Part 2 is thus concerned with the basic relationship between God and people, exploring it negatively through criticism of bad offerings and positively through praise of good offerings (v. 14) combined with a right attitude (v. 15).

Part 3 is addressed to the wicked (v. 16a). The sins in verses 17-20 are breaches of the Ten Commandments (theft, adultery, bearing false witness), and they are conscious sins, not momentary acts of human weakness, for the perpetrators are in league with others. They reject ("hate") instruction (v. 17), run with thieves, join with adulterers (v. 18), and sit with slanderers (v. 20). As God was not silent ("does not keep silence," v. 3) about sin offerings in part 2, so God is not "silent" now about the sins

(vv. 21-22). Repeated words tie the condemned sacrifices in part 2 with the condemned conduct in part 3: "covenant" begins each section (vv. 5 and 16); "silence/silent" opens (v. 3) and closes (v. 21) the two sections as does "rebuke" (vv. 8 and 21). Parts 2 and 3 both conclude positively with an exhortation and promise (vv. 14-15 and 23). They are verbally linked to each other: "those who bring thanksgiving as their sacrifice *(zōbēaḥ tôdāh)*" in verse 23*a* reprises "offer . . . a sacrifice of thanksgiving *(zēbaḥ tôdāh)*" in verse 14, and "honor me *(yĕkabbĕdānî)*" in verse 23*a* reprises "you shall glorify me *(ûtkabbĕdēnî)*" in verse 15.

Exegetical Analysis

Theophany and summons to Israel (vv. 1-6)

"The mighty one, God the LORD" is better rendered "Yahweh, the God of gods" (so NAB), meaning that as the Most High among all heavenly beings, Israel's God has the right to summon the whole earth. "God shines forth" means "appears in a storm theophany" as in Deut 33:2; Job 37:15; Ps 94:1. At Sinai God appeared in a storm (Exod 19:16-19) and does so again here "out of Zion." God "does not keep silence," because keeping silence would make people think they were observing the commandments satisfactorily (v. 21*a*). Since the "heavens" and "earth" witnessed the original agreement, they are summoned to testify about any sins the original signatories might have committed (v. 4). In lists of witnesses in Hittite and West Semitic treaty texts, Heaven and Earth (and other cosmic pairs such as Abyss and the Springs, Day and Night) are listed following the patron gods of the parties to the treaties and the great gods and the gods of the cult places. Biblical monotheism eliminated such witnesses or reduced them to metaphors. Heaven and Earth are invoked in Deut 4:26; 30:19; 31:28, and Mountains and Hills are invoked in Mic 6:1-2. NRSV "faithful ones" (v. 5) is misleading. It does not refer to the sincere faith of the assembly but to their "objective holiness" that derives from being party to a covenant with God, as is clear from the parallel verse. A better rendering is "consecrated ones" (NIV) or "devotees" (NJPS). The whole congregation is "consecrated," even those guilty of serious sins (vv. 17-20). The latter are rebuked with severity because they have profaned their holy state as God's people. "The heavens" (v. 6) testify, their testimony being simply an affirmation of the Lord's own judgment.

Instruction on proper sacrifice and attitude toward God (vv. 7-15)

Criticism of sin sacrifices is a staple of prophetic preaching, for example, Isa 1:10-17; Jer 6:20; Amos 5:21-24. Such criticism is not a rejection of sin offerings as such but of offerings unaccompanied by sincere repentance. When offered improperly, they dishonor God and pervert the relationship between God and the people. The harsh rebukes of this passage are a means of instructing the people and helping them to see what is essential in the relationship. Direct and even aggressive rebukes and questions characterize covenant renewal ceremonies in Ps 81, Deut 32, Josh 24, and 1 Sam 12. In Josh 24, which reflects a ceremony of renewal, Joshua accuses the people of being unwilling to live up to the covenant: "You cannot serve the LORD, for he is a holy God. He is a jealous God; he will not forgive your transgressions or your sins. If you forsake the LORD and serve foreign gods, then he will turn and do you harm, and consume you" (Josh 24:19-20). In 1 Sam 12, Samuel's description of the people's behavior is so unsparing that they cry out, "We have sinned" (v. 10). Samuel accuses the people in verse 17 of doing wickedness in the sight of the Lord by asking for a king. After divinely sent thunder and rain, Samuel says, "you have done all this evil, yet do not turn aside from following the LORD" (v. 20). In such texts, therefore, severe rebuke precedes affirmation. Psalm 50 is no different.

Rebuke of violations of the Decalogue and final exhortation (vv. 16-23)

The transition to part 3 is clearly marked by verse 16a: "But to the wicked God says." Though not every member of the congregation is guilty of the serious covenant breaches named in this section, the entire congregation must listen to the rebukes. Each individual is inescapably in the community and must hear what God says to it.

Part 3 is linked closely to part 2. In the earlier section sin sacrifices were rebuked because they were a substitute for conversion. This section condemns the sins themselves. The sins mentioned are all against the neighbor. Sins directly against God were perhaps already covered in part 2, which was concerned with basic attitude. "But now I rebuke you" nicely states the aim of this liturgy, for the intent of the instruction is to change conduct. The aim of the leader, speaking as covenant mediator, is to lead the people back to observance of the covenant and loyalty to God. Verse 22 concludes part 3 and sums up matters forcefully: Accept this message or I'll tear you to pieces! The vocabulary of the final verse (v. 23) harks back to the positive summary at the end of part 2 (vv. 14-15), saying in essence: Let your religious practice fit the relationship between you and me.

Theological and Ethical Analysis

The psalm acknowledges both the covenant God established with the holy community and the reality of sin. To speak of the relationship is inevitably to speak of sin, conversion, and forgiveness. The biblical God is always ready to forgive and give a fresh start, and that is the whole point of this psalm. The poem begins with the worldwide dominion of the Lord, invoking the primordial witnesses of human conduct toward God—Heaven and Earth. Such a scene inspires fear, and the first words spoken in God's name do nothing to allay that fear: "Gather. . . . Hear, O my people. . . . I will testify against you" (vv. 5-7). The tone changes, however, into something more positive. Instead of outright condemnation or easy forgiveness, God leads the people through a process carefully designed to reveal to them divine "justice" (including the divine initiative in making the covenant) and the people's deviation from the original relationship. The language is occasionally harsh but never loses sight of its purpose.

Not condemnation, not easy dismissal, but a process that leads to conversion and fresh and enlightened commitment.

The psalm enables an individual or community to hear the divine word that defines them as God's people (vv. 14-15) and not to mistake external worship for their relationship to God.

PSALM 51

The poem is one of the seven penitential psalms of the church, along with Pss 6, 32, 38, 102, 130, and 143. They were in liturgical use from early Christian times because of their suitability for expressing contrition and the desire for forgiveness. The superscription attributes it to David after the prophet Nathan confronted him over his adultery with Bathsheba and murder of Uriah (2 Sam 12:1-15), a reminder that all human beings, even the most revered, must beg God for forgiveness. One cannot simply presume forgiveness, for the biblical God is all-seeing and just. One needs a great poem like this one to bring one properly before God.

Literary Analysis

The structure of a poem has to be sufficiently visible to guide pray-ers through it. This poem has two sections of approximately equal length, verses 1-8 and 9-17, plus a prayer at the end for Jerusalem, verses 18-19. The sections are marked off in such a way that they would be visible to ancient readers. The two main sections are formally interlocked by the repetition of "blot out" in the first verse of each section (vv. 1d and 9b) and of "wash" after the first verse (v. 2a) and before the last verse (v. 7b) of section 1. Section 1 is further defined by the verbs of seeking forgiveness that appear only in the outer frames, verses 1-2 (all in the imperative mood) and verses 7-8 (all in the imperfect tense). Between these two frames are five bicola (vv. 3-6) introduced by "for" (v. 3a) expressing the sinner's confession and openness to divine reproof. The section is further defined by the initial Hebrew consonants that occur in pairs in verses 4 (*l*), 5-6 (*h*), and 7-8 (*t*). Section 2, simpler in construction, is framed by the repetition in verses 10 and 17 of the triad "heart," "God," and "spirit."

The two sections are differentiated by their content as well as by the formal features noted above. Section 1 asks forgiveness for sin that is reckoned as a past act having personal and social consequences. Section 2 details the effects of forgiveness. Forgiveness brings interior renewal, nearness to God, an enlivened spirit, joy, all of which inspire the teaching of sinners (vv. 13-15), which is of more value than sacrifice (v. 17).

The verbs for forgiveness in section 1 suggest that stain is the underlying metaphor for sin: "blot out" (vv. 1*d* and 9*b*, lit. "to wipe clean"); "wash" (vv. 2*a* and 7*b*); "cleanse," "clean" (vv. 2*b* and 7*a*), all refer to cleansing and purifying what is soiled or defiled. The two other verbs for forgiveness, "have mercy" (v. 1*a*) and "purge" (v. 7*a*), are general, being defined by the other verbs. The vocabulary in section 2 suggests that the underlying metaphor for forgiveness is "admittance" (removal of barriers), making possible an encounter with God whose "spirit" (v. 11) reanimates the psalmist's principle of activity ("heart," "spirit," vv. 10, 12).

Exegetical Analysis

Forgive me, O God, because of your mercy,
I acknowledge my sin (vv. 1-8)

The appeal for forgiveness is based primarily on God's "steadfast love" and "mercy"; only verses 3-6 mention the psalmist's contrition that might win divine favor. The conjunction "for" (v. 3*a*) shifts the topic from seeking forgiveness (vv. 1-2) to expression of sorrow (vv. 3-6) where the psalmist gives up all excuses. Verse 3*a* describes the psalmist's constant experience of the consequences of his sins—the sense of alienation, sadness, and experience of ostracism. "Sin" (v. 3*b*) can mean the consequences of the act as well as the act itself. "When my mother conceived me" (v. 5*b*) means that at no time was the psalmist ever without sin. Psalm 88:15 describes a similar experience: "Wretched and close to death from my youth up," that is, I have always been afflicted.

Though the sense of verse 6 is somewhat uncertain, it probably expresses the painful realization of the gap between God's demands and the sinner's state. The realization provokes a renewed petition for forgiveness in verses 7-8. To hide one's sins from God can be acutely painful (cf. Ps 32:1-5 and Prov 28:13). The phrase "you desire" (v. 6*a*) is derived from the liturgy, that is, God is pleased with (accepts) an offering, for such is the meaning of the two other occurrences of the verb in the psalm (vv. 16 and 18). The confession of the "truth"—the previously unacknowledged sin of the penitent—is well pleasing to God, like a properly offered sacrifice. Though "Teach me wisdom" (v. 6) is taken by some as a statement rather than a petition ("you teach me wisdom"), NRSV makes acceptable sense. In summary, the first section shows the sinner painfully aware of defilement, open to God's reproof, and profoundly desirous of cleansing.

Renew me, restore me to the community, and let me proclaim your praises (vv. 9-17)

As already noted, the three words "heart," "God," and "spirit" in verses 10 and 17 frame section 2 and set the tone. As section 1 asked to be freed from defilement, section 2 asks to be empowered to respond to God. "Heart," the thinking-deciding center of a person, and "spirit," one's divinely given breath, are given prominence, for they are the principles of human activity. The phrase "create in me a clean heart" has much in common with the prophetic hope of restoration from the exile as in Ezek 36:26, "A new heart I will give you, and a new spirit I will put within you; and I will remove from your body the heart of stone and give you a heart of flesh." See also Jer 31:33-34. "Spirit" (lit. "air in motion") in Ps 51 has a double reference. One is to God's spirit or breath, which animates human beings as in Gen 2:7, Ezek 37:10, and especially Ps 104:29-30, "When you hide your face, they are dismayed; when you take away their breath, they die and return to their dust. When you send forth your spirit, they are created; and you renew the face of the ground." The other reference of "spirit" is to human breath, which is parallel in Ps 51 to "heart," as in Pss 34:18; 78:8; Prov 17:22. The psalmist plays on both meanings, that is, I can fully "breathe" when your breath touches me. The psalmist, conscious that sin merits death in the sense of exclusion from God's life-giving presence, prays for "life" in the sense of readmittance to God's presence and renewal of heart and spirit. Such renewal brings "joy" (v. 12), which perhaps refers to joyous celebration in the Temple.

In anticipation of being heard and forgiven, the psalmist in verse 13 promises to teach God's ways to sinners. What gift can the psalmist give to God for the transformative forgiveness just received? There is only one thing God lacks that the psalmist can give—the praise of humans on earth. The psalmist will encourage "transgressors" to give praise by teaching them "your ways" (v. 13) and will also personally sing God's praises (vv. 14-15) as only those with "a broken and contrite heart" (v. 17) can do. Other psalmists also share their experience of a gracious and forgiving God (e.g., Ps 34:11-12). In verse 14, deliverance from *dāmîm,* "blood guilt" (the usual meaning in the Pentateuch) or "bloodshed, violent behavior" (the usual meaning in Psalms) is puzzling. Context suggests the psalmist wants to be publicly recognized as forgiven, to be admitted to the community and to be able to teach "transgressors." Verse 15 is the invitation to praise in the Liturgy of the Hours (official morning and evening prayer in some Christian denominations) for the Daily Office of the Western church. The assertion in verse 16 that God has "no delight in sacrifice" is not a rejection of animal sacrifice as such. It is "dialectic negation," contrast-by-negating to express emphasis.

Prayer for Jerusalem (vv. 18-19)

The prayer is usually reckoned as an addition designed to reassure worshipers that when Jerusalem is rebuilt animal sacrifice will be restored. An editor apparently interpreted the statement that a "broken spirit" is an acceptable sacrifice (v. 17) to be a prediction that animal sacrifice is a thing of the past. The destruction of the Temple in the sixth century BCE may have suggested that idea to some. Canonically, the verses function to emphasize public prayer as a complement to personal prayer.

Theological and Ethical Analysis

Though sin is not a fashionable topic in some circles, the Bible speaks often and insistently about it. The biblical vocabulary of sin is large and subtle, the product of much reflection on the all-too-common rebellion of human beings against God's blessings and demands. When one sins seriously, how does one manage the journey back to God and find cleansing, interior renewal, and a restored relationship? To guide the process of repentance is the purpose of this great psalm.

It would be easy to guide repentance by playing off human wretchedness against divine holiness and inaccessibility. Psalm 51 does not take that route. Instead, the penitent is taught to give up defensive excuses, rely purely and simply on God's mercy, and deepen the desire for God's presence. Romans 3:4 cites Ps 51:4 to show the universal sinfulness of the human race that is the prelude to God's salvation.

PSALM 52

Literary Analysis

Though scholars differ on its proper classification (some refusing to classify it at all), Ps 52 is best taken as a song of trust. Its denunciation of the false hero and announcement of punishment for the "mighty one" (v. 1) is done from a secure stance of trust. According to some, the song may even have arisen in a ritual for beleaguered sufferers. The poem uses the language of polar opposite "types," which is common in Wisdom literature; it contrasts the wise and the foolish person, the righteous and wicked person, in order to focus on their respective fates: prosperity or punishment. A good example is Prov 11:28, *"Those who trust in their riches* will wither, but *the righteous* will flourish like green leaves" (words identical to Ps 52 are italicized). Psalm 36 is similar in logic and ideas. It too opens with an intensely drawn portrait of a malefactor (Ps 36:1-4, cf. Ps 52:1-4), expresses confidence in divine judgment (Ps 36:5-6, cf. Ps 52:5-7), and concludes with an appreciation of the safety of the Temple and God's care of the trusting (Ps 36:7-9, cf. Ps 52:8-9).

Psalm 52 maximizes the contrasts between the types of the righteous and the wicked: the opening boast of the wicked (v. 1) versus the scornful reaction of righteous onlookers (vv. 6-7); the exclusion from "the land of life" (i.e., the Temple, v. 5) versus the psalmist's admittance to the Temple (v. 8); the uprooting of the wicked (v. 5c) versus the psalmist's rootage in the soil (v. 8a). The succession of themes suggests three stanzas: denunciation of the arrogant scoundrel (vv. 1-4); divine judgment and the reaction of the righteous in joyous celebration (vv. 5-7); reaction of the psalmist in trust and proclamation (vv. 8-9).

Exegetical Analysis

Denunciation of the arrogant scoundrel (vv. 1-4).

Desiring to see divine justice realized, the singer denounces an individual who represents its polar opposite—rampant injustice. The intensification of language, especially that focus on malicious words enlarges and deepens the portrait of evil, as in Ps 36:1-4; Prov 6:12-15. In Wisdom literature, speech is the most revealing human act, for it expresses the heart. The address "O mighty one" is ironic, for the word normally means brave in battle, heroic; it can even be applied to God. This "mighty one" takes pride in destroying others not by the sword (which might win some honor), but by malicious and lying words. Ruining reputations and making outcasts, the "hero" has sold out to a violent and god-despising way of life. To the psalmist, people who are confident that they have the resources to live outside the limits actually live in a danger zone. Their prosperity lasts only for the moment. The brevity of their flourishing is underlined by the four-times repeated phrases expressing the opposite state: permanence ("all day long," v. 1; "forever," v. 5a; "forever and ever," v. 8b; "forever," v. 9a).

NRSV and other translations rightly emend verse 1b (v. 3b in the Masoretic Text). The Hebrew reads, literally, "God's steadfast love (ḥesed) is all day long." The syntax of the line is awkward as is its placement in the poem. Pronouncing judgment at this point would ruin the pronouncement in verses 6-7. For its emendation of this line, NRSV ("mischief") draws on the Septuagint rendering, "lawlessness." "Lawlessness" reflects Hebrew ḥāmās, which is similar enough to ḥesed to confuse scribes. The emendation "against the godly" (also NRSV) is derived from the Syriac version.

Divine judgment and the reaction of the righteous in joyous celebration (vv. 5-7)

Divine justice must be seen by humans in order to be true justice. The axiom was even more true in antiquity than today. A scoundrel running rampant erodes the credibility of the God of justice as well as poses danger to the vulnerable. Verse 5 is thus both a prayer and a hope. God's punishment of arrogance brings joy and reassurance to the righteous. Divine intervention and the righteous rejoicing in response to it are two sides of the same coin. The taunt of the righteous in verse 7 specifies the malice of the wicked as trust in riches rather than trust in God.

Four verbs for divine punishment occur in verse 5: "to break down" (as a structure), "to snatch up quickly" (as coals of fire), "to pull up" (as from the land), and "to uproot" (as a plant). The underlying metaphors are tearing down (of human constructions) and rooting out (of natural plantings).

In verse 5c NRSV's "the land of the living" is best rendered "the land of life." Hebrew ḥayyîm can be the substantive plural of the adjective "living" (i.e., "living ones") and the abstract plural "life." In Pss 27:13 and 116:9, "the land of life" is the Temple.

Such a designation befits the dwelling of the Creator of all living things. The sinner is uprooted from the Temple and excluded from the domain of life. The singer, on the other hand, is "like a green olive tree in the house of God" (v. 8a), that is, like a tree in the garden of God. It is very probable that "tent" (v. 5b, there is no "your" in the Masoretic Text) refers to the Temple, as in Pss 15:1 and 61:4, not to the individual's dwelling.

Judgment takes place in Zion. The "hero" is broken and uprooted from the sacred precincts. The righteous person, on the other hand, is as firmly rooted as the trees in the garden of God, which was on the Temple grounds.

Reaction of the psalmist in trust and proclamation (vv. 8-9)

"But I" (v. 8a) in the Psalter denotes a break with the preceding section; it also signals a contrast between the psalmist and evildoers (e.g., Pss 5:7; 13:5; 31:14). What greater contrast can there be than that between the quietly trusting psalmist (the olive tree) and the boastful hero of the opening verse! The olive tree is rooted in the garden of God. The image calls to mind other passages on the planting of God (Pss 1:3; 92:12-15; Jer 17:5-8). "I trust" in God (v. 8b) contrasts with arrogant trust in wealth (v. 7c). Instead of boasting about self, the psalmist boasts about God, giving praise for blessings bestowed on the faithful.

Theological and Ethical Analysis

Few things are more discouraging to believers in a just God than to see the prosperity and good reputation of those who use their power for selfish ends. Such people do what they wish; they set the standards; and their tongues slash any who oppose them. It often happens that speaking up for the poor and for the gospel brings down the scorn of the mighty. This psalm was written for people overwhelmed by the power of such enemies.

In using this prayer, one must be cautious about painting oneself as a helpless victim and one's enemies as God's enemies. High position and influence are not bad in themselves, and can even be means of promoting the common good and furthering the cause of God. Prestige and power can easily go awry, however, with disastrous results for those committed to justice and peace. That is what has happened in the psalm. For the victims of the powerful wicked the psalm is a perfect prayer, full of passion for divine justice, full of childlike trust in God's care and ultimate triumph.

PSALM 53

Exegetical Analysis

This psalm categorizes human responses to God's governing the world as basically two: contemptuous dismissal of God's involvement with the world and loyal waiting for God's justice. The two dispositions are forever at enmity.

Psalm 53 is virtually the same as Ps 14, and the reader is referred to the commentary there. Despite the similarities, Ps 53 is distinctive and worthy of comment on its own terms. Psalm 14 described the arrogant thinking and exploitative actions of "fools," and how the just and active God scrutinizes them and finds them guilty. They deserve the name "fools" because they do not understand the nature of reality (Ps 14:4). Judgment is coming when they will learn the just God is on the side of the righteous and the poor.

Psalm 53:5, a verse that is not in Ps 14, lends Ps 53 a special tone: Visible and shameful judgment will be visited upon the wicked after they have been killed. The judgment of sinners will be so thorough that their bones will be scattered to the four winds, and they will be deprived of proper burial. A battlefield covered with the unburied bones of the slain, bleached by the sun, was an image of total defeat and hopelessness. The Assyrian annals of Shalmaneser III report enemy skulls erected into pillars and enemy corpses scattered over the battlefield. Jeremiah 8:1-2 predicts the bones of false officials, priests, and prophets will be disinterred and scattered "like dung on the surface of the ground." Other severe judgments are Ps 141:7, "Like a rock that one breaks apart and shatters on the land, so shall [the wicked's] bones be strewn at the mouth of Sheol"; Ezek 6:5, "I will lay the corpses of the people of Israel in front of their idols; and I will scatter your bones around your altars." In the Bible, the ultimate end of a reality provides its evaluation. The scattered bones of the wicked show how God evaluates their lives.

PSALM 54

Literary Analysis

Psalm 54 is an individual lament. It consists of a dialogue between the pray-er and God that is based on the conviction stated in verse 4, "God is my helper." All the components of the genre are here: the petition (vv. 1-2), the complaint (v. 3), the statement of trust (vv. 4-5), and the promise of thanksgiving by an offering and praise (vv. 6-7). The psalmist makes no claim of innocence, which other psalms of the genre sometimes make.

The structure is simple: "your name" in verses 1 and 6 frames the poem; "God" occurs three times in the first part (vv. 1-3, *'ĕlōhîm*) and three times in the second part (vv. 4-7) though in three different names: "God" (v. 4*a*, *'ĕlōhîm*), "the Lord" (v. 4*b*, *'ădōnāi*) and "LORD" (v. 6*b*, *YHWH*). The structure is otherwise determined by the well-known conventions of the genre, that is, the petition (vv. 1-2) is followed immediately by the complaint, introduced by the word *for* (v. 3*a*), which is then followed by the statement of trust (vv. 4-5) and the promise of thanks (vv. 6-7).

There are some indications that the king is the speaker. The absence of an assertion of innocence suggests the king, whose claim upon God would have rested on the dynastic promise rather than on personal innocence. The enemies, according to verse 3*a* of the Masoretic Text, are "foreigners" (which NRSV and other translators emend to "insolent"). Needless to say, if the original singer were the king, the poem is usable by all members of the community, because the king represents Israel.

Exegetical Analysis

Petition and complaint: Save me, for enemies attack (vv. 1-3).

The superscription refers to the incident recounted in 1 Sam 23:15-29, when the fugitive David hid in Ziph, and residents of Ziph reported his whereabouts to Saul. Scribes may have made the connection between the psalm and the Samuel passage because the phrase "seek his life" occurs both in 1 Sam 23:15 and Ps 54:3*b*.

"Name" (vv. 1*a*, 6*b*) is that which "presents" a person to others; the name of a god displays an aspect of the god's power to the one who invokes it. "Name" in this psalm is particularly forceful; it is parallel with "might" (v. 1, uniquely in this sense) and frames the entire poem. To those who invoke it, the name is a pledge of help on the way. The psalmist wants to be vindicated, that is, shown to be in the right in a conflict with foes. God is the judge in such conflicts. The loser will be ashamed in the sense of being publicly shown to be in the wrong.

As noted, NRSV and other translators emend the Masoretic Text, "strangers, foreigners" (v. 3*a*, *zārîm*) to "insolent" *(zēdîm)* on the basis of several Hebrew manuscripts, the targum (the later translation into Aramaic), and the parallel passage in Ps 86:14. Copyists sometimes confused the two words because the letters *d* and *r* are virtually indistinguishable in some scripts. It is difficult to judge which word was original. The similar Hebrew nouns *zārîm* and *zēdîm* both occur in parallelism with "ruthless" *('ārîṣîm*, v. 3*b*). *'Ārîṣîm* and *zēdîm* are parallel in Ps 86:14 ("the insolent" and "ruffians") and Isa 13:11*cd* (NRSV: "the arrogant" and "insolence"). *'Ārîṣîm* and *zārîm* are parallel in Isa 25:5 and 29:5. Though both readings are possible, the Masoretic Text "foreigners" is more likely. If that reading is correct, it would be likely that the king is the speaker.

COMMENTARY

God is here to help me and I will give thanks! (vv. 4-7)

"But surely" is a strong statement of trust, suggesting that "God is right here to help, and I am fortunate enough to count God as my powerful friend" (v. 4). The psalmist's confidence is underlined by the dual occurrence of divine names in verse 4 ("God" and "the Lord") and by the reversing of the phrase "enemies seek my life" (v. 3*b*) in the phrase "God upholds my life" (v. 4*b*). Verse 5*a* describes poetic justice in that the evil intended for the other comes back upon the head of the evildoer. There are many examples of poetic justice in the Psalter, for example, Pss 7:16 and 12:3. Biblical scholars sometimes term the phenomenon the "deed-consequence connection," which is a satisfactory term as long as one does not mean by it automatic causality. It is better to say that such consequences are "typical" rather than inevitable. Life will remain unpredictable for humans, which is why verse 5 is a prayer rather than a plain statement of fact. The request in verse 5*b* ("put an end to them") seems brutal, but it simply parallels verse 5*a*, which asked that "their evil" (their attempt to seek the psalmist's life, v. 3*b*) be turned back on their heads. "Since they tried to kill me, kill them!" Verse 5*b* is virtually the same as Ps 143:12. Psalmists made use of a common stock of expressions.

The perspective is theocentric; the final verses assume that God will act in a certain sense from self-interest, that is, for the sake of the voluntary "freewill" offering that will be made and the praise to be given (v. 6). The promise is made as if the rescue had already happened. In effect, the promise is a vow.

Theological and Ethical Analysis

The psalm exhibits earnest zeal for the triumph of justice, which makes it both admirable and a bit unsettling. The singer comes to God beset by truly dangerous enemies whose intent is murder. If the psalm is royal, the fate of the nation hangs in the balance, as well as the life of the king. The singer wants justice right now. The upholding of the psalmist will consist in the removal of the enemy. Rescue will be the verdict on the rightness of the psalmist's cause. Retribution is left in the hands of God; the psalmist relies completely on the Name to bring about justice. As so often is the case, the individual lament restates an individual's suffering in terms of the reign of the just God. One sometimes hears the assurance from a friend, "Please use my name when you meet so and so." This psalm has similar confidence in the divine Name. The Name is the supreme source of help in danger.

PSALM 55

Literary Analysis

The poem is notable for its poignant wish to flee from trouble ("O that I had wings like a dove!" v. 6), its sorrowful accusation against a former friend ("It is not enemies who taunt. . . . But it is you, my equal . . . with whom I kept pleasant company," vv. 12-14), and, unfortunately, its difficult logic. Some interpreters have expressed the opinion that verses 18b-23 were mistakenly inserted at the end of verses 1-18a; their reasoning has rightly not been accepted by other scholars. Jewish tradition has found unity in the poem by correlating it closely to Ahithophel's betrayal of his friend David and the latter's flight from Jerusalem during Absalom's rebellion (2 Samuel 13–19). It will be shown below that there is a structural unity to the poem, even though unanswered questions and several uncertain lines remain.

The genre of the psalm is that of individual lament. It opens with an urgent cry for divine help (vv. 1-2b, 16-17), vividly complains of inner anguish (vv. 3-5) and threats of enemies (vv. 9-11) especially of former friends (vv. 12-14, 20-21), and prays for the punishment of the enemies (vv. 9, 15) while maintaining a lively hope for justice (vv. 16-19; 22-23). As in other laments, the threat is left unspecified so that almost any sufferer can enter into its sentiments. Certain concrete details do occur: The psalmist finds the city dangerous because of calumny (implied in "confound their speech" in v. 9) and yearns for the security of the wilderness where there are no people; special danger comes from a former friend (vv. 12-14, 20-21) who abused their intimacy for the purposes of betrayal. Such details should not hinder later pray-ers from making the sentiments of this psalm their own.

The logic of the psalm is not visible at first reading and requires comment. Hebrew words in verses 1-3 ("O God" and "bring trouble [mût]") are echoed in the concluding verses 22 and 23 ("be moved [mût]" and "O God"). This inclusio signals that the psalm is concluded. Structurally, the psalm falls into two parts, verses 1-15 and 16-23. The first and last lines of part 2 (vv. 16 and 23) both begin with the independent personal pronoun ("I" and "you") followed by the divine name 'elōhîm. Most important, the beginning and concluding verses in Hebrew in parts 1 and 2 have been made parallel to each other.

Beginning of part 1: verses 1-3		Beginning of part 2: verse 17	
"Give ear"	A	"I utter my complaint" (hāmāh)	C'
"in my complaint (śîḥ)	B	"moan" (śîḥ)	B'
"I am distraught" (hāmāh)	C	"he will hear"	A'

Conclusion of part 1: verses 12-15		Conclusion of part 2: verses 20-23	
false friend	A	false friend	A'
descent into Sheol	B	descent into pit	B'
"alive" (in prime of life)	C	"not live out half their days" (i.e., in prime of life)	C'

The poem possesses a dramatic movement. Part 1 opens with a plea to be heard (vv. 1-2a), describes emotional pain that can only be relieved by flight (vv. 2b-8), and depicts the oppression of the city, as well as the betrayal of a friend (vv. 9-15). Part 2 strikes out in a more positive direction, for God will rescue the psalmist and punish the enemies.

Exegetical Analysis

Emotional distress, flight, oppression in the city
by a former friend (vv. 1-15)

Laments often open with a request that God pay attention to the prayer, and so here in the opening tricolon (vv. 1-2*a*, contrary to NRSV division). Several words will be reprised in the beginning of part 2, as noted in the outline above. The description of the psalmist's emotions in verses 2*b*-5 is unusually detailed. The word NRSV translates as "troubled" is, literally, "to wander about" in an agitated way, which seems to be a symptom of severe depression. Similar symptoms are described in Job 30:28; Pss 35:14; 42:9. In terrible pain and near collapse, the psalmist can only envision flight to the wilderness, that is, far from the city and its violence (vv. 6-8). In part 2, the sufferer will be able to imagine a more creative solution: waiting for God to come to the city to establish justice. The process in the psalm goes from anguish and despair to courage and hope.

Verse 9 marks the halfway point in part 1, the shift being signaled by the command in the imperative mood, "confuse." The city here is imagined as a place where evil has a home, is "in its midst" (vv. 10*b*, 11*a*, 15*c*, all with *qereb*). In a series of striking personifications, the poet portrays "violence and strife" walking about the city, patrolling its walls, never leaving the plazas. No wonder the sufferer thinks the wilderness more hospitable than the city. The citizens of the wicked city are not the ones who inflict the most damage, however, but an individual, a once loved friend whose hostile words are hardest to bear (vv. 12-14). So pervasive and rampant is the malice of the city and the former friend that only death can adequately deal with it (v. 15).

God will redeem me and punish my enemies.
Cast your troubles on the Lord (vv. 16-23)

The phrase "but I" (v. 16) often denotes a contrast between the present and preceding sections of a psalm and between the psalmist and evildoers (e.g., Pss 5:7; 13:5; 31:14). Here the evildoers are the inhabitants of the wicked city and "you," the ex-friend (v. 13*a*). The psalmist turns to God afresh, and the result is an enlivened attitude and a certainty of being heard, which differs considerably from the desperate and hesitating request of the opening verse. "Battle" in verse 18 suggests to some commentators that the issue is national rather than personal and that the singer is the king. Though the suggestion is plausible, it cannot be demonstrated. In any case, the sentiments are perfectly suitable for a private person.

Verses 20-21 most probably refer to the enemy mentioned in verses 12-14, though the Hebrew of verse 20 is obscure. The psalmist again reminds God of the great scandal of the perfidious friend. Verse 22 is the singer's transformed response to the scandal. The words can be interpreted either as the psalmist's faith statement, a kind of "self talk" (like Pss 42:5, 11; 43:5), or as an oracle of salvation given by a liturgical officiant, which the psalmist accepts as the word of God. As noted in the introduction, oracles of salvation are normally not transmitted in the individual laments. The final verse, reprising the final verse of part 1 (v. 15), wishes death upon the enemies. In both cases, the wish is for a *premature* death that will advertise to all that it is God who has cut them down, not ordinary mortality. The psalmist wants justice to be seen by all.

Theological and Ethical Analysis

There is something strangely modern in a poem that begins with a depiction of the self shattered by injustice in the form of a corrupt city and false friend and ends with that same self calm and hopeful, having gone through a process of healing. The language for the emotions in verses 4-8 displays serious pathology in the form of agitation and depression. The psalmist grasps at straws, such as flight to the wilderness that might provide one kind of safety, only to bring threats from a hostile environment. The root cause for the distress is only revealed in verses 9-14 as a corrupt and oppressive society and a friend who has turned into a betrayer. Without social support, it is no wonder that the psalmist has slipped into desperation. When part 1 ends, the process is not finished. Only in part 2 is the business brought to a proper conclusion.

At first reading, the psalm seems exaggerated, the product of a highly rhetorical culture. Though the emotional temperature is high, the feelings are universal. The poem hides nothing from God out of the conviction that one's inner and outer life belong wholly to God. It invites people to initiate their prayer by expressing their anxieties, hurts, and disenchantment and bringing them before God. The prayer is not interested merely in airing such feelings, however, but in being guided to new levels of hope and action. Despite the call for divine vengeance, the psalm leaves the execution to God. It maintains, however, a passion for justice and for personal healing.

PSALM 56

Literary Analysis

Psalm 56 is an individual lament, displaying the customary components of the genre: petition plus complaint (vv. 1-2, 5-7), statements of trust and hope (vv. 3-4, 8-11), and promise of praise (vv. 12-13). Noteworthy are the large number of lines allotted to assertions of trust and promises of thanksgiving offerings (vv. 2c-4, 8-13) and the vivid image of God's caring, a bottle for tears (v. 8).

The structure of the poem is largely determined by its two refrains, verses 3-4 and verses 10-11. There are eighteen Hebrew words before its first occurrence (vv. 1-2) and eighteen Hebrew words after its second occurrence (vv. 12-13). The verses in between divide neatly into verses 5-7 (complaint plus petition) and verses 8-9 (statement of hope).

Exegetical Analysis

In the superscription "The Dove on Far-off Terebinths" is probably the name of a melody. The historical reference is to

1 Sam 21:11-15, when the Philistines seized David in the city of Gath. The references in the poem to the multitude of enemies and their enduring hostility may account for the scribes' choice of the Samuel passage.

Petition plus complaint (vv. 1-2b)

A single verb of petition is followed by an extended complaint. In verses 5-7, the sequence is reversed: An extended complaint is followed by a brief petition. The verb "to trample" is unusually vivid; basically it means to breathe heavily (as in Isa 42:14); in a specialized sense it is "to hasten toward" (Eccl 1:5) and "to rush at with hostile intent" as here. The psalmist's enemies are multiple, as shown by the words "people," "enemies," and "many" in verses 1-2, and the attacks are constant ("all day long"). The sufferer makes only one petition, "be gracious to me," evidently believing that God's merciful regard is enough to guarantee safety. "God" in verse 1 is the first of its nine occurrences in the poem; "the LORD" (v. 10b) and "Most High" (v. 2c) each occur once. The large number of divine names shows the strong bond the psalmist feels toward God.

Refrain: I trust in you (vv. 2c-4)

The refrain is repeated in verses 10-11, but does not match its mate in every detail; biblical symmetry is not necessarily identical. The refrain itself is intricate, as can be seen even in translation: The words of verse 3a are reversed in verse 4b. There is also persistent alliteration of the Hebrew consonant aleph. The tight connection of verses 3a and 4b throws into relief the distinct final colon, "What can flesh do to me?" "Flesh" is a biblical expression for human beings on their own, without divine help to aid them. The rhetorical question adds a note of defiance.

An ancient exegetical tradition, represented in Jerome's Psalms from the Hebrew (fourth century) and Ibn Ezra (twelfth century), takes the Hebrew word mārôm, "elevated site; heaven," as a divine name, "Most High." The interpretation is accepted by NRSV, REB, NJPS, and NAB, though it should be pointed out that a number of scholars reject it. Arguments in support of the translation "Most High" are that the usual meaning "elevated site" does not make sense in the context and that the Hebrew word *mārôm* can mean "heaven," a surrogate for the divine name.

Complaint plus petition (vv. 5-7)

Reversing the order of verses 1-2, the complaint is followed by the petition (v. 7). "All day long" (v. 5*a*) picks up the same phrase from verse 2, emphasizing the unrelenting nature of the attacks. The rest of the complaint develops the hostility hinted at in the opening verses—"their thoughts are against me," "they lurk," "they hoped to have my life." The enmity against the psalmist is organized and focused. The term for enemies, "the peoples" (v. 7*b*), suggests that the singer is the king praying for help against the nations arrayed against Israel.

Statement of trust: You note my sufferings and so I trust (vv. 8-9)

Verse 8 is one of the most memorable images in the entire Psalter: God keeps count of "my tossings," putting "my tears in your bottle," as a shepherd keeps track of his animals by putting pebbles in a bag. There is an obvious play on words, "my tossings" *(nōdî)* and "your bottle" *(nō'd)*, giving the statement a proverbial feel. NRSV "tossings" (buffetings) is rendered by others as "wanderings" (forced dislocation).

Verse 9 logically follows verse 8: Because you know so well my suffering on your behalf (v. 8), you will defeat my enemies and show that you are my God (v. 9). The reasoning is like David's when he bore patiently the curses of Shimei in 2 Sam 16:12, "It may be that the LORD will look on my distress, and the LORD will repay me with good for this cursing of me today." The psalmist knows the value of suffering patiently borne.

Refrain: I trust in you (vv. 10-11)

Like the first refrain (vv. 3-4), the two cola of verse 10 are tightly linked in sound and sense, giving emphasis to the final colon, "What can a mere mortal do to me?" Despite the incessant and vicious attacks, the singer is defiant.

Promise of offerings in the Temple (vv. 12-13)

Like Ps 54:6-7 and other psalms, the singer promises to fulfill vows that were uttered in anticipation of a rescue. The promise is both a motive for God to act and, even more, an expression of love for God; one simply must give praise. The repeated mention of the name of God and the certitude that God has recorded every suffering make it clear that the promise is a genuine prayer, not mere bargaining. The best clue to the meaning of the phrase "light of life" (v. 13d) is the nearly identical phrase in Ps 116:9, "I walk before the LORD in the land of the living," where "land of the living" (better, "land of life") refers to the Temple. Buttressing the argument that the occurrence of the phrase in Ps 56:13d refers to the Temple is the phrase "before God" in verse 13c, since it can mean "in the sanctuary," as in Ps 96:6. The singer longs for the security of the Temple after being beset by enemies for so long a time. To be saved is to be brought into God's presence in the Temple.

Theological and Ethical Analysis

The poem is remarkable in that long-term and highly personal attacks have not diminished the psalmist's affectionate and personal relation to God. Complaint flows into petition (vv. 1-2, 5-7), and in the refrains fear is transformed into trust. It is the refrains that give the poem its structure and tone. Other laments show the sufferer on the ropes, spent and despairing. This lament shows a sufferer who knows the importance of endurance and is able to maintain poise and orientation. The poem helps one to recognize how important each person is to God even when God seems absent. The psalmist seems to have no doubt of God's passionate commitment and ability to rescue.

PSALM 57

Literary Analysis

Psalm 57 is an individual lament, which ends with an extraordinary confession of confidence (vv. 7-11). Especially memorable are its metaphors of "the shadow of your wings" and of waking the dawn with musical praise (vv. 1c, 7-8).

In structure, a refrain in verses 5 and 11 divides the poem into two virtually equal parts: verses 1-5 (41 Hebrew words) and 6-11 (38 Hebrew words). Another set of verses near these refrains also link the two parts, for the hoped-for sending of "steadfast love" and "faithfulness" (v. 3c) is answered by a praise of those virtues in verse 10; the set of verses states the question: Can God's love and fidelity in heaven protect the psalmist on earth?

It must be noted that some scholars have doubted that the psalm was originally unified. For them, verses 7-11 were appended later, for it occurs also in Ps 108:1-5. They note that the lyrical tone of Ps 57:7-11 differs sharply from the anguished lament in verses 1-6, and that there are differences in vocabulary in the two parts. For example, in verses 1-6, "my soul" occurs three times to designate the self (vv. 1, 4 [NRSV: "I"]; v. 6), whereas in verses 7-11 "my heart" (v. 7) and "my honor" mean the self (v. 8a, NRSV: "my soul"). Such differences do not, however, prove lack of unity, for liturgical poetry reuses traditional material, and terminology need not be uniform. Psalms 57 and 108 have their own emphases. In the case of Ps 57, it is anticipated triumph.

Exegetical Analysis

The superscription refers to David's flight from Saul, which is told in 1 Sam 22–24. First Samuel 24 has verbal and thematic similarities to Ps 57: David cuts off "a corner (*kanap*, 1 Sam 24:4) of Saul's cloak," which is the word for "wings" in Ps 57:1; David ends up being blessed by his persecutor (cf. Ps 57:7-11). The meaning of the term *miktam* is unknown; it is applied to six psalms, 16, 56–60; the latter forming a group linked in words and themes.

I take refuge in the shadow of your wings. Send forth your steadfast love (vv. 1-5)

Twice in verse 1 the psalmist asks God to "be merciful." Repetition of words is a feature of the poem, especially of the first part; "take refuge," "will send," "my soul," "heaven(s)," "steadfast love," "faithfulness," "my heart is steadfast" are all repeated. Repetition adds intensity and reenforces unity.

The references to "refuge" and "in the shadow of your wings" (v. 1c) lead some scholars to believe that the situation in life is a troubled individual seeking asylum in the Temple like Adonijah in 1 Kgs 1:49-53 and Joab in 1 Kgs 2:28-35. The phrase "your wings" would refer to the wings of the cherubim (animal guardians) protecting the throne of God in the Holy of Holies (1 Kgs 6:27; 8:6). Good arguments against this assumption exist, however. The wings of the cherubim are not the wings of Yahweh; the cherubim carry the throne, they do not represent Yahweh. Ancient representations of animal throne-guardians show them shielding their clients with their paws rather than their wings. It is more likely that the image is a bird hovering protectingly over its nestlings, keeping predators away by the rapid fluttering of its wings. This image of divine protection is apt: The god's arms stretch, winglike, over a client. In Egypt, the wing motif was part of the iconography of solar deities or the sun itself; the winged sun represented the sun's daily course across the heavens, repelling evil by its light and bestowing life. As solar elements were not prominent in Yahwistic religion, the psalm image is rather that of God providing protection like a mother bird (see Deut 32:10-12).

The danger from which God shelters the psalmist is associated with the night (v. 4), when the psalmist lies down to sleep. It is at night that lions look for food (see Ps 104:20-23). Night can symbolize danger and human vulnerability. To lie down in trust that God will protect one in the night is a great thing (Pss 3:5-6; 4:8). The metaphor system of night and danger is in the background all the way to verse 8c where the singer calls forth the sun with its danger-dispelling rays, "I will awake the dawn."

A second metaphor for divine protection is used in verse 3. The verb "to send forth" occurs twice, first in verse 3a (without an object) and second in verse 3c with the objects "steadfast love" and "faithfulness." These are, so to speak, messengers sent from the divine throne to protect the psalmist. Similarly, two messengers appear in Ps 43:3ab, "O send out your light and your truth; let them lead me." Beyond the inherent danger of night, danger is depicted in two further metaphors: wild animals and war. The lion has spears and arrows for teeth and a sword for its tongue. The tongue-sword defames others as it does in Ps 64:3 and Prov 12:18.

The refrain in verse 5 is an appeal to the divine character: Establish justice by rescuing me so that heaven and earth will recognize you as Most High. Such actions show forth God's grandeur and glory.

I eagerly await the dawn of your justice (vv. 6-11)

The second part of the psalm, like the first, begins by speaking of danger metaphorically. The metaphor here is that of an animal trap. The trap was a net stretched taut to catch an animal's foot. Once entangled, the animal was easy prey for waiting hunters. Another type of trap consisted of a pit hidden by leaves or lattice work into which an animal would fall. A linguistic problem is presented in verse 6b, "my soul was bowed down," for it is not parallel to verse 6a. Falling into the pit one has dug to trap others is a common metaphor for divine retribution (e.g., Ps 141:10; Prov 1:18-19; Eccl 10:8). The psalmist believes firmly that God's justice will be done.

The final section (vv. 7-11) is unexpected in a lament because of its robust confidence. Convinced that the trap set by enemies is sure to be thwarted (v. 6), the psalmist cries out to God, "My heart is steadfast," that is, I am undaunted, and decides to sing now the thanksgiving that less bold spirits sing *after* their rescue. It is night, when wild animals are about (v. 4). Too impatient to wait passively for the dawn, the psalmist orchestrates a musical performance to speed the morning light (vv. 7-8). Not content to sing only to those nearby, the singer wants to be heard by the whole world (v. 9). As verse 3 prayed that "steadfast love" and "faithfulness" be sent from heavens as guides on earth, so verse 10 acknowledges their effectiveness and omnipresence. The second occurrence of the refrain (v. 11) is both a prayer and an expression of triumph.

Theological and Ethical Analysis

Like the preceding psalm, this one manages to express hope in the midst of danger. Psalm 57 is exceptional for its boldness, however. Its ardor and enthusiasm are palpable in spite of the dangers. The sufferer finds God even amid the violence and predatory instincts of others. It is night; the hunt is on; war is being waged, but the sufferer's imagination has been transformed by faith. Powerful guides named Steadfast Love and Faithfulness have been sent, and rescue is sure. Other psalms vividly portray the destruction of feeling and resolve that attacks often bring. This poem shows the resolution and audacity that opposition can unleash.

In few psalms is such a keen awareness of threat juxtaposed to a keen sense of God's power and grandeur. The psalmist does not desire only personal rescue but the triumphant appearance of the Lord.

PSALM 58

Literary Analysis

The psalm has the same superscription as Pss 57 and 59 but without any reference to an incident in David's life. Like them, it is an individual psalm of lament, though it is unusual in its rhetoric. Jewish tradition relates the phrase in the superscription, "Do not destroy," to David's refusal to "destroy" Saul on the grounds that he was the anointed of the Lord (1 Sam 26:9; cf. 1 Sam 24:6). "Do not destroy" is possibly the title of the melody of the psalm. The psalm divides into three parts. The complaint in verses 1-5 is framed as a judgment against unjust gods and their human agents. The psalmist's petition is contained in verses 6-9, which use a variety of metaphors for the hoped-for punishment—broken teeth, water disappearing into the dry ground, grass trodden down, a snail that dissolves, and a premature, stillborn baby. The statement of trust in verses 10-11 expresses hope for a world that is definitively and directly ruled by the just God, where there are no longer evil powers and their human minions.

Exegetical Analysis

Judgment Against the Gods (vv. 1-5)

The meaning of verses 1-2 is debated. In verse 1, does "you gods" refer to high-ranking earthly beings (as in 2 Kgs 24:15 and Ezek 17:13) or to the heavenly beings who were thought to govern the human race (as in Pss 29 and 82)? This commentary follows the latter interpretation. In the passages in which "gods" refers to human beings, context makes a metaphorical meaning unmistakable; there is no such context here. Used alone, the word must refer to gods. Moreover, this interpretation comports with the ancient conception, found even in some biblical passages, that every nation is governed by a particular deity. Israel's particular deity is Yahweh, who is also the "Most High" over all other deities. Deuteronomy 32:8-9 concisely expresses the belief: "When the Most High apportioned the nations, / when he divided humankind, / he fixed the boundaries of the peoples / according to the number of the gods; / the LORD's own portion was his people, / Jacob his allotted share."

As is now widely recognized by scholars, Israel came only gradually to monotheism in the modern sense of the term. There was a stage in which the existence of other divine beings was taken for granted though it was believed that Yahweh was the absolute head of the pantheon. An example of this view in the Psalter is the command in Ps 29:1 to worship Yahweh as the supreme God: "Ascribe to the LORD, O heavenly beings [lit. "sons of gods/god"], / ascribe to the LORD glory and strength." Psalm 82 goes a step further and declares the other gods dethroned for failing to fulfill their responsibilities of ruling the world justly, and decrees for them mortality like human beings. Unlike Pss 29 and 82, the words of Ps 58:1-2 are not uttered in heaven but by a human being on earth concerning the malfeasance of these so-called gods.

The reference to gods here is an instance of the homology of heavenly and earthly realities taken for granted in the culture. There was a correspondence between heavenly and earthly institutions, for example, earthly temples and rituals imitated heavenly palaces and their ceremonies, just as statues imitated the gods and made them present to worshipers on earth. Heavenly beings influenced earthly affairs through various mediators. See, for example, Judg 5:19-20, "The kings came, they fought. . . . The stars fought from heaven." Similarly, the visions of Daniel 7–12 draw parallel scenarios of nations on earth and their angelic patrons. In the New Testament, powers and principalities are said to influence the conduct of human beings (e.g., Eph 6:12; Col 1:16). Here the psalmist boldly stands up to the wicked on earth and their heavenly patrons, echoing perhaps the divine judgment against them uttered in Ps 82:2, "How long will you [gods] judge unjustly?" The psalmist's question presumes that heavenly powers "judged" (that is, ruled) incompetently by allowing evil to run rampant on earth and that they should be unmasked as malicious frauds. The verbs of Ps 58:2 even suggest the heavenly beings encourage human sin: "devise" and "deal out" suggest aiding and abetting human wrongdoing.

The scene is a cosmic trial like Ps 82 and, in much adapted form, like Isa 40:12-31; 41:1–42:9 and other passages. God is imagined as summoning the entire universe, heavenly and earthly, to judgment. Judgment here has the biblical connotation of bringing about justice as well as declaring someone guilty or innocent. God will actually put down the wicked and uphold the righteous. The origin of the biblical scene may have been mythic stories of the exaltation of the Storm God after his victory over chaotic forces. Unlike Ps 82 and the Isaiah passages, however, Ps 58 has transposed the scene to an earthly plane: A human speaker judges the earthly agents of the heavenly patrons and looks to the Lord to carry out the sentence.

Evidence for the negative assessment of the gods is presented in verses 3-5. The so-called gods whose duty was to supervise divine justice on earth never corrected the wicked on earth. "From their birth" wicked people were allowed to do whatever they wanted (v. 3). Poison is at the core of their being and they pour it forth at will, confident that no one will challenge them (vv. 4-5).

The petition that God directly intervene (vv. 6-9)

Living in a universe that seems corrupt and dangerous, the psalmist cries out to the God who rules that universe, echoing the sentiments of Abraham's prayer in Gen 18:25: "Shall not the Judge of all the earth do what is just?" The appeal is to the divine character. How can you allow anyone, in heaven or earth, to stand in the way of your just rule? The plea to smash their teeth is found also in Ps 3:7 and is part of the metaphor system of lions for enemies (though some believe it refers to the fangs of the serpents in the previous verse). It is possible that the smashing of teeth in verse 6 refers primarily to the angelic rulers, and the gradual decline and decay in verses 7-9 refers to their human agents, that is, when God finishes off the heavenly patrons of evil, their human agents collapse.

The general sense of verses 7-9 is clear enough—may the wicked lose their strength and disappear—but textual corruption and rare words make the verses (except vv. 7a and 8b) all but untranslatable. Comparison of fleeting human life to water in verse 7 is found in Ps 22:14 and 2 Sam 14:14, "We must all die; we are like water spilled on the ground, which cannot be gathered up." NRSV emends verse 7*b* because the Masoretic Text is corrupt (lit. "Let [God] aim his arrow that they may languish [be cut down?]"). Verse 8 provides two images of decline and decay—the snail that was thought to leave behind its own substance in a slimy trail, and the semi-formed or decomposed stillborn fetus. Verse 9 is unintelligible; literally the text reads, "before your pots can understand the thorn, like alive like wrath, may he sweep them away." NAB's emendation is bold but better than most: "Suddenly, like brambles or thistles, / have the whirlwind snatch them away."

The hope of the righteous (vv. 10-11)

The hope of the pray-er is a bloody one: The vindicated righteous person will shout in joy when the wicked are punished. The shocking image of washing in blood recalls the fate of the blood-filled chariot of the slain King Ahab in 1 Kgs 22:38: "They washed the chariot by the pool of Samaria; the dogs licked up his blood, and the prostitutes washed themselves in it, according to the word of the LORD that he had spoken." The violent, that is, sudden and unexpected, death of the wicked is itself the sign of divine intervention and becomes the occasion for the proclamation that virtuous conduct is rewarded and that the Just One lives. When justice is done on earth in the sense that the wicked are being thwarted and the righteous prospering, people acknowledge that the Lord lives.

Theological and Ethical Analysis

The prayer blazes with indignation and with zeal for the coming of God's reign. Unlike other personal laments, it does not cite immediate and particular distress as the reason for praying. Instead, what brings this psalmist to prayer is the enormous gap between people's belief in a just and supreme God and their experience of evil triumphant. The pray-er recognizes that evil is not simply discrete acts of malice but something large and systemic and prays for the system to be destroyed. Only the one God with universal power, Yahweh the God of Israel, can accomplish it. One gets the sense that the poet is disturbed intellectually as well as emotionally at the injustice that seems to prevail in the world. How is it possible that evil succeed if God is all-powerful and good? The questions plague the psalmist and inform this prayer.

The passion of prayer expresses itself in dramatic either-or statements: People fall into two neat groups, righteous and sinners, and each group is rewarded or punished in dramatic fashion. One prays for the unhindered reign of God, while recognizing that it is God's reign and not our own that is to come. One can hope that the enemies of God's justice be publicly unmasked so that God's friends can rejoice, but one has to recognize that such vindication takes place through agencies and timetables chosen by God.

Few psalms in the Psalter are so aware of the systemic nature of evil, its deep roots, and its stubborn persistence. The nature of evil is mysterious and can only be expressed in metaphors. The psalm expresses the anguish of living in an evil age. More significantly, it voices the plea for justice and hopes for the triumph of grace over wickedness.

PSALM 59

Literary Analysis

Though usually classed as an individual lament, Ps 59 is as much concerned with attacks on Israel and "the city" (vv. 6, 14) as it is with personal danger. The enemies are "all the nations" (vv. 5, 8). Similarly in verse 8 the Lord laughs and holds all the nations "in derision," as in the royal Ps 2:4, "He who sits in the heavens *laughs;* the LORD has them *in derision*" (identical words in italics). Furthermore, the singer hopes God's punishment will be "known to the ends of the earth" (v. 13). The singer in verse 11*a* speaks of "my people" as the king does in 1 Sam 15:30; 1 Kgs

22:4; 1 Chron 29:14. For these reasons, it is best to view the psalm as a communal lament uttered by the king or in his name. The poem is divided into two parts (vv. 1-10, 11-17) by refrains in verses 9 and 17. Each refrain concludes a section consisting of petition-complaint-(anticipated) thanksgiving. Like Ps 55, the psalm leads pray-ers twice through the same process. The second displays a calmer and more confident attitude than the first. Thus, petition (vv. 1-5); complaint (vv. 6-7); refrain: expression of trust (vv. 8-10); petition (vv. 11-13); complaint (vv. 14-15); refrain: expression of trust (vv. 16-17).

There are many repetitions in the poem, for example, "deliver" in verses 1*a* and 2*a*; "evil" in verses 2 and 5; "sin" in verses 3 and 12; the root *śgb* in the verb *śāgab* ("deliver," v. 1) and in the noun *miśgab* ("fortress," vv. 9, 16, 17). The refrains (vv. 9 and 17) are also repetitions. Moreover, the complaint in verses 6-7 is repeated in verses 14-15. The repetitions add intensity and provide structure.

Exegetical Analysis

For the technical terms in the superscription, see the introduction. The allusion is to 1 Sam 19:11-17 when Saul sent messengers to David's house to kill him; David's escape before dawn provides a context for Ps 59:16*b*, "I will sing aloud of your steadfast love in the morning."

Petition: Deliver me from my enemies who attack without cause. Rouse yourself (vv. 1-5)

The epithets for the enemies in verses 1-3*b* are too conventional to permit precise identification. The enemies lay an ambush, a verb that can be applied either to personal attack (Ps 10:8) or to war (Judg 9:34; 16:2; Lam 4:19). The denial of "transgression," "sin," and "fault" in verses 3*c*-4*a* can be interpreted either as declarations of personal innocence (as in Ps 26:1 and 73:13) or as the king's declaration he has done nothing to provoke an invasion by foreign nations.

The metaphor of waking the deity in verses 4*b*-5 may surprise modern readers: God is imagined as a sleeping warrior needing to be awakened by a frightened client-people. The same figure is used in Pss 44:23; 78:65; 121:4; and Isa 51:9. The singer's descriptions of God are appropriate for the present crisis: God of hosts (i.e., the heavenly armies) and God of Israel, that is, the God who has made a covenantal commitment to the people.

Complaint: The enemies surround the city
like hungry dogs (vv. 6-7)

The complaint is closely linked to the immediately preceding petition (vv. 4*b*-5), for "the dogs" are "the nations" and the plotters of evil. In the Bible, dogs are generally regarded as base creatures (1 Sam 17:43), lapping up the blood of the slain (1 Kgs 21:19)—apt symbols of enemies (e.g., Ps 22:16 and Isa 56:10-11). Isaiah 56:9-12 depicts foreign invaders as wild animals and Israelite defenders as useless watchdogs who prefer to sleep rather than bark and wake the populace. In Ps 59:6-7, the dogs symbolize the invaders prowling outside the walls of the city. Neither in this refrain or the next (vv. 14-15) do they attack; they only howl and bellow with tongues like swords (cf. Ps 64:3), thinking, "Who will hear us?" Like the comparable expressions in Isa 29:15, "Who sees us? Who knows us?" the rhetorical question presumes God will not or cannot stand up to human arrogance. One is reminded of the attacks on Zion depicted in Pss 2, 46, and 48. The divine response to such attacks in Ps 2:4 ("He who sits in the heavens laughs; the Lord has them in derision") is particularly close in vocabulary to Ps 59:8. Though scholars differ on whether Ps 59 contains an implicit reference to Zion, the likelihood is that it does.

Refrain: expression of trust (vv. 8-10)

"But you" in verse 8*a* signals a shift in tone from fear and anger to anticipated triumph as the psalmist reflects that God rules *all* the nations and that this God is "*my*" strength and fortress (v. 9). "Fortress" in verse 9 is the first of three occurrences of the term. The refrain in verse 9 will be repeated in verse 17 with the significant change "I will sing praises to you" (v. 17) for "I will watch for you" (v. 9), that is, a movement from expectation to celebration.

Petition: Consume my enemies and show the nations your universal rule (vv. 11-13)

The petition in verses 1-5 asked only for rescue, and the petition in verses 11-13 asks for the destruction of the enemies so that the nations might see the justice of God. There is movement from concern for personal safety alone to concern for the sovereignty of God. Verse 11*a*, "Do not *('al)* kill them" seems to contradict verse 13*b*, "consume them until they are no more." Aware of the problem, some scholars and NAB propose reading the adverb of negation in *'al* ("not," in the Masoretic Text) as *'ēl* ("God"). All the ancient versions and most modern interpreters, however, rightly accept the Masoretic Text. The singer's request that God *not* kill the attacking army all at once is apparently made in awareness that Israel will never be free of attackers. Israel must learn that it will always be under attack yet ultimately saved by a God who is ever a shield protecting them. NRSV's translation "make them totter" in verse 11*b* is interpreted by NJPS and REB as "make wanderers of them," which is the meaning of the verb in Num 32:13 and 2 Sam 15:20. The second interpretation presumes that the enemy, repulsed in its attack on the city, will survive so that its defeated condition will advertise to the nations the sovereignty of the Lord (v. 13*cd*). The reason for their punishment, according to verse 12, is their arrogant words. The enemy had thought, "Who will hear us?" (v. 7*c*), that is, nobody will ever contest our arrogant words against the city.

As noted, verse 13*ab* (kill them!) is in tension with verse 11*a* (spare them!), though many commentators pass over the problem in silence. H. J. Kraus takes verses 11-13 as a sequence of actions: Do not kill the enemies immediately (so their punishment will be visible), scatter them, and (finally) annihilate them completely. Perhaps the best solution is to suppose that "consume" refers to the malicious impulses of verse 12.

Complaint: The enemies surround the city like hungry dogs (vv. 14-15)

The complaint again uses the metaphors of war and savage animals. The army surrounds the walls of the city of God and is compared to a pack of wild dogs, sleeping during the day and rising up to scavenge and feed at night. They are outside the city walls and are heard by the citizens within. Their barking is incessant and bothersome but ultimately harmless to those within the "fortress," that is, the walled city.

Refrain: expression of trust (vv. 16-17)

"But I" marks a transition in the poem from anxiety to hope and proleptic thanksgiving like the transition marked by "but you" in verse 8. The psalmist looks forward to dawn when the rising sun will chase away night, symbol of chaos and the absence of God. The "mighty" (*'azîm*, v. 3) strove against me, says the psalmist, but I "sing of your might" (*'uzz*, v. 16*a*). The psalmist calls God, "my strength" (*'uzz*, vv. 9 and 17). "Fortress," which occurs in verses 16 and 17 for the second and third time in the poem, occurs also in two Zion songs, Pss 46:7, 11 (NRSV: "refuge") and 48:3 (NRSV: "defense"). The refrain in verse 17 makes a significant change from the refrain in verse 9: "I will sing praises to you" instead of "I will watch for you." The change is an important clue to the development of the psalm, for verses 11-17 depict the same process as verses 1-10, though with more hope that justice will be done.

Theological and Ethical Analysis

The poem is notable for its sustained metaphors of evil (armies surrounding a walled city and dogs scavenging around the walls at night) and metaphors of security (a walled city and a God who is "my strength" and "my fortress"). The Bible itself contains horrific accounts of sieges including starvation, famine, and cannibalism. They were everyone's worst nightmare, and the psalmist prays to be delivered from them. Though the city is most probably Jerusalem, the poet leaves it unnamed, thereby making it an apt symbol for any beleaguered community.

The doubled structure of the poem leads the sufferer twice through the same process in order to change attitudes from a simple desire for personal rescue to a passion for justice, hope, and eagerness to sing praise. The emotions awakened by the psalm are powerful and, it must be added, potentially dangerous as well, for the desire to see one's enemies punished and God's glory established easily leads to oneself taking on the role of judge and executioner. The psalmist is passionate and zealous but is careful to allow God to be the judge.

PSALM 60

Literary Analysis

The poem is a community lament over the defeat of Israel's army (v. 10*b*) and encroachment upon Israel's borders (vv. 6-8), which harms land (v. 2) and people (v. 3). Invasions inevitably destroy crops and wipe out domestic animals, which were the bases of Israel's economy as an advanced agrarian society. Community laments usually cite the divine act that established the order that is now threatened. Such citations remind God of the *lèse majesté* ("loss of majesty" or royal dignity) that would result if an enemy were to succeed in ruining that order. The divine act cited in the psalm takes the form of an oracle declaring that God is the owner of the land of Israel (vv. 6-8). The implication is that the land is for the use of God's special people, Israel. For the enemy to destroy or capture it seems to invalidate God's original grant. The areas listed in the oracle in verses 6-8 appear to be the boundaries of the old Davidic Empire. Some of the territory was lost to the Israelites in the period after David. The psalmist asks God to live up to the venerable promise. The oracle is also used in Ps 108:6-13.

The poem has three parts, each roughly of the same length:

verses 1-5; 6-8; and 9-12. The phrase "O God, you have rejected us" appears both in verses 1 and 10 as a refrain uniting the first and third parts. The oracle is the centerpiece of the poem.

Exegetical Analysis

Complaint and petition (vv. 1-5)

The superscription (probably secondary) attempts to provide a historical context for the psalm. The struggles with Aram-naharaim (a region in the eastern part of modern Syria, meaning Aramaeans) and Aram-zobah (an Aramaean city-state) are told in 2 Sam 8:3-8 and 10:6-13. Joab was David's general, and the story is told in 2 Sam 8:13-16.

The complaint is that God has abandoned the people to their enemies. Metaphors from warfare ("broken our defenses," cf. 2 Kgs 14:13) and natural disasters are used. Though "quake" occurs mostly in theophanies where God's thunder shakes the earth, it here refers to an earthquake as a metaphor for war's devastation, as in Jer 4:24. The once-solid ground is rent with huge fissures. The ground of Israel's being is shaken by invasion. Verse 3*b* accuses God of forcing the people to drink wine that made them reel. The wine symbolizes the intent of the master who forces underlings to drink it to the bitter dregs (Ps 75:8; Isa 51:17, 22; Zech 12:2). Psalm 75:8 is particularly illustrative: "For in the hand of the LORD there is a cup / with foaming wine, well mixed; / he will pour a draught from it, / and all the wicked of the earth / shall drain it down to the dregs." Verse 4 is uncertain. The verb is in the perfect tense (NRSV: "you have set up") but is most likely a "precative perfect," that is, one expressing a prayer. If the text is sound, it must mean something like "Please set up a banner for those loyal to you, so they rally around it out of range."

The ancient oracle (vv. 6-8)

Community laments typically cited an ancient divine act or word in virtue of which they could demand that God act now.

Though the warrant in most laments is a primordial deed establishing the present order, in this case it is a promise God made "in the sanctuary" (v. 6a).

The oracle seems to have been originally spoken at a moment of military triumph, for "exultation" in passages such as 2 Sam 1:20 and Ps 149:5 occurs in a context of victory. The oracle not only asserts total ownership of the land but also its distribution to the people ("I will divide up," "portion out," v. 6). As noted, the place names suggest border areas of the Davidic Empire. According to 2 Sam 8, in the north, the Aramaic states Damascus, Hamath, and Zobah paid tribute. In the east and southeast, David subjected Ammon, Moab, and Edom. In the southwest, he defeated the Philistines. The Aramaic city-states are not mentioned in the poem. Shechem is a city forty-one miles north of Jerusalem, lying in the heart of Israel in the key pass between Mounts Ebal and Gerizim. It was important in the old tribal confederacy and the northern kingdom (Josh 24; Judg 9:22-25; 1 Kgs 12:1). Though the precise location of the "Vale of Succoth" is unknown, it is in middle or northern Transjordan where the tribal holdings of Gilead and Manasseh are also located. Ephraim and Judah represent respectively the northern and southern kingdoms. The oracle moves from northern to southern Transjordan place names. Moab is east of the Dead Sea, between the Arnon and Zered rivers, and Edom lies south of it, on the eastern side of the Arabah. Philistia, homeland of the Philistines, is a twelve to fifteen-mile swath of land extending from Joppa south toward Egypt.

The Divine Warrior is victorious and does what every victor does: apportion out the conquered territory to loyal troops (v. 6). Ownership and dominion are implied in every phrase, from "divide up" (v. 6b) to "I shout in triumph" (v. 8c). "Hurl my shoe" may refer to the legal gesture of claiming ownership attested in Ruth 4:7, "Now this was the custom in former times in Israel concerning redeeming and exchanging: to confirm a transaction, the one took off a sandal and gave it to the other." Given the contemptuous tone of the claim of Moab in the immediately preceding phrase, "hurl my shoe" may simply be a boast rather than a legal gesture.

Complaint and petition (vv. 9-12)

"Who will bring me" is an implicit prayer, O that I might be led! The verbs "bring" and "lead" refer to Yahweh leading the people in Ps 77:20 ("led") and Jer 31:9 ("lead"); the context suggests leading in war. The speaker, perhaps the king as commander of the army, expresses the wish that Yahweh lead the army to conquer the nation of Edom. The next verse ("Have you not rejected us, O God?") is a reprise of verse 1 and shows the present state of wrath. God's wrath means withdrawal: no going out with the army, no victory. The last two verses make clear Israel has learned an important lesson through bitter experience: Human help is worthless. The final petition comes from suffering and is full of feeling.

Theological and Ethical Analysis

Though the original context of the poem is located in very specific historical circumstances—an oracle of the Divine Warrior supporting the army's defense of the land—every member of the holy people can pray it. The drama is timeless. The community knows that its God has made a promise to protect it from enemies, and it recites the well-known promise to prove it. Yet the community has seen the triumph of their enemies as if the promise meant nothing. It would be easy for the people to conclude the promise has had its day, like other human words, and devise other means of self-defense. The psalm does not take that route. Instead, it pressures God to act by citing the ancient promise. It protests against the people's apathy and God's passivity, holding up to God the gap between divine promise and present reality.

Living between promise and fulfillment is the situation of believers of every age, not just the original pray-ers of this psalm. The time in between can be long indeed with no sign being given that the promise will ever be honored. Those who rise from their own apathy and do not let God off the hook can pray this psalm, which asks that God defend their gift from encroaching enemies.

Psalm 61

Literary Analysis

The psalm is an individual lament that complains of being far from God's dwelling ("from the end of the earth") and expresses longing to be led to the Temple. Danger from enemies is mentioned only once and conventionally (v. 3*b*); the real anguish is separation from God and the holy community. "Rock," "refuge," "tower," "tent," and "wings" (vv. 2-4) refer to the Temple and its precincts. Similar ardent longing is found in Pss 27, 42–43, 63, and 84. Portraying God as hearing vows (v. 5*a*) and the psalmist as fulfilling them (v. 8*b*) is a concrete way of describing the mutual relationship of deity and devotee. Praying for the long life of the king (vv. 6-7) is equivalently praying for the prosperity of the community, for the king is its representative before God and among the nations.

Considerable difference of opinion exists about the structure of the poem. Some scholars propose sections consisting of verses 1-4 and 5-8, whereas others propose verses 1-2, 3-4, 5, 8 (vv. 6-7 are judged an addition). The genre, too, is disputed. Some have seen here a memorial of an answered prayer, whereas most scholars rightly take it as an individual lament with an elaborated statement of trust (vv. 3, 8). It is true that the psalm can be variously outlined. The most satisfactory structure is to divide the psalm between verses 1-4 and 5-8, marked by the rubric "selah" in verse 4. The first verse of each section (vv. 1 and 5) contains "hear/heard" and "O God." Part 1 is wholly concerned with arriving at the longed-for sanctuary; part 2 is rather concerned with the present and future relationship with God in the sanctuary. Furthermore, part 2 is framed by the repetition of "vows" and "your name" in the first and last verses (vv. 5, 8).

Exegetical Analysis

Lead me to your Temple (vv. 1-4)

"From the end of the earth" means a remote place, as in Deut 28:49; Isa 5:26; 43:6; the psalmist feels far from the center. The psalmist follows the ancient practice of praying toward Jerusalem (1 Kgs 8:35; Dan 6:10). Though "lead me to the rock" is corrected by some scholars to "place me on the rock" (cf. Ps 27:5), it is clear that the distant pray-er wants to be guided along the right route to the Temple, as in Ps 43:3, "O send out your light and your truth; / let them lead me; / let them bring me to your holy hill / and to your dwelling." As in Psalms 42–43 and 63, the psalmist feels far from God and longs for the Temple, which is symbolized by the "tent," a traditional term for the Temple (2 Sam 6:17; Pss 15:1; 27:5-6), and "the shelter of your wings" (Ps 91:1, 4). "Wings" can refer to the wings of the cherubim guardians of the Ark in the Holy of Holies as in 1 Kgs 8:7, "For the cherubim spread out their wings over the place of the ark, so that the cherubim made a covering above the ark and its poles" (cf. 1 Kgs 6:27; 2 Chron 3:11; 5:8; Ps 36:7). The wings of the cherubim are not necessarily identical with "[the Lord's] wings," however, for the cherubim's task is to guard and carry the throne rather than represent the Lord. "Your wings" can be a metaphor for God as a bird protecting its nestlings by fluttering its wings (see comment on Ps 57:1; Deut 32:10-11; Isa 31:5). Because of the Temple imagery this interpretation seems less likely. "Rock," a common metaphor for God, is associated with the tent in Ps 27:5, "For he will hide me in his shelter / in the day of trouble; / he will conceal me under the cover of his tent; / he will set me high on a rock." "Refuge" can also refer to the Temple, as in Pss 46:1 and 91:1-2.

The use of the perfect tense of the verb "to be" in verse 3 is better translated "you have *been* my refuge" (so REB and NJPS) rather than NRSV's "you are my refuge." The translation is important. The psalmist has chosen the Lord as a personal God. That choice means two things: (1) The psalmist wants to go to the Lord's own shrine and take part in its rituals; (2) the psalmist expects to be protected and blessed by this God even outside the sacred precincts. That protection, which the psalmist has experienced and desires to experience again, only deepens the desire for the special place of divine presence and disclosure.

*You, who are my God, give life to the king
of your people (vv. 5-8)*

"You [God] have heard my vows" (v. *5a*) is a unique phrase in
the Bible. It is often interpreted as hearing the prayer uttered in
verse 1, but that is unlikely, for a vow is not a prayer. Moreover,
vows is plural and *prayer* in verse 1 is singular. The phrase rather
means that God has entered into an agreement with the psalmist
like that with Jacob's vow in Gen 28:20-22: "If God will be with
me, and will keep me in this way that I go, and will give me bread
to eat and clothing to wear, so that I come again to my father's
house in peace, then the Lord shall be my God, and this stone,
which I have set up for a pillar, shall be God's house; and of all that
you give me I will surely give one tenth to you." God "heard," that
is, accepted, Jacob's vow by guiding him safely home; Jacob for his
part fulfilled the vow by giving honor to Yahweh by erecting a pil-
lar-house and paying a tithe. It is likely that the psalmist's vow, like
Jacob's, is concerned with his safe return to the sanctuary.

The verbs in verse 5 are in the perfect tense, which normally
designates a past action. In this case, however, the perfect tense
has one of its less common meanings—the precative or "prayer"
use: "hear my vows" and "give me the heritage." This interpretation is suggested by the mention of "heritage" in the parallel verse
in *5b.* "Heritage" refers to the land (e.g., Deut 2:5, 9, 19). The
verse states that the psalmist hopes to share the land with fellow
Israelites. Though the Hebrew word for "heritage" is sometimes
corrected to a nearly identical word for "wish, plea" (so REB,
NAB, NJPS), NRSV rightly retains the Masoretic Text.

The request of part 2 (v. 7), that the king live long and his reign
be permanent, may strike modern readers as odd in a psalm that
has been concerned up to this point with the desire to reach the
sanctuary. The king here represents the people, and their prosperity was bound up with his. His long life not only means political
stability and cultural continuity but is itself a sign of the fertility
that only God can grant. Prayers for the long life of the king were
in any case part of royal protocol in the ancient Near East (e.g.,
1 Sam 10:24; 1 Kgs 1:31; 2 Kgs 11:12; Neh 2:3). God's "stead-

fast love and faithfulness" are personified as a pair of servants sent from the heavens to guard the king, as in Ps 43:3, "O send out your light and your truth; / let them lead me; / let them bring me to your holy hill / and to your dwelling." In the final line, references to singing praises and paying vows sum up the pious duties of a worshiper of God.

Theological and Ethical Analysis

The psalmist speaks from a place far from the Temple and the holy community. Even in separation, it is possible to declare that "you have been my refuge and strong tower." It is the mix of experiencing God in a remote place yet knowing God is present in a particular place that gives the poem its special urgency and drama.

The poem describes the drama of life, which is a search for the place where God is especially present and discloses God's self. God is not present in the world in an undifferentiated way, like a gas that fills space, but rather is found in particular moments and in particular places. The poem shows us a pray-er who builds on the experiences of God as a refuge and a strong tower and relies on these special moments and experiences to hope for a time of arriving at the shrine where Israel gathers to worship and rejoice.

Saint Augustine gives a christological reading of the poem:

> The praying person who cries from the ends of the earth is therefore wrung with pain, but not deserted. Christ willed to prefigure us, who are his body, in that body of his in which he died and rose again, and ascended into heaven, so that where the head has gone in advance, the members may confidently expect to follow him. (Boulding 2000, 194)

PSALM 62

Literary Analysis

The poem is a song of trust uttered by someone beset by powerful and influential enemies. The sufferer focuses outward as well as inward, for there are two kinds of statements in the psalm. One is an exhortation to the self (vv. 1-2, 5-7), the other a rebuke to enemies (vv. 3-4) and an exhortation to the community (vv. 8-10). The inner dialogue shows the vulnerability of a believer caught in an unjust world. As John Calvin observes in his commentary on the Psalms, "David felt an inward struggle and opposition, which he found it necessary to check; Satan had raised a tumult in his affections" (Calvin 1999, 146). The psalmist's faith is "in process," going from inner dialogue (vv. 1-2) to denouncing the unjust (vv. 3-4) to teaching the uninstructed (vv. 8-10) to praying to God (vv. 11-12). The psalmist is not content simply to unmask the attackers but seeks a change in their hearts.

The structure is established by both form and content. The Hebrew particle *'ak* is the first word in verses 1, 2, 4, 5, 6, 9, which NRSV variously renders as "alone," "only," and "but." The particle *'ak* can affirm ("truly, surely, yes") or restrict ("only, alone"); it can qualify an entire sentence or a single word. NRSV and most translators prefer the restrictive sense. In this psalm, each verse of the refrains in verses 1-2 and 5-6 begin with *'ak*. The entire opening refrain recurs, with but slight variation, in verses 5-6. The three parts of the psalm are verses 1-4, 5-10, and 11-12. The word "God" appears seven times in the poem.

Exegetical Analysis

I hope in God alone as I stand up to my enemies (vv. 1-4)

The root meaning of "waits" (v. 1) is "to be silent," which suggests that the sense is "to be resigned, inactive" in the face of threats when expecting help from God. The images of "Rock" and "fortress" (v. 2) are often used of God as support and defense of the people. "Rock" is the protection against attackers afforded by the heights of massive rock formations. "Salvation" is specific: deliverance from the threatening enemies right now.

Instead of speaking *about* the enemies, the psalmist in verse 3 speaks *to* them as if they were standing there. This poetic device adds vividness as in Pss 2:10-11; 4:2; 11:1; 14:6; 75:4-7. The victim of the enemies is described metaphorically as "a leaning wall" (v. 3c), an effective symbol of imminent collapse (see also Isa 30:13). As verse 4 indicates, the malice of the evildoers is hidden; their "plan" is destruction of others, their pleasure is in "falsehood." No one is aware of their real selves, for their courtesy is a mask. "Bless" in verse 4c can mean "to greet" as well as "bless." The psalmist, who has been their victim, strips away their polite facade with powerful and courageous words.

I hope in God alone as I witness to the community (vv. 5-10)

The repetition of the refrain, with an additional verse (v. 7), suggests the psalmist is still struggling, feeling both trust and fear. Even the most robust psyche would be confused and disheartened by enemies intent on murder. The earlier assertion, "I shall never be shaken" (v. 2b), was not a final report, but a statement of hope.

In verse 8, the psalmist addresses a new group, "O people!" Instructing others in the way of the Lord is a common response in the psalms, especially in thanksgivings where the rescued person seeks to increase the circle of God's admirers, out of gratitude as in Ps 40:10: "I have not hidden your saving help within my heart, / I have spoken of your faithfulness and your salvation; / I have not concealed your steadfast love and your faithfulness / from the great congregation." The situation in Ps 62 is different, however. The psalmist evidently fears that the unchecked intimidation by the wicked will lure others to their path. In complete opposition to their arrogance is the psalmist's own style of absolute trust in God. The actions proposed in verse 8—trusting, pouring out one's heart, making God a refuge—is what the psalmist has been practicing. The positive exhortation to "trust [bāṭaḥ] in him" (v. 8a) will be repeated in negative fashion in verse 10a, "put no confidence [bāṭaḥ] in extortion."

The translation of the parallel phrases in verse 9, "low estate" and "high estate," reflect a common scholarly assumption. NRSV and most translators distinguish běnê-ʾādām (lit. "sons/members of humankind") and běnê-ʾîš (lit. "sons/members of man") as referring, respectively, to common people and the upper class. This interpretation relies on a similar use in Ps 49:2. Other scholars regard the phrases as synonymous (e.g., NJPS: "men," "mortals"). In each interpretation, the verse declares all human beings a breath *(hebel)* that is so insubstantial as to rise when weighed in a balance. "Breath" is a favorite word in Ecclesiastes, where it was traditionally translated as "vanity" in the phrase "Vanity of vanities! All is vanity" (Eccl 1:2*b*).

The transition to the reflection on the vanity of humans in verse 9 and the warning against unjust wealth in verse 10 may seem abrupt to modern readers. The reasoning is elliptical and needs to be spelled out. The choice for the psalmist is not between relying or not relying on God for protection, but between relying on God or relying on *something else* for protection. The "something else" in this case is human strength and the wealth it amasses. Thus the psalmist in verse 8 urges hearers positively to "trust in [God]" and in verses 9-10 urges them negatively not to trust in human beings or in their wealth. The acquisition of the wealth is characterized as "extortion" and "robbery" (v. 10), which seems to allude to the attackers in verses 3-4. Similar denunciations of reliance on powerful human beings and their wealth is found in Psalm 49, Prov 10:2, 11:4, and Ecclesiastes. An apt commentary on Ps 62:10 is the taunt in Ps 52:7,

> "See the one who would not take
> refuge in God,
> but trusted in abundant riches,
> and sought refuge in wealth!"

The word of God the psalmist lives by (vv. 11-12)

Once, twice is an instance of parallelism of numbers, which is a common device in Semitic poetry. Amos 1:3 is a good example: "Thus says the LORD: / For three transgressions of Damascus, / and for four, I will not revoke the punishment" (see also Prov 6:16-19; 30:15). One should not add up the numbers literally. The fixed pair "power/might/strength" *('ōz)* and "steadfast love" (*ḥesed*) expresses the essence of God's relationship to Israel as in Ps 59:16, 17 ("But I will sing of your *might;* / I will sing aloud of your *steadfast love* in the morning") and Exod 15:13 ("In your *steadfast love* you led the people whom you redeemed; / you guided them by your *strength* to your holy abode"). In Ps 62, the psalmist acknowledges that the relationship is totally in the hands of God ("to God," "to you") and is confident in divine justice ("you repay").

Theological and Ethical Analysis

The moral hero is an ambiguous figure today, admired on the one hand for self-reliance and for standing up to powerful people, yet regarded with suspicion, on the other, for moral superiority and refusal to compromise. This psalmist is not that kind of moral hero. The inner struggle, the unashamed reliance on God rather than self, the willingness to speak to one's enemies, keep the pray-er human and humble. In a sense, the pray-er is strong by being "weak," evoking Paul's famous words: "God chose what is weak in the world to shame the strong; God chose what is low and despised in the world, things that are not, to reduce to nothing things that are, so that no one might boast in the presence of God" (1 Cor 1:27*b*-29).

PSALM 63

Literary Analysis

Psalm 63 expresses ardent longing to dwell safely in the Temple. Similar songs of longing for the Temple are Pss 27, 42–43, 61, and 84. The house of the deity offered safety from enemies and enhanced one's life. An example of safety from enemies is David's general Joab, who was pursued by enemies for having backed the wrong son of David. He "fled to the tent of the LORD and grasped the horns of the altar" (1 Kgs 2:28*b*). (Unfortunately,

Joab's enemies disregarded the sanctity of the place and struck him down.) The superscription attributes the poem to David when he hid from Saul in the Wilderness of Judah (1 Sam 23:14-15 and 24:1). The psalmist, however, desires not only protection from enemies (vv. 9-10) but also communion with God expressed in the metaphors of seeing, praising, and eating (vv. 2-5).

Though the broad context is clear, the psalm has elicited diverse analyses. Hermann Gunkel (1929, 266-67) believed the sequence of verses had been disturbed and rearranged them in what he considered their original order: 1-2, 6-8, 4-5, 3, 9-11. The threefold stanza arrangement of NRSV, commonly but by no means universally held, presumes the psalmist is already in the sanctuary ("I have looked upon you in the sanctuary," v. 2a). This interpretation does not, however, cohere with other psalms of longing in which being in the shrine lies in the future as a hope. NRSV also does not satisfactorily explain the expression "to pray upon one's bed," which in its other occurrences in Pss 4:4; 36:4; 149:5; and Hos 7:14 designates a private attitude *in contrast* to public performance of ritual.

Two key interpretative questions must therefore be answered before one can interpret the psalm as a whole: (1) Is "looking upon you" in verse 2 a future hope (NJPS: "I shall behold You in the sanctuary") or a statement that one is already in the Temple (NRSV and most translators)? (2) What is the meaning of the phrase "when I think of you on my bed" in verse 6, and does it begin a new section?

Regarding the first question, in other psalms of longing for the Temple such as Pss 27:4-6; 42:2-3, 5, 11; and 84:1-2, visiting the shrine is a future hope. These parallels suggest that "looking upon the Lord" in the sanctuary in Ps 63:2 is also a future hope. Thus the Hebrew verb in the perfect tense, which NRSV renders "I have looked upon" should be rendered either as a precative (prayer) perfect, "O, that I might look upon," or a perfect of certainty (Gunkel, pp. 267-68), expressing a hope so strong it can be expressed as a present state. In either case, "I shall behold you" is the appropriate translation. An even more compelling case for translating the verb in the future tense is that the neighboring verbs in verses 3-5, "will praise," "will bless," "will lift up," are all in the imperfect tense expressing future time.

The other preliminary question is the meaning of "thinking of you upon my bed" in verse 6. Though NRSV is not alone in taking verse 6 as a subordinate clause in the sentence that begins in verse 5 (so also NJPS), others rightly take the verse as beginning a new section (REB). The first reason for taking verse 6 as beginning part 2 is the acrostic mechanism of *aleph-kaph* (the first and last letters of the first half of the Hebrew alphabet) in verses 1-5 and 6-7. Verse 1a begins with the letter *aleph* and verses 2c-5 begin with the letter *kaph*. Similarly, verse 5 begins with *aleph* and verse 6 begins with *kaph*. The repetition of letters signals a fresh beginning. The second reason for postulating a new section is the meaning of the phrase "thinking of [better: remembering] you upon my bed." It symbolizes spontaneous private conviction in contrast to commanded ritual performance. See, for example, Ps 4:4b-5a, "ponder it on your beds, and be silent. / Offer right sacrifices" (i.e., repent sincerely, then offer sacrifices) and Ps 149:5b, "Let them sing for joy on their couches" (in contrast to praising in the assembly of the faithful, v. 1). In the examples, remembering in private is contrasted with the same kind of public ritual mentioned in Ps 63:2-5. Verse 6 is a fresh start: "I call you to mind on my bed / and meditate on you in the night watches" (REB). Thus verses 6-8 describe a private sentiment like that of verse 1. Although both parts of the poem have the same starting point, private conviction (vv. 1 and 6), each develops it differently. Part 1 expresses the hope of being in the Temple; part 2 acknowledges God has always been the psalmist's God.

In summary, the poem has two rather than three parts: hope of "seeing" God in a sanctuary (vv. 1-5) and awareness that God is present even now (vv. 6-11). "God" occurs in the first and last verses of the poem; "my soul/life" occurs twice in the first part (vv. 1, 5) and twice in the second part (vv. 8, 9).

Exegetical Analysis

I long to see you in the Temple (vv. 1-5)

The comparison of desire to thirst is found in Ps 42:1-2 ("As a deer longs for flowing streams, / so my soul longs for you, O God. My soul thirsts for God, / for the living God. / When shall I come and behold / the face of God?"). See also Ps 143:6. "Soul" *(nepeš)* in its most basic meaning refers to the throat area where the vital signs (moisture, breathing, warmth) are especially visible. Thirst is experienced most acutely in the throat. Verse 2 shifts the metaphor from desire as thirst to enjoyment as looking. The metaphor of seeing God in a theophany is found in Exod 24:11, "God did not lay his hand on the chief men of the people of Israel; also they beheld God, and they ate and drank." Seeing is also implied in references to seeking God's face in 2 Chron 7:14; Pss 24:6; 27:8; Hos 5:15. The closest parallels to verse 2, however, are references in Pss 27:4 and 42:2 to seeing God in the Temple.

In Ps 63, looking is only one of several ways of experiencing God in the Temple; other ways mentioned in the poem are singing, using the divine name, and enjoying a repast. "Glory" (v. 2*b*) has an element of radiance and majesty not conveyed by English "glory," which commonly connotes that which elicits praise and honor. The glory of the Lord touched down on Mount Sinai in Exod 24:16; it filled the tabernacle in Exod 40:34 and the house of the Lord in 1 Kgs 8:11.

"Better than life" in Ps 63:3*a* is a unique phrase and not altogether clear. Context suggests that the psalmist states that enjoying God's love in the Temple is better than mere survival in the wilderness. Verses 3 and 4 are closely linked, so verse 3*b* could be considered parallel to verse 4*a*. "My soul" in verse 5 refers back to the thirsting throat ("soul") in verse 1, drawing part 1 to a close. To have one's longing for God satisfied is compared to having one's hunger and thirst satisfied; compare Ps 107:9, "For he satisfies the thirsty, / and the hungry he fills with good things."

I know you are my God, protecting me in danger (vv. 6-11)

As noted above, the phrase "when I think of you upon my bed" begins a new section. The verbs "think" and "meditate" are better rendered as "recite" or "remember," for they mean recalling, sometimes audibly, a specific act, not pondering or meditating. The verbs are so used in Ps 77:11. In Ps 63, the psalmist remembers "you" (v. 6*b*) who is specified in verses 7-8: you have been my saving God and I have been your loyal and responsive friend. The relationship is defined by reciprocal acts; God acts ("help," "upholds") and the psalmist responds ("sings," "clings"). The psalmist remembers the past divine acts that give assurance of God's present love and protection.

Divine assistance consists primarily in protection from enemies. The final section of the psalm (vv. 9-11) therefore prays that the psalmist's enemies die suddenly and prematurely. Their sudden death, which cannot be explained by "natural" causes, will send a clear signal that they were slain by God. The psalmists imagined evil concretely as embodied in particular people. The timetable and mode of destruction, however, is left entirely in the hands of God.

The mention of the king in the final verse can be interpreted in two ways. The entire psalm might have been recited by the king, perhaps as representative of the people or of the army on campaign. Or, the psalm might view the king, in typical ancient Near Eastern fashion, as the representative of divine justice who would be pleased by the destruction of evildoers.

Theological and Ethical Analysis

The Old Testament is realistic, recognizing the absence as well as the presence of God in the world. This confession celebrates the desire for God that can be as powerful as thirst for water. The poet is driven by a thirst for seeing God in the Temple, with all that implies about taking part in worship and feasting. The desire acts like a powerful magnet, drawing the psalmist ever forward.

The movement described in part 1, right down to the metaphor of eating in the holy place, is nicely caught in the hymn, "The God of Abraham Praise."

> The heavenly land I see, with peace and plenty blest;
> a land of sacred liberty, and endless rest.
> There milk and honey flow, and oil and wine abound,
> and trees of life forever grow with mercy crowned.
> (*The United Methodist Hymnal* [Nashville: The United Methodist Publishing House, 1999], hymn 116.)

Christians will see in the rich food offered in the sanctuary a symbol of both the preached word and the eucharistic bread of life, which answer the deepest thirst of the human soul. The reference to the watches of the night (v. 6) makes it a natural choice for morning prayer.

PSALM 64

Literary Analysis

Psalm 64 is an individual lament that asks God for protection from murderous and arrogant enemies and from the society that supports them. What distinguishes this lament from others is its outrage at the secrecy of the evil and its insistence that the conspiracy be unmasked, for the enemies assume no one can see them and bring them to justice. The pray-er asks for public vindication so all can see it and the righteous can rejoice in the actions of their just God.

The poem has two parts, verses 1-6 and 7-10. Part 1 contains the petition and complaint; part 2 is the statement of hope and exhortation to the righteous. Another division is possible: petition and complaint, verses 1-5 (40 Hebrew words); statement of hope and trust, verses 6-10 (39 Hebrew words). The reasons for adopting this division (vv. 1-5, 6-10) are two: (1) the nearly identical number of Hebrew words in each section, forty and thirty-nine; (2) the meaning and implication of the Hebrew verb in verse 6*a*, *ḥāpaś*, "to search out."

The translation of the verb *ḥāpaś* in REB, NAB, and many commentaries as "to think out, devise," unduly stretches the meaning of the Hebrew. The verb means rather "to scrutinize, pursue, investigate, bring to light," as in Prov 2:4; 20:27; and Lam 3:40. NRSV correctly recognizes the meaning of the verb, though it unfortunately adopts an unsupported emendation in verse 6*a*, "Who can search out our crimes?" A literal reading of verse 6*a* makes the best sense (though there are uncertainties in the rest of the verse): "they will search out the evil deeds, / the hidden plot [lit. "that which is to be searched for"] that they completed, / what lay deep within, buried in the heart." The opening verb, "They will search out," is an instance of the impersonal "they." The impersonal construction is a Hebrew way of describing divine activity; it is equivalent to "it will be searched out" or "one will search out." The psalmist is here expressing the confidence that secret schemes will be exposed.

An important feature of the rhetoric is the repetition in part 2 of key words from part 1: "arrows/arrow" in verses 3*b* and 7*a*; "tongues/tongue" in verses 3*a* and 8*a*; "suddenly" in verses 4*b* and 7*b*; "shoot" in verses 4*a*, 4*b*, and 7*a*; "fear" in verses 4*b* and 9*a*; "see" in verses 5*c* and 8*b*. In every instance, the second occurrence reverses the first; for example, God will "shoot arrows" at those who have shot arrows at the righteous; those who use their "tongues" to attack the righteous and declare God's indifference will be brought to ruin because of their tongue, that is, their words. The repetition underscores the hope that the evil of the enemies will be frustrated.

The psalmist appeals to the divine character by underscoring the enemy's attacks on the blameless and by quoting their boast that no one will ever punish them. If the world is ruled by a God who is just and wise, the "blameless" (v. 4*a*) should be able to count on divine protection. The boast that no one is in charge of the world is a direct attack upon God's justice and commitment. God must act for the sake of justice.

Exegetical Analysis

Petition and complaint (vv. 1-5)

The verb "hide" in verse 2*a* is from the same root *(str)* as "from ambush" (i.e., hidden places) in verse 4*a*. The complaint underscores the concealed malice of the wicked. The psalmist wants to be hidden from it. The wicked use calumny to destroy the psalmist. They wield their tongues like swords, their words are like arrows (v. 3). Their victim will lose standing in the community with consequent social and economic loss. To see how disastrous a fall from social prominence can be, see Job's description of his own downfall in Job 29–30. The evil the psalmist complains about may be broader, however: Society is hostile to virtue and loyalty to God. The boast "Who can see us?" in verse 5*c* is important in the psalmist's argument, for it is a reminder that some are calling into question God's capacity to rule the world justly, as in Isa 29:15, "Ha! You who hide a plan too deep for the Lord, / whose deeds are in the dark, / and who say, "Who sees us? Who knows us?" The bold question ends part 1, setting up an expectation for the hope expressed in part 2.

Statement of hope and trust (vv. 6-10)

As explained above, in verse 6 the psalmist expresses his or her firm hope in the form of a boast that matches the boast of the wicked: The secret schemes of the wicked will be tracked down and exposed to the light of day. Though the wicked boasted that no one sees them (v. 5*c*), their plans will be made public. Flushed from their "ambush" (v. 4*a*), God will "shoot his arrow at them." In the Bible, the adverb "suddenly" can often mean what is caused by unnatural causes and therefore "divinely" caused. As a public event, the ruin of the wicked functions as a judgment that upholds the aggrieved righteous person and puts down the wicked oppressors. Those watching the unexpected downfall of the wicked "shake with horror," that is, are struck with awe at witnessing a divine deed (v. 8). The phrase "then everyone will fear" (v. 9*a*) reverses verse 4*b* where the wicked shot their arrows without fear.

To tell others what God has done in this context is to make them understand that God acts justly, exactly the opposite of what the wicked said in verse 5, and what their actions implied. The last verse commands jubilation, for "to rejoice" connotes exterior expression as well as inner feeling. After God has acted, those who earlier doubted God's power to save can now "take refuge in him." Those who in the time of trial did not give in to apathy and did not lose their hope in God can rejoice and exult (NRSV: "glory"), for they have struggled and known anguish.

Theological and Ethical Analysis

Though experiencing profound pain from a hostile society and vicious personal attacks, the psalmist waits courageously for divine protection that has not yet arrived. The enemies' words are destroying the psalmist's world, eroding the respect and affection of neighbors. It is not one but many enemies who are engaged in the destruction, and they operate anonymously with a complete disregard for justice. Faced with such opposition, the psalmist's reaction could easily have been despair and collapse, for friends tend to depart when one is defamed. Instead, the psalmist holds steady. What is the reason for the steadiness? It is undaunted hope in a God who, though not yet acting, is just and an unfailing friend of the blameless. So the sufferer does not yield but fights back with the certainty of faith.

The psalm is particularly suitable for those who are the victims of hidden malice. The wicked operate in secrecy and the prayer of the psalmist is that they be exposed to public view and God's scrutiny.

PSALM 65

Literary Analysis

Scholars have variously classified Ps 65 as a hymn, a communal song of thanksgiving, and a communal lament. The different assessments arise largely from the different interpretations given to key verbs in verses 4c-5. The two verbs (NRSV: "we shall be satisfied," "you answer us") are in the imperfect tense. They can be read either as expressing a present or future action (so NRSV) or expressing a wish. If they are taken in the latter sense, the translation of verse 4c is, "May we be filled with the good things" (so REB, NAB, and NJPS), and the translation of verse 5a is, "Answer us with victory" (so NJPS). The Hebrew syntax of verse 4c suggests petition ("May we be filled with the good things") rather than statement; verse 5a is more ambiguous. It must be admitted, however, that the petitions, if they are such, do not seem urgent and suggest a ritual rather than a prayer of genuine distress. The interpretation adopted here is that the psalm is a communal thanksgiving, perhaps originally accompanying a ritual for harvest thanksgiving.

The festival that best matches the themes of the psalm is Tabernacles, which is also called Booths and Ingathering (sukkôth, Exod 23:16; 34:22; Deut 16:13-15). It is the third of the three annual pilgrim festivals and is celebrated in the early fall (late September or early October). The festival gives thanks for the harvest of the threshing floor and winepress and also commemorates the exodus in that the booths in which people live during the festival represent the tents in the wilderness. The feast is marked by intense joy; Jewish tradition calls it "the time of our rejoicing" (cf. Deut 16:15; Ps 65:8, 12-13). In the description of the feast in late sources, the Feast of Water-Drawing took place during the festival (b. Sukkah 53a; cf. Ps 65:9-11). According to these sources, one of the readings at the feast is Zech 14:16-19 in which verse 17 declares, "If any of the families of the earth do not go up to Jerusalem to worship the King, the LORD of hosts, there will be no rain upon them." Psalm 65:9-10 mention the river of God raining down upon earth. The festival is characterized by public rejoicing, giving thanks for life-giving water, and concern for the nations. All these concerns are found in Ps 65.

Exegetical Analysis

Jerusalem, the place for praise, vows, and the
forgiveness of sin (vv. 1-4)

The first two verses in Hebrew begin with "to you" (v. 1*ab*), which emphasizes the centrality of God and dependence of the people on the divine bounty. The point of verses 1-2 is that every act of obeisance—praise, vow, or pilgrimage—must have God as its object and the Temple on Mount Zion as its location or goal. Even the nations recognize that Zion is the dwelling of the God who created and sustains the whole world (vv. 5, 8). The Hebrew verb rendered "forgive" (v. 3) is rare in the Psalter (occurring only in Pss 78:38; 79:9) though common in priestly language; it means atonement through ritual. Similarly liturgical is the verb "bring near" (v. 4*a*), which indicates a divinely permitted approach to the sacred precincts; it is equivalent to forgiveness (cf. Exod 12:48; 40:32; Lev 16:1). The initiative to come near comes from God, not from human beings, because it is God who chooses and makes one "happy" (v. 4*a*). "Happy" means blessed or fortunate because of God's favor. As already noted, "we shall be satisfied" is best taken as a petition ("May we be filled with good things") rather than a statement. The community recognizes that creation order and bounty are to be found in the Temple and asks to share in it.

Enjoyment of the bounty of the creation victory
symbolized by the Temple (vv. 5-8)

"You answer us" means to respond favorably to prayers and rituals. Though it is possible to translate the verb *answer us* as a petition (contrary to NRSV), the meaning is ultimately the same: that God answers the community's prayers by deeds rather than by words. God answers by deeds in 1 Sam 7:10 (thunder), 1 Kgs 18:37-38 (fire); Hos 2:21-23 (Heb 2:23-25; fertility). "Awesome deeds" inspire wonder in those beholding them. In Ps 106:22, the deeds are the exodus miracles. The words "deliverance" and "salvation" in Ps 65:5*ab* refer to the creation victory described in verses 6-7. They occur as a fixed pair also in Isa 45:8 (NRSV: "righteousness" and "salvation") and 51:8. "Hope" in verse 5c has an objective sense—that in which one can put one's hope. In this case, it is God whose great deeds demonstrate supreme might. All the verbs in verses 6-7 are participles ("establishing," "silencing"), characteristic of the hymn genre, though they are often translated in the past tense, as here. The verses praise God as creator of the world who placed the vast mountains into their sockets (v. 6a; see Pss 89:12; 90:2). As often in the Bible, creation is conceived in mythological terms as a battle in which the Storm God repels Sea with the weapons of wind, rain, lightning, and thunder. The same sequence of actions and vocabulary is found in Ps 89:9-13: "sea," "waves," "you still them," "praise" (i.e., "shout for joy" in Ps 65:8b), "strong" (i.e., "might" in Ps 65:6b). This great victory strikes the peoples with awe and makes the world rejoice.

Celebration of the fertility provided by the rain that God gives (vv. 9-13)

The appearance of the Storm God to human beings in Canaanite and biblical literature is usually accompanied by thunder, lightning, wind, and by the rain that pours from the clouds scudding eastward from the Mediterranean Sea. Agricultural societies of the area depended on this rain, which fell in the period from late September to late May. In this section the poet concentrates exclusively on water and fertility as the precious gifts of God. A close parallel to the verses is Isa 30:23, 25, which promises the creative action of God: "He will give rain for the seed with which you sow the ground, and grain, the produce of the ground, which will be rich and plenteous. On that day your cattle will graze in broad pastures. . . . On every lofty mountain and every high hill there will be brooks running with water." In the psalm, the source of water is called "the river (or channel) of God," which is the ultimate source of the water reaching the earth in the form of rain. Genesis 2:6, 10 speaks of a river that rises from the vast subterranean waters; Ps 46:4 and Isa 33:21 envision a cosmic river in Zion. The "river of God" could be any one of these sources, or it may be a heavenly source that the God of storm delivers to earth in rain. At any rate, the water makes the grain grow (v. 9d) and softens the earth so seeds can sprout (v. 10).

Verse 11b has in view the cloud-chariot of God "who rides upon the clouds" (Ps 68:4; cf. Ps 68:33; Deut 33:26; Hab 3:8). The Ugaritic texts also call the Storm God "Rider of the clouds." Psalm 65:11b thus describes God's chariot of rainclouds pouring rain upon the earth as it courses through the skies. The "richness" (v. 11b, lit. "fatness") with which the tracks "overflow" is metonymy for water, the result (fatness) standing for the cause (water).

The final two verses (vv. 12-13) are a sustained metaphor: The earth, covered with ripe wheat and rich flocks, is compared to human beings, beautifully attired and singing joyous songs. The rain of God issues not only in abundant vegetative and animal life but in the joy and song of people made happy by the abundance of food.

Theological and Ethical Analysis

Though the origin of the psalm seems to have been a thanksgiving festival, the purpose of the poem now is to enable readers of other places and times to give thanks for the bounty of creation. The poem is a model of how to give thanks in a biblical way. It envisions God in a particular place where the community assembles and where the vast gulf separating human beings and God is overcome by divine initiative. In the psalm, God is an active being who convokes the assembly, takes away sin, and inspires the desire to be filled with the goodness of the Temple (vv. 1-5). The God who faces the community does not speak to them in words but addresses them through what their eyes see and their hands touch: the abundantly alive world from which they draw their very being (v. 5). The world is not static; it is dynamic and full of forces of which one, chaotic and anti-human, must be defeated and contained so that life can go on (vv. 6-7). Aware of this, people put their trust in God and stand amazed at the power they see (vv. 5, 8). The element that best expresses the subtlety and control of God is water (vv. 9-13). The poet is astonished at this means of fertility and life. Its source is God; it makes the wheat grow, softens the hard soil for the growth of vegetation, and supports the flocks and herds. The outlook is strangely modern, for the world is not the predictable clockwork of deism but the balance and control of multiple forces, reminding one almost of the perspective of particle physics. God acts everywhere enabling life and order to prevail, providing joy and color as well as food.

PSALM 66

Literary Analysis

Psalm 66 seems at first reading a strange blend of several genres: a hymn of praise in verses 1-4, a communal thanksgiving in verses 5-12, and an individual thanksgiving in verses 13-20. Gunkel views Ps 66 as a unified composition that moves in clear stages:

> The community offers praise for that which the individual members have experienced from YHWH's gracious help (66:1-12). As the choir becomes silent, an individual voice is raised to sing a thanksgiving song for the deliverance to which the choir's song alluded (66:13-20). The performance makes one consider how YHWH's goodness, which the community praises, is reconfirmed in every individual case. (Gunkel 1933, 316)

This analysis explains much if the speaker is the king. The psalmist's "I" in verses 13-19 would be compatible with the "we" of verses 5-12, for the king represents the people. In that case, the salvation that benefited the community in verses 8-12 would be the same as that mentioned in verses 13-20. Even apart from the question of the speaker, the psalm is a unity: The people regard themselves as given identity by the exodus, which continues to affect and define them in present crises.

The poem has five parts which are clearly marked off by their distinct themes as well as by the rubric "Selah": verses 1-4; 5-7; 8-12; 13-15; and 16-20. NRSV reflects the same division. The invitation to praise invites the entire world to praise God's "awesome deeds" and "great power" (vv. 1-4). Part 2 (vv. 5-7) asks the nations to view the works of God, chief of which is the exodus (v. 6). By bringing about the exodus, God has become sole ruler of the world. Both Israel ("we," v. 6c) and "the nations" (v. 7bc) are summoned to acknowledge that rule. Part 3 (vv. 8-12) repeats the invitation to praise God, but this time because of a contemporary saving event, which, however, is not specified. This new event has "kept us among the living" (v. 9) and brought us into "a spacious place" (v. 12c). God severely tested Israel, making them go "through fire and through water" (v. 12b), but the people have been brought through it safely. The psalmist links the contemporary crisis and rescue to the ancient paradigm. Both rescues, the exodus and its contemporary instantiation, reveal God as ruler of the world. For this reason, the nations are bidden to give praise. Part 4 (vv. 13-15) promises the payment of the vow that the psalmist (or the community) made in the period of danger. Part 5 (vv. 16-20) is the thanksgiving itself, for thanksgiving in the Bible is the proclamation of the story so that hearers can give praise to God.

Exegetical Analysis

Let the entire world give praise to God (vv. 1-4)

The entire world, not just Israel, must acknowledge the glory or preeminence of God, for the work of the God of Israel affects every nation. It establishes God's utter sovereignty, which entails the obeisance of everyone. The section is marked off by the repetition in verse 4 of words from verses 1-2: "all the earth" and "sing . . . his name."

See the work that made God ruler of the world (vv. 5-7)

The grand saving act of God in the Old Testament is the exodus. It can be described either in historical language, as in most of the book of Exodus, or in suprahistorical (cosmic) language, as often in Psalms and Isaiah 40–55. This psalm combines both perspectives, seeing the exodus both as founding Israel and as establishing the authority of God over the nations (v. 6ab).

Crossing the Red Sea stands for the whole exodus (the liberation from Pharaoh, the Sinai experience, the taking of the land). To have participated in that great event made Israel rejoice, for its God's grandeur appeared to all the nations (v. 7ab). Let none of the nations rebel against so powerful a God (v. 7c).

O peoples, bless our God who has again saved us (vv. 8-12)

The psalmist in this section is giving thanks for a *recent* rescue, not the exodus from Egypt that was mentioned in verses 5-7. The psalm praises God "who has kept us among the living," that is, enabled the psalmist's own generation to survive. The present rescue is considered a repetition or renewal of the classic rescue, the exodus, which the Bible often regards as the act of salvation. Like the original exodus, this saving act also establishes God's utter sovereignty over all peoples, which is why they are given the command, "Bless our God" (v. 8a). The text does not identify the national distress or the rescue. Though one tends to think of the sixth-century exile and restoration, almost any significant national setback and rescue might have been the original situation. At any rate, any communal tragedy could serve as the occasion for reciting it.

Because the psalm wishes to establish the sovereignty of Israel's God, it must explain why the chosen people were brought so close to extinction before help arrived. An ancient Near Eastern people would normally conclude that defeat meant its national god was overcome by the god(s) of the conquering nation. How could Israel's God have allowed such devastation? The psalmist's answer: God tested Israel to determine whether its heart was true (vv. 10-12). "Tested" normally means to discern the true situation, as Joseph did with his brothers in Gen 42:15-16. "Tried" can mean both discernment and purification, as in Prov 17:3; Isa 1:25; 48:10. Explaining the underlying goal of the testing is important for the psalm, and it devotes several lines to the task. "Spacious place" (v. 12c) is, literally, saturation with water, a good metaphor for prosperity in the context of an agricultural society.

I will offer thanksgiving sacrifices (vv. 13-15)

The psalmist shifts from first person plural to first person singular in declaring the intent to offer the animal sacrifices that were promised in the vow. Does the shift in grammatical number signify that the offerings will be made on behalf of the psalmist as an individual rather than on behalf of the people? The preceding passages about the sufferings and eventual triumph of the people (vv. 8-12) consistently used first person plural verb forms and the personal pronouns "we," "us," and "our." In view of the constant use of the first person singular pronoun "I" from verse 13 to the end of the poem, it is likely the psalmist made a personal vow in the national distress. The psalmist is fulfilling the vow because God saved the people (and the psalmist).

Vows are a transaction between God and a human being. In essence, the one who makes the vow says that if you, O God, bring me through this crisis, I will do something for you, such as make you my God, erect a house for you, or offer you sacrifices. For examples of other biblical vows, see Gen 28:20-22; Num 21:1-3; Judg 11:30; 1 Sam 1:11; 2 Sam 15:7-8.

I will tell the story of my rescue to others (vv. 16-20)

Ritual sacrifice of animals is not enough. The psalmist wishes to go further and enlarge the circle of God's admirers and worshipers. The narrative of rescue will let others know that God hears the prayers of clients and acts on their behalf. In ancient times, the "God question" was not the existence of the gods but their ability to benefit or "save" their worshipers. The psalmist declares from personal experience that the God of Israel is such a saving God.

How does one bless God? God can bless human beings by bestowing what they do not have—health, wealth, family, and reputation. God lacks only one thing, freely given worship by all peoples. This the psalmist attempts to supply by telling the story of God as the One who comes to the aid of human beings.

Theological and Ethical Analysis

The poem underscores the absolute freedom of God, who without hindrance turns the sea into dry land, makes the chosen people Israel go through fire and water, and then brings them to salvation. The effect of these acts is to establish God as the sole sovereign of the world, for there is no power that can hinder the sovereignty of God. In responding to the historical exodus and to the present act of salvation, the psalmist expresses both gratitude and the desire that all nations offer their obeisance and praise. The acts are the mighty acts of the one God, who is also God of Israel. The psalm is a blend of thanksgiving and invitation of the nations.

The poem insists that saving events of every age "renew" the great saving event of the exodus. That event created Israel, and every saving intervention since that time reaffirms the original creation. The psalmist is aware also of the link between individual and community. In few psalms is the psalmist more acutely conscious of participating in the community and its salvation. Christians regard the work of Jesus as a new exodus and can similarly regard the divine guidance of the church as deriving from that founding moment. When Christians pray verses 8-9, "[God] turned the sea into dry land," they know the power and effect of the act continues up to the present day.

Giving thanks is always a delicate task, especially when it is a benefit granted to the community. "Thank you" is not enough, and the psalm does not take that route. Instead, the psalmist fulfills a ritual, the vow, and more important, tells the story of God's saving work so that others throughout the world may join in the praise of the merciful God.

PSALM 67

Literary Analysis

Psalm 67 is a communal petition, asking God to bestow blessings on the nation Israel. It is not, however, a lament, as one might expect. There is no danger mentioned and thus no lament. Instead, one finds confidence in being chosen as a people, awareness that election requires gracious help, and desire that the nations see God as the bestower of Israel's prosperity. Israel is meant to be an icon of God's goodness for all the world to see. The poet's argument is thoroughly theocentric: It is God who stands to gain by blessing Israel because the nations will see its prosperity and celebrate such wise and generous governing.

The structure uses chiasm and repetition of themes: "May God . . . bless us" (v. 1); "Let the peoples praise you, O God" (v. 3); "Let the nations sing" because "you judge . . . with equity" (v. 4); "Let all the peoples praise you, O God" (v. 5); "May God . . . bless us" (v. 7). The psalm will be commented on according to the NRSV stanza divisions: verses 1-3, 4-5, 6-7.

Hebrew words for "nations" *('am, gôy, lĕ'ōm)* occur seven times. "Earth" occurs four times, which suggests universality, like the four rivers of Gen 2:10, the four beasts in Dan 7, and "the four quarters of the earth" that Mesopotamian kings boasted they ruled.

Translators differ on how to translate the verbs. Syntactically, all the verbs are in the imperfect tense in Hebrew except the verb "has yielded" in verse 6a. Verbs in the imperfect tense can be rendered as referring to events in the present or the future or as expressing a wish or prayer. NRSV, REB, NAB, and others translate the verbs in verses 1-5 as expressing a wish, and the verbs in verses 6-8 as descriptive. NJPS takes the verbs in verses 1-2 and 6-7 as prayers, and verses 3-5 as descriptive, stating what will happen if Israel receives blessings. The advantage of the NJPS interpretation is that it provides a motive for God to bless Israel: If Israel prospers, the nations will acknowledge the Lord's sovereignty. All the interpretations are syntactically possible. NJPS seems to make the most sense, however.

Exegetical Analysis

Favor your people that your salvation may be seen (vv. 1-2)

To "favor" is to show graciousness toward someone. To "bless" is to endow someone with power in the forms of vitality, progeny, and prosperity. "Make his face shine" is a metaphor in which the face is a light (like the moon or the stars) casting its light upon another, that is, looking approvingly upon another. The same idiom is found in Num 6:25; Pss 31:16; 80:3, 7, 19; 119:135; Dan 9:17. The language is that of the Aaronite blessing in Num 6:24-26: "The LORD bless you and keep you; / the LORD make his face to shine upon you, and be gracious to you; / the LORD lift up his countenance upon you, and give you peace." The main point of part 1 is that the nations will see the prosperity of God's particular people and acknowledge its origin in a particular God, Yahweh. The nations would have worshiped many gods, and the excellence of each was judged by the power each possessed and could grant to clients. Israel's prosperity will startle them and make them reflect what god gave such great benefits. "Known" means acknowledged by the nations. "Your way" *(derek)* means "your authoritative way," for the parallel is "saving power," and the Semitic root *drk* has the meaning "rule, power" in Ugaritic texts and some biblical texts.

The nations will acknowledge it is you who rules
the world (vv. 3-5)

Verse 4 is the center of the chiastic arrangement of the poem because it is the only three-line verse in the poem. As noted above, it is best to take the verbs in verses 3-5 as expressing result, what happens when God blesses Israel. The nations will acknowledge God as the God, that is, the most powerful God. Their acknowledgment is portrayed primarily in cultic terms, as giving praise consists in rites and songs and engaging in public rituals of rejoicing. The reason for the celebration is that "you," God of Israel, "judge" and "guide" (i.e., rule) all the nations on earth.

Favor your people so that your salvation may be seen (vv. 6-7)

Part 3 is a prayer like part 1. "Yielded" (v. 6a) is the only verb in the perfect tense and is translated by NRSV and most others as stating the simple fact that the earth has borne fruit. It is preferable, however, to take the verb as precative (prayer) perfect, "May the earth yield its harvest." Blessing includes fertility, so that verse 6b is perfectly parallel. Parts 1 and 2 (respectively, 12 and 13 Hebrew words) form a prayer frame around the center, the expression of hope for divine blessings.

Theological and Ethical Analysis

The assumption of the psalm, that the holy community's prosperity is a means through which God's sovereignty becomes visible to the world, may be jarring to Christians especially of a liberal or individualist stripe. Contemporary Christianity in the West does not have the distinct boundaries of, say, Judaism, so that church members do not readily draw lines between themselves and the world. Furthermore, many Christians are almost predominantly concerned with their personal relationship to God or Jesus rather than with the mission of the church. The psalm is concerned with the role of the holy community. How does one pray this psalm today?

The first point to be made is that the psalm is not about privilege, but about awareness that the church's very being is a gift. The gift is daily received. Unless God's face shines on the community, it can communicate nothing. One is reminded of the similar combination of "pride," humility, and gratitude in Mary's Magnificat, "for he has looked with favor on the lowliness of his servant. Surely, from now on all generations will call me blessed" (Luke 1:48). Second, it is the light from God's face first felt in the church, and not human greatness, that reminds others of God's grandeur and guidance. Matthew 5:16 is in the same spirit: "In the same way, let your light shine before others, so that they may see your good works and give glory to your Father in heaven." The psalm leaves to God how the nations will respond. The psalmist is nonetheless convinced of Israel's special role toward the nations and of God's desire to be known by all the nations of the world.

PSALM 68

Literary Analysis

Psalm 68 is perhaps the most difficult in the Psalter, for its context and dramatic logic are not clear to modern readers, and there are a large number of uncertain words and phrases. To some scholars of a previous generation, the poem was understood simply as a list of poems catalogued by their opening lines ("incipits"). Most scholars today, however, believe the poem is a song of victory incorporating themes from the exodus from Egypt, conquest of Canaan, and proclamation of divine kingship at the holy mountain, variously called Sinai or Zion. Mythic and historical perspectives are fused; the mythic language gives a cosmic and universal dimension to the acts of God in history.

Given the difficulties of the poem and the limits of this commentary, it is advisable to state at the beginning some assumptions governing the interpretation of this commentary. This commentary assumes that Ps 68 is a communal thanksgiving, probably reflecting a liturgical ceremony representing Yahweh's march from the southern mountains to defend the people against infertility and attack. Yahweh is depicted as a warrior, using the weapons of storm. The ceremony reflected in the psalm depicts the Lord's battle, victory, and entry into the Temple in Jerusalem. The battle-victory is described in cosmic as well as historical terms, for it is waged against "the depths of the sea" (v. 22b), "wild animals," and "the herd of bulls" (v. 30), as well as against "the kings of the armies" (v. 12). At stake is the governance of the universe, for all nations come bearing tribute to the victorious deity. The original ritual might have been a procession involving the armies of Israel and the ark-throne of the Lord. Psalms such as 24, 47, and 118 are similarly based, remotely or immediately, on liturgical ceremonies. Such psalms made ceremonies in the Temple available to pray-ers in all places.

The outline is determined by the progress of the procession and the responses of the worshipers. This commentary accepts the stanzaic structure of NRSV and places them within larger units for ease of commentary.

Exegetical Analysis

Sing exultantly to God setting out to battle for justice (vv. 1-6)

Numbers 10:35-36 provides a clue to the context of the opening lines, "Whenever the ark set out, Moses would say, 'Arise, O LORD, let your enemies be scattered, / and your foes flee before you.' And whenever it came to rest, he would say, 'Return, O LORD of the ten thousand thousands of Israel.' " The holy war begins with the ark-throne (Exod 25:21-22) going out at the head of the army while the people sing in anticipation of victory. The ark played a role in war as in 1 Sam 4 when the people brought it into the battle against the Philistines. Yahweh's weapons are wind and fire (Ps 68:2). War in the psalm is more than a skirmish between God and enemies such as the Pharaoh or the Canaanites; it is a conflict between "righteous" warriors (v. 3) and "the wicked" who resist the will of God (v. 2c). The warriors are "joyful" (v. 3a) in the anticipation of victory. Verse 4 applies to the Lord an epithet of the Canaanite storm god, Baal ("who rides upon the clouds"), who was imagined as mounted on the storm clouds dark with water moving eastward toward Palestine from the Mediterranean Sea.

The ultimate purpose of the intervention of God is revealed by the epithets and hymnic participles in verses 5-6—to establish justice. According to the verses, God cares for the unprotected, the poor, and the oppressed. "Orphans" and "widows" were traditional categories of vulnerable people; such people were unconnected to the family system that provided support and protection in that culture. God became their family protector and legal advocate, giving also a supportive family structure ("home," v. 6a) for the "desolate," that is, those left to their own devices. God ensured the safety of another defenseless class, "prisoners" (v. 6b). Divine justice has a negative function too—forcing "the rebellious" from their land (v. 6c).

The Divine Warrior's triumphant march, making the earth fertile and secure (vv. 7-14)

The verses describe a single scene: God marching to Palestine from the southern mountains. The scene is familiar from ancient poetry: Deut 33:2-5; Judg 5:4-5; Hab 3:3-15 and, in a modified version, Exod 15:13-18. According to the ancient poems, Yahweh originally resided in a mountain south of Palestine. (The location of Sinai/Horeb in the Sinai peninsula is a later and nonbiblical tradition.) When Israel was in danger and called out, Yahweh came armed with weapons of storm (rain, thunder, wind, lightning). The march became a paradigm for other divine rescues. In liturgical terms, it is a past event that is capable of being renewed. Accounts of "the march from the south" differ according to use. Here it brings plenteous rains (vv. 9-10) as well as victory (vv. 11-14), and God takes up a new residence in Jerusalem (vv. 16, 17, 24, 29, 35). An effect of the intervention is fertility. The Rider of the Clouds pours water from the clouds upon the parched earth (vv. 9-10). The journey has a military purpose, for the Hebrew verbs rendered "went out" and "marched" (v. 7) can connote war, as in Judg 5:4. Thus the goal of the march is both *cosmic* and *historical*, that is, the defeat of sterility (vv. 9-10) and of encroaching enemies (vv. 11-14). Ancients did not make a dichotomous distinction between *cosmic* and *historical*, for drought and encroachment are both enemies of justice, that is, the peaceful order intended by the deity for a favored people.

"Heritage" (v. 9*b*) refers to the land that belongs by divine grant to Israel, as in Jer 3:19 and Ps 105:11. "Your flock" is a metaphor for the people, like "sheep" and "flock" in Ps 78:52. Verses 11-14 depict God's victory indirectly by citing only the victory tidings ("The kings of the armies, they flee, they flee!" v. 12*a*) rather than describing how the victory happened. Omitting the account of battle underscores the ease of victory. Only the spoils of victory are mentioned. In Judg 5, the statement that "[the kings] got no spoils of silver" (Judg 5:19*d*) means they lost the battle.

God takes up residence in the holy mountain, Jerusalem (vv. 15-23)

"Bashan" (v. 15*a*) is the area east of the river Jordan between Mount Hermon in the north and Gilead in the south. "Mountain of Bashan" (v. 15*a*) is possibly Mount Hermon (9,232 feet), the northern limit of Bashan. In an apostrophe to the mountains (vv. 15-16), the poet personifies them as human beings seeking the prestige of being chosen by God and then growing jealous because another mountain is chosen. Verse 17 returns to the narrative, telling of the triumphant arrival of God at "the holy place" in Jerusalem (v. 17*c*). God moves from the southern mountain, Sinai, to Jerusalem. Psalm 50 also witnesses to the transfer of the divine residence from Mount Sinai to Mount Zion, for the Lord "shines forth" out of Zion (Ps 50:2) in a ceremony renewing the covenant made at Sinai. From this point onward, Ps 68 is concerned with the arrival of the Divine Warrior and the celebration of victory. Arriving at the holy mountain, God ascends it in triumph, as in Ps 47:5, "God has gone up with a shout, the Lord with the sound of a trumpet." Plunder and prisoners are brought in (v. 18). The jubilant crowd acclaims God's benefit toward themselves (vv. 19-21). The reference to Bashan and the "bringing back" in verses 22-23 are obscure. NRSV and most translators assume that the object of "bring back" is the heads of the enemies shattered in verse 21. In that case, enemy corpses are carried back to the shrine so that people can bathe their feet in the blood. The grisly scene may have a parallel in the Ugaritic texts where the goddess Anat, the bellicose consort of the storm god Baal, wallows knee-deep in warrior's blood, neck-deep in soldier's gore (*CTU* 1.3.ii). The reference to the "tongues of your dogs" (Ps 68:23*b*) evokes 1 Kgs 22:38*b*, "The dogs licked up [Ahab's] blood, and the prostitutes washed themselves in it, according to the word of the LORD that he had spoken." The grim scene symbolizes complete victory.

The procession of the tribes of Israel (vv. 24-31)

As noted, the march seems to have been reenacted liturgically in a procession in the precincts of the Temple. There are three references in the poem to processions (vv. 1, 7, 17). The phrase, "Israel's fountain" (v. 26), though sometimes corrected to "assembly of Israel" (so REB and NAB), makes sense as it stands, for God is a "fountain of living water" in Jer 2:13 and 17:13. Four tribes are mentioned: Benjamin, Judah, Zebulun, Naphtali. Why these four tribes? Perhaps because they represent the northern (Naphtali, Zebulun) and southern (Judah) boundaries of the land. The number four would represent the totality of the tribes, as in the four directions and the four quarters of the universe. It is not clear, however, why Benjamin, the smallest tribe, located just north of Judah, was included.

"Summon your might" (v. 28) might seem an unnecessary request in a celebration of a victory of such scope, but the Bible does not consider evil ever definitively vanquished in history. Renewed efforts against it will always be required. "Wild animals" and "herd of bulls" (v. 30) are metaphors for the enemies that perennially surround and threaten Israel. Their location in the "reeds" is perhaps an allusion to the lagoons of Egypt. The psalm here and elsewhere (e.g., vv. 7-14) deliberately blends cosmic and historical language. National enemies embody chaotic forces that threaten God's life-giving order. Divine order is something that goes beyond Israel, however, for the psalm commands the nations to bring tribute (vv. 18, 29, 31).

Nations of the world, bring your tribute to the
victorious God in the Temple (vv. 32-35)

Verse 33 echoes verse 4, bringing the psalm to its conclusion. Other themes mentioned in the beginning are reprised in verses 33-35, "rider in the heavens" (v. 4) and thunder ("his mighty voice") from the storm theophany in verses 8-9. "His sanctuary" is mentioned once again as the goal of the march/procession (v. 17). Where the victorious God takes up residence is the royal center of the world; other kings come with their tribute.

Theological and Ethical Analysis

Psalm 68 celebrates Yahweh as the Storm God maintaining and defending the integrity of creation against diminishment and attack. The poet makes God a warrior whose storm clouds make the soil able to sustain animals and humans and whose sword smites all enemies. The poem uses the ancient topos of the march from the south according to which God goes out to do battle for the holy people and then returns in triumph. Psalm 68 identifies the march with the exodus-conquest, the founding event of Israel. The ritual celebration of the event makes it possible for the entire people to participate in the event. The psalm text transposes the communal celebration into a form usable by worshipers in every age.

Modern readers may be disturbed by the violent imagery used of God and by the nationalistic point of view. Though the violence cannot be denied, it is important to remember that the violence directed against "the wicked" (v. 2), "the rebellious" (vv. 6, 18), "his enemies" (v. 21), and "the wild animals" (v. 30) has a positive purpose. Its purpose is to preserve divine order. An aspect of divine order is to make the earth fertile and supportive of life (vv. 9-10). Israel worshiped a *saving* God, and saving often took the form of military action. The nationalist outlook is simply part of the biblical perspective—God chooses a particular people and enters into a relationship with them. The question is whether God's commitment to the human race is lessened by a commitment to one group. This psalm is clear about God choosing one people and one shrine (vv. 15-16) in preference to others. It does not claim, however, that the enemies are against God simply because they are against Israel. The enemies are not identified with a national group and their crime is that they have rebelled against God. Readers must nonetheless recognize how easily psalms such as these may be misused by people who identify their own interests as God's.

Christian readers will appreciate how God's actions are incorporated into the one great act of the exodus. The exodus has two aspects: liberation from bondage followed by the formation of a community. In this sense, the death and resurrection of Jesus is an exodus, the destruction of death and the formation of a new people. Psalm 68 thus refers to the new exodus of Christ. Ephesians 4:8 applies Ps 68:18 ("You ascended the high mount") to the descent of Christ to hell, his ascension, and giving of gifts: "Therefore it is said, 'When he ascended on high he made captivity itself a captive; / he gave gifts to his people.' "

PSALM 69

Literary Analysis

The poem is one of the longest and most deeply felt individual laments in the Psalter. The allusion to rebuilding the cities of Judah (v. 35b) indicates a sixth- or fifth-century BCE date and suggests a context in which the psalmist, contrary perhaps to the populace discouraged by the destruction of the Temple and by the exile, remains loyal to the Lord and hopeful of restoration. At any rate, the psalmist complains of having many enemies (v. 4), including relatives (v. 8), and of suffering constant public shame (shame is mentioned nine times, vv. 6-7, 9-12, 19-20). The sufferings remind one of Jeremiah, with the difference that the psalm has a livelier hope than Jeremiah of rebuilding Jerusalem and repossessing the land (vv. 30-36). The strong hope at the end of the poem is a counterbalance to the bitter feelings in the earlier verses. There are similarities to Pss 22 and 102.

The structure is complex and carefully arranged. On the most obvious level, alternation of the pronouns "you" (vv. 5 and 19) and "I" (vv. 13 [NRSV: "But as for me"] and 29) in initial position help mark the five major divisions: verses 1-4; 5-12; 13-18; 19-28; and 29-36. Marvin Tate (1990, 193) has noticed that beginning with verse 14 the poem reprises words and consonantal roots from parts 1 and 2, which can be shown graphically.

*Verses 1-13*a	*Verses 13*d-29
verse 1 "Save me" (yšʿ)	verse 13d "your faithful help" (yšʿ)
verse 2 "I sink"	verse 14 "sinking"
"deep" (mire)	verse 15b "the deep"
"deep waters"	verse 14 "deep waters"
"flood sweeps over me"	verse 15a "the flood sweep over me"
verse 4 "those who hate me"	verse 14c "those who hate me" (NRSV: "enemies")
"my enemies"	verse 18 "my enemies"
verse 5 "you know"	verse 19 "you know"
verse 6 "be put to shame"	"my shame"
"be dishonored"	"dishonor"
verse 7 "reproach"	verse 20 "reproach (NRSV: "insults")
verse 9 "insults of those who insult you"	
verse 10 "insulted"	
verse 13a "but I" (NRSV: "but as for me")	verse 29 "but I"

The doubling of words lends intensity to the plea, and serves to unify the poem.

Exegetical Analysis

The waters rise, my strength fails, and enemies abound (vv. 1-4)

The troubles are likened to waters inexorably rising to throat level while the sufferer is unable to find any footing. Suffocating waters are also mentioned in Pss 32:6; 88:7, 17; Jonah 2:3-5. The scene is nightmarish, the sufferer feels helpless and doomed. The theme of waters unifies verses 1-2; the mention of bodily organs unifies verses 3-4*b* ("throat," "eyes," "hairs of my head"). The sufferer is exhausted, with a throat sore from constant vocal prayer and with eyes failing from looking intently for aid. The reference to restitution in verse 4*ef* does not necessarily imply that the psalmist has been accused of theft. It is a proverbial statement to the effect that the psalmist's enemies are using an outrageously unfair standard for their accusations.

As is true in most individual laments, it is difficult to learn what precisely the sufferings are. Possibly it is sickness, which onlookers reckon as punishment for sin like the friends of Job; verses 10-12 and 26 can be so interpreted. The most striking suffering, however, is shame; the word or its near-synonyms are mentioned nine times as afflicting the sufferer. Shame here refers primarily not to the painful emotion from consciousness of guilt (the common modern meaning), but something more "objective," the pain and diminishment experienced by those who act against the dominant culture's values and accepted behaviors. It is the opposite of honor, which is granted by the culture to those who conform to it. It may be that the shame is connected to championing the Temple in some way, perhaps its rebuilding, which was controverted as one learns, for example, from the prophet Haggai (520 BCE). Such a controversy may lie behind the statement "It is zeal for your house that has consumed me" (v. 9*a*). At any rate, the psalmist has suffered for remaining God's loyal servant and uses that loyalty to persuade God to give aid (vv. 7-12).

Help me lest it appear that your loyal servants
are left to their own devices (vv. 5-12)

Though verse 5 seems at first sight to be an admission of sin, it is in reality an affirmation of innocence as is clear from the immediately following statement (v. 6) that if God abandons the psalmist people will be scandalized by the failure to rescue this innocent and loyal servant. Verse 6 can be paraphrased: "Let those who pin their hopes on you not be disappointed because of (your abandonment of) me." Next follow protestations of loyalty to God and the listing of its high social costs (vv. 7-12). Verse 12 is a merism: "those who sit in the gate" are the town elders who make its decisions and "the drunkards" are the lowest level of society.

The precise form that the psalmist's zeal took is not mentioned. Perhaps it was insistence that Temple ritual be accompanied by just behavior outside the Temple, as in Isa 1:2-20. Reference to the town gate in verse 12 recalls the popular rejection of prophetic reproof in Amos 5:10-12.

Let my prayer be acceptable to you, for the waters are rising (vv. 13-18)

As noted, with verse 13 the poem begins to replay the opening verses, which has the effect of intensifying these lines. The unit is defined by the repetition at its beginning (v. 13) and end (vv. 16-17) of the words "answer me," "LORD," and "steadfast love." The psalmist urges God to act, this time arguing from the divine character (steadfast love and mercy) rather than from the scandal that would result if God were not to act, as in verse 6.

My enemies have taken away my honor and broken my heart. Avenge me (vv. 19-29)

The psalmist, still smarting from insults and pain inflicted by others, asks God for revenge, for there is no one else to turn to (vv. 19-20). The justice is "poetic justice" as often happens in the Bible. Because the enemies poisoned the food that symbolizes fellowship, let their table be a snare to them and their guests (vv. 21-22). Let them who attacked me suffer ill health (v. 23). As they destroyed my household, let theirs become desolate (v. 25). Those whom God afflicted with illness had to bear further pain when their illness was attributed to their sins. As the enemies ostracized me, let them be ostracized (v. 28) and even deprived of life. Such sentiments disturb modern readers, to be sure, but the psalmist is convinced that these people have attacked "God's" servants and so deserve to be punished by God. But most important, the psalmist leaves all to God, both the punishment and the timetable.

When you rescue me, I will give you thanks and
rejoice in the rebuilding of your people
and land (vv. 30-36)

The final part is signaled by the pronoun *I*, which, alternating with *you*, guides the reader through the poem. The bold statement of divine preference for prayer over animal sacrifice in verse 31 is a hint perhaps of why the singer suffered hatred from others—insistence on the proper disposition of worshipers.

When the singer is rescued the oppressed will rejoice, for they will recognize that God "hears the needy" and, consequently, they will be heard. The psalmist is conscious here as in verse 6 of being an example, living a life that can scandalize or edify the community. The last verses (34-36) broaden the perspective of the poem to include the entire universe and the fortunes of Israel. God's saving this needy person is only an instance of a larger saving purpose.

Theological and Ethical Analysis

Through carefully chosen words and arguments, the sufferer turns an experience of desperation, despair, and rage into a prayer directed toward God. So faithful is the prayer to human experience and so sure-footed with regard to God that it is suitable for others, even those far from the original experience. In the drama of the poem, life is on the brink, water is rising neck-high, all human help is useless, and the only hope is God.

In the Gospel of John, Jesus cites Ps 69:9 as he drives the money changers from the Temple, "Stop making my Father's house a marketplace!" (John 2:16). Romans 11:9 uses Ps 69:22-23 as an explanation for Jewish rejection of Jesus. It should be remembered that the Romans verse is only one statement, and not the final one, in Paul's reflections on the relation of Christians and Jews.

The psalm as a whole can be used by Christians in a variety of situations: Those who feel choked by life, those whose labors on behalf of God and God's work have earned them the enmity of the community and struggle to deal with the ensuing bitterness, and those who carry the inescapable responsibility of being an example for the community.

PSALM 70

Literary Analysis

This individual lament is neatly divided into a prayer that the enemies be punished (vv. 1-3) and a prayer that all who seek God, among whom is the psalmist, will sing for joy at a timely deliverance (vv. 4-5). The same poem (with a few variants) is the final section of Ps 40:13-17. Phrases and even whole sections of one psalm could be incorporated into another. The reader is referred to the commentary under Ps 40.

An unusual feature is the emphasis put on shaming enemies (four words for shaming occur in vv. 2-3). The point is that everybody will see that the enemies' designs on the psalmist's life have been frustrated and will recognize that the hand of God has done this. Another noteworthy feature is that God-seekers in general are mentioned (v. 4) before the singer's own need (v. 5). Finally, great stress is laid on a speedy rescue, for the imperative verb "make haste" occurs twice and the same sentiments are expressed in the verb "do not delay."

Exegetical Analysis

Shame my enemies! (vv. 1-3)

The words "God," "help," and "make haste" will be echoed in the final lines (v. 5), bringing closure to the poem. Shame, important in the preceding Ps 69, plays a key role here as well. Different from the modern meaning of shame as the painful consciousness of sin or impropriety, the ancient notion of shame presumed a coherent culture and widely accepted moral code that, when broken, brought dishonor upon the violator. Such dishonor was serious, for it showed the violator to be in the wrong and damaged his or her social standing in the community. In the psalm, when the schemes against the psalmist are blocked, people recognize that the schemes have no validity and so heap scorn on the planners of the evil. The prayer is that the enemies' schemes be *publicly* frustrated so that the frustration will function as a judgment-in-act. Everyone will see and declare the enemies to be in the wrong and the psalmist in the right. "Aha, Aha" are malicious cries of triumph that the psalmist hopes will be proved foolish by God's judgment.

Enable your followers to rejoice in your salvation;
hasten to help me! (vv. 4-5)

There is a wordplay on "seek" in 2*b* and 4*a*: "seek my life"; "seek [God]." The psalmist hopes that God-seekers will "rejoice." The context shows that the joy is that of a public celebration of a saving intervention of God. Mentioning the public celebration first is a shrewd rhetorical move on the part of the singer, for it reminds God that any rescue of the righteous poor elicits a worshipful response from onlookers. People will "say evermore, 'God is great!' " (v. 4*d*). To declare oneself "poor and needy" (v. 5*a*) is the best way to attract the attention of the God who is ever inclined to be merciful.

Theological and Ethical Analysis

Even more, it seems, than the desire for personal vindication is the singer's desire that God's justice be done and be seen. Indeed, the psalmist uses this desire for divine justice to persuade God to act, reminding God ever so gently of the joyous celebration that will take place (v. 4) when the wicked are put down and "the poor and needy" (v. 5) are upheld. Moreover, the psalmist associates joy with the triumph of justice, for it leads to celebration and worship. Despite the desperation that one can sense behind the urgent pleas, the psalmist never loses sight of the primacy of God and of God's glory.

PSALM 71

Literary Analysis

This psalm is an individual lament of a person of mature years (vv. 9, 18, 20) facing attack from enemies (vv. 10-11, 13). Despite the dangers posed by enemies, they are described with comparative mildness. The psalmist is consistently able to draw strength from the knowledge that God has never failed in the past (vv. 6, 17, 20-21). The poem is marked by a rhythm of petition/complaint and trust/praise: petition (vv. 1-4); trust/praise (vv. 5-8); petition/complaint (vv. 9-13); trust/praise (vv. 14-17); petition (v. 18); trust/praise (vv. 19-24).

The psalm recycles material from other psalms, especially Pss 22 and 31. There are links to Ps 70 as well, leading some commentators to suggest it continues the preceding psalm.

The structure is not clearly marked, which has resulted in a wide variety of strophic divisions by translators. The poem is a succession of units each containing a plea, complaint, and act of trust or promise of praise. This commentary uses divine names and the personal pronoun I as section markers.

Part 1	Part 2
Verses 1-3	Verses 14-16
("Lord," 25 Hebrew words)	("But I," 24 Hebrew words)
Verses 4-11	Verses 17-21
("O my God," 60 Hebrew words)	("O God," 46 Hebrew words)
Verses 12-13	Verses 22-24
("O God," 16 Hebrew words)	("I," 32 Hebrew words)

Symmetry seems to be an important factor in the structure. Parts 1 and 2 have virtually the same word count (respectively, 101 and 102 words). The second and third divisions of parts 1 and 2 are nearly alike in their number of words (respectively, 76 and 78 words).

Exegetical Analysis

I take refuge in you, my rock and refuge (vv. 1-3)

The metaphors are apt for someone fleeing danger and seeking a safe hideout—"rock of refuge," "strong fortress," and "rock and fortress." The psalmist compares God to a massive and abruptly rising rock formation. Such massive rocks are found in the wilderness regions that one would typically repair to in times of danger. The word *righteousness (ṣĕdāqāh)* is used in an objective sense—that which is done by the righteous God, that is, beneficial actions. The word is important in the psalm, occurring five times, always with the possessive pronoun "your" ("your righteousness," "your righteous acts," vv. 2, 15, 16, 19, 24). The poet's images of God as rock and refuge are born of a lifelong companionship with God.

Rescue your servant from enemies who accuse you of abandoning me (vv. 4-11)

The psalmist's claim on God dates back to birth, for it was God who "took me from my mother's womb." The implicit argument is that you gave me life, so you must preserve it. "My praise is continually of you" (v. 6c) means something like "I always acknowledged you as my God. Consequently, I am an example of how you care for your friends (v. 7); to abandon me is tantamount to agreeing with my enemies that you toss aside your friends" (vv. 9-11). Though adopted by nearly all scholars, "portent" (v. 7a) is not a good translation of *môpēt*, which means "a wonder," a special divine intervention like the plagues in Egypt. The English word "portent," however, connotes an impending calamity, an omen. The Hebrew word is positive. Its true sense is shown by the parallelism: "I have become an example for others, [that] you have been a secure refuge" (similarly NJPS and Ehrlich). To have been rescued many times throughout a long life is a good advertisement for God's fidelity. Moreover, the psalmist has always been careful to give thanks for every benefit received (vv. 6c-8) so that it would be against God's own interest to cast off such a loyal servant (vv. 9-13). The singer's "old age" (v. 9a) is an additional argument, for it was a virtuous thing in the ancient East to care for the elderly, especially one's parents. Neglect of them came under harsh criticism (Prov 19:26; 20:20; 28:24).

Be near, O God, frustrate my enemies (vv. 12-13)

To pray that one's enemies be shamed is basically to pray that they and their plans be frustrated. Shame is not primarily the modern sense of painful consciousness of guilt, but more objectively, the censure that attaches to those who spurn the dominant culture's values and accepted behaviors. It is the opposite of the honor that is granted by the culture to those who conform to its values.

I will never cease praising your mighty deeds (vv. 14-16)

"I" introduces a fresh section. The singer is remarkably buoyant, finding joy in identifying the beneficial acts of God, both personal and public, whose "number is past my knowledge."

From my youth you have been my faithful and saving God (vv. 17-21)

"You have taught me" (v. 17a) through what I have experienced. The relationship of the psalmist and God is expressed through verbs of mutuality—God acting and the psalmist responding in praise. Such reciprocity has always characterized their life together. Like many other older people, the psalmist is concerned with "the generations to come" (v. 18d), giving thought to how to communicate an appreciation of God to the next generation. The clause "O God, who is like you?" (v. 19*d*) must be understood against a background where polytheism was the dominant paradigm and where one chose one's god on the basis of the god's power to save. "Who is like you?" has an experiential tone that modern readers easily miss. In verse 20, one learns that the singer's life has been marked by ups and downs, descents and ascents. The pray-er has experienced "deaths and resurrections" under the guidance of God. The final stance (v. 21) is positive, restoration of honor.

I will spend my days praising you, certain my
enemies will be defeated (vv. 22-24)

The final section is almost ecstatic in its appreciation for the Lord's guidance and protection. The praise given in response is public, involving musical instruments ("harp," "lyre") and bodily expression ("lips" and "tongue"). The poet is confident, as always, that enemies have been frustrated (v. 24*bc*).

Theological and Ethical Analysis

Though some commentators believe the references to old age are figurative, their very number and significance argue otherwise. The singer is elderly. Old age can be regarded as an affliction, as in 2 Sam 19:34-35 and Eccl 12:1-8. It can also be regarded as a blessing, as in this psalm. Though the sufferings reported in the poem are not slight—attacks by enemies and calumny—the psalmist possesses the poise and equanimity to deal with them. That poise comes from having seen much over a long life: sufferings, yes, but more significantly, God's care of those who are loyal and trusting.

The psalmist said "I am an example to many." This poem is a model for people of mature years for how to use the fruits of their experience. It is also, more broadly, a prayer for anyone who has seen God active in their life and wishes to further the relationship.

PSALM 72

Literary Analysis

This prayer for the Davidic king may have been used at his coronation. It would also have been appropriate for other royal ceremonies like the similar Pss 2, 20, 21, and 110. The one who is ultimately praised in the adulation given to the king is his dynastic God, the ruler of the universe. The Israelite king is only the instrument of divine justice, ensuring that creation bounty is available to all, especially the poor. The king is the symbol of divine rule, the receiver of the offerings of the kings of the nations. Ancient scribes did not stint in their praise of the king. The rhetoric of ancient Near Eastern royal poetry thoroughly marks this poem. Its language is grand and full of hyperbole. German scholars aptly call it *Hofstil*, "court style."

The poem has five stanzas. These are largely determined by topic: verses 1-4, the king as instrument of divine justice; verses 5-7, the longevity of the king who is the exemplar of health and fertility; verses 8-11, the universal sovereignty of the king; verses 12-14, the king as instrument of divine justice; verses 15-17, the king's need of prayer. The divine name appears only once in the psalm; "God" is the authoritative first word. Verses 18-19 is the doxology that ends Book 2; it is not part of the psalm.

Exegetical Analysis

The king as instrument of divine justice (vv. 1-4)

The poem is one of only two attributed to Solomon (the other being Ps 127) because of similarities in this psalm to the portrait of Solomon in 1 Kings: He was a "king's son" (Ps 72:1), renowned as a wise judge (1 Kgs 3; 4:29-34), and visited by the queen of Sheba (1 Kgs 10, cf. Ps 72:15).

The king was, according to ancient Near Eastern royal ideology, the chief judicial officer. His decrees and legal decisions embodied the order that the gods designed for the world. An example is the summary of David's reign in 2 Sam 8:15, "So David reigned over all Israel; and David administered *justice* and *equity* to all his people." The italicized words (in Hebrew) are the same nouns as in Ps 72:1. The actions described in the next verse (v. 2) are the *result* of God endowing the king with justice (so NAB, NJPS, REB). NAB goes further and takes verses 3-4 also as result clauses.

What do justice and righteousness mean here? Hebrew words for justice are notoriously fluid and hard to define especially out of their contexts. Here, the standard by which something is judged just or unjust is not extrinsic to God (as a law code or a custom would be); the standard is within God. Justice often has to do with safeguarding creation order, which was by definition "just" in the sense that it conformed to the divine will. Deviations from that original order cannot be allowed to stand. Doing justice often has to do with correcting such deviations, particularly when they lead to deprivation of poor people. The existence of the poor is an affront to the generous God who created a bountiful world. Biblical justice is interventionist, in contrast to the modern Western notion of justice as disinterested decisions. "Justice" in verse 1 is literally plural, "judgments," and probably refers to the legal decisions a king makes. Royal justice favors the poor; it is not simply maintenance of the status quo. The psalm mentions the poor no less than seven times (vv. 2, 4, 12-13).

At first reading, verse 3 seems concerned with fertility rather than justice, which is the topic of the surrounding verses. Fertility is related to justice, however, for the king's leadership in the practice of justice makes the cosmos more fruitful and hospitable to human beings. Covenant blessings and curses such as those in Deut 28 are experienced as fertility and infertility. The gist of Ps 72:3 is: Give your justice to the king to make the world more just, so the earth can give its bounty. Isaiah 48:18 is comparable: "O that you had paid attention to my commandments! / Then your prosperity would have been like a river, / and your success like the waves of the sea."

The king as effective symbol of our health and fertility (vv. 5-7)

Creation in the ancient Near East included human society and its institutions (such as kingship) as well as earthly and astral elements that moderns associate with creation. The king's good health, longevity, and sexual potency were important symbols for the people. Like verse 3, verse 7 mixes the language of fertility ("flourish") and of justice ("righteousness," "peace").

The universal sovereignty of the king (vv. 8-11)

"Sea to sea" and "the River" are not geographical locations. The language is mythic, expressing sovereignty over the whole universe, like the language in Ps 89:25 ("I will set his hand on the sea / and his right hand on the rivers") and Zech 9:10e ("his dominion shall be from sea to sea, / and from the River to the ends of the earth"). The king does not conquer the nations. Rather, as representative of the Most High God, he receives their tribute, which is ultimately intended to honor God. The tribute acknowledges that they and their patron gods are subordinate to the Lord and to his lieutenant, the Davidic king.

The king as instrument of divine justice (vv. 12-14)

These verses are a vivid statement of the king as servant of the poor. "For" in verse 12a shows that the Davidic king's authority over the kings of the world comes from carrying out God's justice. The king has a special concern for the poor and is expected to act on their behalf. Verse 14b in NRSV, "precious is their blood in his sight," is much clearer in NJPS: "the shedding of their blood weighs heavily upon him."

The king's need of prayer. Reprise of the themes
of fertility, long life, and universal dominion (vv. 15-17)

The cry "Long live the king!" was shouted at the accession of a new king (1 Sam 10:24; 2 Sam 16:16; 1 Kgs 1:31, 34, 39). "May gold be given to him" is an equivalent acclamation, for only a king would be given such a rich gift. "Sheba" is in southwest Arabia, a kingdom "at the ends of the earth" (v. 8*b*).

As exalted as the Davidic king is, he is still a human being and has no less need of divine help than the lowest slave. A diplomatic way of stating his needy state is to exhort all to pray for him (v. 15*cd*). The final verses reprise parts of the opening section: Verse 16 picks up verse 3 (mountains and earth bearing fruit); verse 17*ab* picks up the wish for long life already expressed in verse 5; verse 17*cd* reprises 8-11 about the nations' recognition. Verse 17*cd* can be translated either as NRSV and NIV do, or "all will pray to be as blessed as he was" (REB, similarly NAB and NJPS).

Doxology (vv. 18-20)

The doxology expresses the hope that the Lord, the God of Israel, be universally acknowledged as the supreme deity, the one "who alone does wondrous things." As if correcting the adulation heaped upon the king in the last psalm of Book 2, verse 18 prays that *God's* name be eternally and universally blessed.

Theological and Ethical Analysis

Modern people are perhaps accustomed to praying directly to God and expecting God to deal directly with them. This psalm goes in another direction, revealing a God so bound up with a particular people as to employ the institutions and genius of that people in governing the world and communicating with human beings. Ancient peoples, indeed most Christians and Jews throughout history, took for granted God's use of human institutions in dealing with the beloved community and with the world. They took for granted the institution of kingship, which historically has often been an instrument of oppression of the poor. This poem is at once a praise of an ideal kingship and an admonition to the king. God is mentioned only once, to be sure, but so decisively that the whole poem hangs from that introductory word.

The king can only succeed if he gives a welcome to the justice with which God has endowed him. His status in the world of the nations depends entirely upon his commitment to be an instrument of God's justice, especially with regard to the poor. He is a sign, a kind of sacrament of God from whom all authority on heaven and earth is derived. In this reading, a poem that seems to be a conventional praise of the king turns out to be something much more.

Jewish tradition has seen in this poem a portrayal of the elder David crowning his son Solomon king. Solomon came close to realizing the grandeur of the poem and, though not fully succeeding, his rule provided a glimpse of what the rule of the Messiah might be. Christians see in Jesus the ideal Davidic king who fulfills the promises of this psalm. In particular, they prize the psalmic vision of the Davidic king inaugurating a universal rule of prosperity and justice and the nations' recognition of God.

SELECT BIBLIOGRAPHY

WORKS CITED

Barré, Michael, and John S. Kselman. 1983. "New Exodus, Covenant, and Restoration in Psalm 23," in *The Word of the Lord Shall Go Forth: Essays in Honor of David Noel Freedman*. Ed. C. L. Myers and M. O'Connor. Winona Lake, IN: Eisenbrauns. 97-127.

Barré, Michael. 1990. "Mesopotamian Light on the Idiom NĀŠĀ' NEPEŠ." *CBQ* 52 (1990) 46-54.

Boulding, Maria, trans. 2000. *Expositions of the Psalms 33–50*. Vol 16 of *The Works of Saint Augustine*. Hyde Park, NY: New City Press.

Braude, William G., trans. 1959. *The Midrash on Psalms*. Vol. 1. Yale Judaica Series 13. New Haven: Yale University Press.

Calvin, John. 1999. *Heart Aflame: Daily Readings from Calvin on the Psalms*. Foreword by Sinclair B. Ferguson. Phillipsburg, NJ: P & R Publishing Co.

Carlyle, Thomas. 1885. *The Works of Thomas Carlyle: Sartor Resartus, Past and Present, The Diamond Necklace, Mirabeau*. New York: John B. Alden.

Crow, L. D. 1992. "The Rhetoric of Psalm 44." *ZAW* 104 (1992) 394-401.

Delitzsch, Franz. 1991. *Psalms*. Vol 5 of *Commentary on the Old Testament* by C. F. Keil and F. Delitzsch. Translated by James Martin. 1872. Reprint, Grand Rapids: Eerdmans.

Ehrlich, Arnold. 1905. *Die Psalmen*. Berlin: M. Poppelauer.

Gunkel, Hermann. 1968. *Die Psalmen*. Göttinger Handkommentar zum

Alten Testament. 1929. Reprint, Göttingen: Vandenhoeck & Ruprecht.

Kraus, Hans-Joachim. 1988. *Psalms 1–59*. Translated by H. C. Oswald. Minneapolis: Augsburg.

McCann, J. Clinton, Jr. 1996. "Commentary on Psalm 8." Vol 4 of *The New Interpreter's Bible*. Nashville: Abingdon Press, 639-1280.

Mowinckel, Sigmund. 1967. *The Psalms in Israel's Worship*. 2 vols. Nashville: Abingdon Press.

Otto, Rudolf. 1958. *Idea of the Holy*. Trans. John W. Harvey. Oxford: Oxford University Press.

Tate, Marvin E. 1990. *Psalms 51–100*. Word Biblical Commentary 20. Waco: Word.

Weinfeld, Moshe. 1991. "What Makes the Ten Commandments Different?" *Bible Review* 6 (1991) 35-41.

Westermann, Claus. *The Living Psalms*. Trans. J. R. Porter. Grand Rapids: Eerdmans.